Bernhard Haslhofer

Mappings in the Web of Data

Bernhard Haslhofer

Mappings in the Web of Data

A Web-based Mapping Technique for Establishing Metadata Interoperability

Südwestdeutscher Verlag für Hochschulschriften

Impressum/Imprint (nur für Deutschland/ only for Germany)
Bibliografische Information der Deutschen Nationalbibliothek: Die Deutsche Nationalbibliothek verzeichnet diese Publikation in der Deutschen Nationalbibliografie; detaillierte bibliografische Daten sind im Internet über http://dnb.d-nb.de abrufbar.
Alle in diesem Buch genannten Marken und Produktnamen unterliegen warenzeichen-, marken- oder patentrechtlichem Schutz bzw. sind Warenzeichen oder eingetragene Warenzeichen der jeweiligen Inhaber. Die Wiedergabe von Marken, Produktnamen, Gebrauchsnamen, Handelsnamen, Warenbezeichnungen u.s.w. in diesem Werk berechtigt auch ohne besondere Kennzeichnung nicht zu der Annahme, dass solche Namen im Sinne der Warenzeichen- und Markenschutzgesetzgebung als frei zu betrachten wären und daher von jedermann benutzt werden dürften.

Verlag: Südwestdeutscher Verlag für Hochschulschriften Aktiengesellschaft & Co. KG
Dudweiler Landstr. 99, 66123 Saarbrücken, Deutschland
Telefon +49 681 37 20 271-1, Telefax +49 681 37 20 271-0, Email: info@svh-verlag.de
Zugl.: Wien, Univ., Diss., 2008

Herstellung in Deutschland:
Schaltungsdienst Lange o.H.G., Berlin
Books on Demand GmbH, Norderstedt
Reha GmbH, Saarbrücken
Amazon Distribution GmbH, Leipzig
ISBN: 978-3-8381-0562-8

Imprint (only for USA, GB)
Bibliographic information published by the Deutsche Nationalbibliothek: The Deutsche Nationalbibliothek lists this publication in the Deutsche Nationalbibliografie; detailed bibliographic data are available in the Internet at http://dnb.d-nb.de.
Any brand names and product names mentioned in this book are subject to trademark, brand or patent protection and are trademarks or registered trademarks of their respective holders. The use of brand names, product names, common names, trade names, product descriptions etc. even without a particular marking in this works is in no way to be construed to mean that such names may be regarded as unrestricted in respect of trademark and brand protection legislation and could thus be used by anyone.

Publisher:
Südwestdeutscher Verlag für Hochschulschriften Aktiengesellschaft & Co. KG
Dudweiler Landstr. 99, 66123 Saarbrücken, Germany
Phone +49 681 37 20 271-1, Fax +49 681 37 20 271-0, Email: info@svh-verlag.de

Copyright © 2009 by the author and Südwestdeutscher Verlag für Hochschulschriften Aktiengesellschaft & Co. KG and licensors
All rights reserved. Saarbrücken 2009

Printed in the U.S.A.
Printed in the U.K. by (see last page)
ISBN: 978-3-8381-0562-8

Abstract

The integration of metadata from distinct, heterogeneous data sources requires *metadata interoperability*, which is a qualitative property of metadata information objects that is not given by default. The technique of metadata mapping allows domain experts to establish metadata interoperability in a certain integration scenario. Mapping solutions, as a technical manifestation of this technique, are already available for the intensively studied domain of database system interoperability, but they rarely exist for the Web.

If we consider the amount of steadily increasing structured metadata and corresponding metadata schemes on the Web, we can observe a clear need for a mapping solution that can operate in a Web-based environment. To achieve that, we first need to build its technical core, which is a mapping model that provides the language primitives to define mapping relationships. Existing Semantic Web languages such as RDFS and OWL define some basic mapping elements (e.g., `owl:equivalentProperty`, `owl:sameAs`), but do not address the full spectrum of semantic and structural heterogeneities that can occur among distinct, incompatible metadata information objects. Furthermore, it is still unclear how to process defined mapping relationships during run-time in order to deliver metadata to the client in a uniform way.

As the main contribution of this thesis, we present an *abstract mapping model*, which reflects the mapping problem on a generic level and provides the means for reconciling incompatible metadata. Instance transformation functions and URIs take a central role in that model. The former cover a broad spectrum of possible structural and semantic heterogeneities, while the latter bind the complete mapping model to the architecture of the Word Wide Web. On the concrete, language-specific level we present a binding of the abstract mapping model for the RDF Vocabulary Description Language (RDFS), which allows us to create mapping specifications among incompatible metadata schemes expressed in RDFS.

The mapping model is embedded in a cyclic process that categorises the requirements a mapping solution should fulfil into four subsequent phases: *mapping discovery, mapping representation, mapping execution*, and *mapping maintenance*. In this thesis, we mainly focus on mapping representation and on the transformation of mapping specifications into executable SPARQL queries. For mapping discovery support, the model provides an interface for plugging-in schema and ontology matching algorithms. For mapping maintenance we introduce the concept of a simple, but effective mapping registry.

Based on the mapping model, we propose a Web-based mediator wrapper-architecture that allows domain experts to set up mediation endpoints that provide a uniform SPARQL query interface to a set of distributed metadata sources. The involved data sources are encapsulated by wrapper components that expose the contained metadata and the schema definitions on the Web and provide a SPARQL query interface to these metadata. In this thesis, we present the OAI2LOD Server, a wrapper component for integrating metadata that are accessible via the Open Archives Initiative Protocol for Metadata Harvesting (OAI-PMH).

In a case study, we demonstrate how mappings can be created in a Web environment and how our mediator wrapper architecture can easily be configured in order to integrate metadata from various heterogeneous data sources without the need to install any mapping solution or metadata integration solution in a local system environment.

Zusammenfassung

Die Integration von Metadaten aus unterschiedlichen, heterogenen Datenquellen erfordert Metadaten-Interoperabilität, eine Eigenschaft die nicht standardmäßig gegeben ist. Metadaten Mapping Verfahren ermöglichen es Domänenexperten Metadaten-Interoperabilität in einem bestimmten Integrationskontext herzustellen. Mapping Lösungen sollen dabei die notwendige Unterstützung bieten. Während diese für den etablierten Bereich interoperabler Datenbanken bereits existieren, ist dies für Web-Umgebungen nicht der Fall.

Betrachtet man das Ausmaß ständig wachsender strukturierter Metadaten und Metadatenschemata im Web, so zeichnet sich ein Bedarf nach Web-basierten Mapping Lösungen ab. Den Kern einer solchen Lösung bildet ein Mappingmodell, das die zur Spezifikation von Mappings notwendigen Sprachkonstrukte definiert. Existierende Semantic Web Sprachen wie beispielsweise RDFS oder OWL bieten zwar grundlegende Mappingelemente (z.b.: `owl:equivalentProperty`, `owl:sameAs`), adressieren jedoch nicht das gesamte Spektrum möglicher semantischer und struktureller Heterogenitäten, die zwischen unterschiedlichen, inkompatiblen Metadatenobjekten auftreten können. Außerdem fehlen technische Lösungsansätze zur Überführung zuvor definierter Mappings in ausführbare Abfragen.

Als zentraler wissenschaftlicher Beitrag dieser Dissertation, wird ein *abstraktes Mappingmodell* präsentiert, welches das Mappingproblem auf generischer Ebene reflektiert und Lösungsansätze zum Abgleich inkompatibler Schemata bietet. Instanztransformationsfunktionen und URIs nehmen in diesem Modell eine zentrale Rolle ein. Erstere überbrücken ein breites Spektrum möglicher semantischer und struktureller Heterogenitäten, während letztere das Mappingmodell in die Architektur des World Wide Webs einbinden. Auf einer konkreten, sprachspezifischen Ebene wird die Anbindung des abstrakten Modells an die RDF Vocabulary Description Language (RDFS) präsentiert, wodurch ein Mapping zwischen unterschiedlichen, in RDFS ausgedrückten Metadatenschemata ermöglicht wird.

Das Mappingmodell ist in einen zyklischen Mappingprozess eingebunden, der die Anforderungen an Mappinglösungen in vier aufeinanderfolgende Phasen kategorisiert: *mapping discovery*, *mapping representation*, *mapping execution* und *mapping maintenance*. Im Rahmen dieser Dissertation beschäftigen wir uns hauptsächlich mit der Representation-Phase sowie mit der Transformation von Mappingspezifikationen in ausführbare SPARQL-Abfragen. Zur Unterstützung der Discovery-Phase bietet das Mappingmodell eine Schnittstelle zur Einbindung von Schema- oder Ontologymatching-Algorithmen. Für die Maintenance-Phase präsentieren wir ein einfaches Mapping-Registry Konzept.

Auf Basis des Mappingmodells stellen wir eine Web-basierte Mediator-Wrapper Architektur vor, die Domänenexperten die Möglichkeit bietet, SPARQL-Mediationsschnittstellen zu definieren. Die zu integrierenden Datenquellen müssen dafür durch Wrapper-Komponenen gekapselt werden, welche die enthaltenen Metadaten im Web exponieren und SPARQL-Zugriff ermöglichen. Als beipielhafte Wrapper Komponente präsentieren wir den OAI2LOD Server, mit dessen Hilfe Datenquellen eingebunden werden können, die ihre Metadaten über das Open Archives Initative Protocol for Metadata Harvesting (OAI-PMH) exponieren.

Im Rahmen einer Fallstudie zeigen wir, wie Mappings in Web-Umgebungen erstellt werden können und wie unsere Mediator-Wrapper Architektur nach wenigen, einfachen Konfigurationsschritten Metadaten aus unterschiedlichen, heterogenen Datenquellen integrieren kann, ohne dass dadurch die Notwendigkeit entsteht, eine Mapping Lösung in einer lokalen Systemumgebung zu installieren.

Acknowledgements

First of all, I would like to express my gratitude to my supervisor, Prof. Dr. Wolfgang Klas, whose expertise and stimulating suggestions helped me during all the time of writing this thesis. I also very much appreciate his guidance through the one or other organisational turmoil, which, at the end, made it possible for me to finish my work. I would also like to thank Prof. Dr. A Min Tjoa for being my secondary advisor and for the time and effort he has invested in judging on the contents of this thesis. Furthermore, I would like to thank Prof. DDr. Gerald Quirchmayr for being a member of my thesis commitee.

A very special thanks goes out to my colleagues, Niko Poptisch, Wolfgang Jochum, Ross King, Stefan Leitich, Bernhard Schandl, and Stefan Zander. They have supported me throughout the past years, were always available for any kind of discussion, gave valuable comments on my work, and helped me in shaping the approach and bringing the text of this thesis into the present form. And most importantly, they have provided a working environment where doing research is not just work, but also great fun.

Things would not run so smoothly without our administrative and technical colleagues. I would like to thank Manu for keeping a large portion of the administrative stuff away from me, and Jan and Peter for taking care that my prototypes keep running.

Bringing up the motivation for a long-term project, such as doing a PhD, is hardly possible without strong support from friends and family. Special thanks to the Verein for the long-term friendship we have, and to my parents for the support they have provided me through my entire life.

Last but not least, my profound gratitude and love goes to Silvia. She closely experienced the effects of being together with a PhD Student during the past years and always gave me the perspective of a life after PhD. Without her love, understanding, and support, finishing this thesis would have been much more difficult.

Table of Contents

1 Introduction   **1**
    1.1 Contributions 2
    1.2 Organisation 4

I Background and Related Work   7

2 Background   **9**
    2.1 Illustrative Example 10
    2.2 Unveiling the Notion of Metadata 13
    2.3 Metadata Interoperability 21
    2.4 Techniques for Achieving Metadata Interoperability 27
    2.5 On the Quality of Interoperability Techniques 35
    2.6 Summary 39

3 Metadata Mapping   **41**
    3.1 What is Metadata Mapping? 41
    3.2 Requirements Framework 45
    3.3 Mapping Solutions 55
    3.4 Analysis of Mapping Solutions 64
    3.5 Summary 74

II Methodology and Concepts   77

4 Towards A Web-based Metadata Integration Architecture   **79**
    4.1 Goals 79
    4.2 Architecture Overview 81
    4.3 Metadata Integration Workflow 87
    4.4 Functional Requirements 89
    4.5 Summary 93

5 Abstract Mapping Model — 95
- 5.1 A Generic Mapping Approach ... 95
- 5.2 Representing Source and Target Metadata ... 96
- 5.3 Generic Graph Model Specification ... 98
- 5.4 Abstract Mapping Model Specification ... 101
- 5.5 The Dynamic Aspects of the Generic Mapping Model ... 104
- 5.6 Summary ... 105

III Implementation and Proof of Concept — 107

6 An RDFS Binding of the Mapping Model — 109
- 6.1 RDFS Overview ... 109
- 6.2 Lifting and Normalising Metadata Schemes to RDFS ... 110
- 6.3 RDFS Mapping Model Specification ... 113
- 6.4 Executing RDFS Mappings ... 121
- 6.5 Maintaining RDFS Mappings ... 137
- 6.6 Implementation Considerations ... 141
- 6.7 Summary ... 145

7 The OAI2LOD Server — Wrapping OAI-PMH Data Sources — 147
- 7.1 What is OAI-PMH? ... 147
- 7.2 Design Considerations ... 151
- 7.3 Implementation ... 153
- 7.4 The Future of OAI-PMH ... 156
- 7.5 Summary ... 157

8 Qualitative Evaluation and Case Study — 159
- 8.1 Comparison with Existing Mapping Solutions ... 159
- 8.2 Example Metadata Integration Scenario ... 166
- 8.3 Summary and Lessons Learned ... 175

9 Conclusions — 177
- 9.1 Summary ... 177
- 9.2 Future Work ... 179

Bibliography — 181

List of Figures

2.1	TV-Anytime metadata describing a video	11
2.2	Proprietary metadata describing a JPEG image	12
2.3	Dublin Core metadata describing a JPEG image	13
2.4	Overview of the three metadata building blocks	15
2.5	Metadata building blocks from a model perspective	19
2.6	Structural and semantic metadata heterogeneities on the model and the instance level	23
2.7	Example for achieving interoperability via a global conceptual model	38
3.1	The main elements of a metadata mapping specification	43
3.2	Achieving metadata interoperability through instance transformation	44
3.3	The four major phases in the metadata mapping cycle	45
4.1	A taxonomy of known architectures for querying heterogeneous data [DD99]	82
4.2	Components of a mediator-wrapper architecture	85
4.3	Metadata integration workflow	88
5.1	The generic mapping model with language-specific extensions	96
5.2	XML metadata represented as three layered, directed labelled-graph	98
5.3	The generic data model from a static perspective	99
5.4	The abstract mapping model from a static perspective	102
5.5	Reflecting the four mapping phases in the abstract mapping model	105
6.1	An RDFS binding of the abstract mapping model	120
6.2	Extending and redefining the RDFS binding of the abstract mapping model with mapping execution behaviour	127
6.3	Run-time execution of SPARQL templates — Overview	132
6.4	SPARQL query template selection	133
6.5	Mapping registry architecture	138
6.6	Mapping registry model	140
6.7	Serving schemes and mapping using HTTP Content Negotiation (adapted from [BP08])	143
7.1	Sample OAI-PMH communication	149

7.2	Size of OAI-PMH repositories	150
7.3	Top 10 metadata formats	150
7.4	Sample OAI2LOD Server response	154
7.5	The OAI2LOD Server architecture	155
7.6	Comparison of OAI2LOD and corresponding OAI-PMH requests	156
8.1	Example metadata integration scenario	169

List of Tables

2.1	A selection of schema definition languages and their characteristics	20
2.2	A categorisation of metadata interoperability techniques	27
2.3	A representative selection of metadata standards	29
2.4	The quality of various interoperability techniques	36
3.1	Requirements framework for the evaluation of metadata mapping solutions	56
3.2	Metadata mapping solutions — categorisation and overview	63
3.3	Metadata mapping solutions evaluation summary	74
8.1	Qualitative evaluation against existing mapping solutions	167

Chapter 1

Introduction

Metadata are machine-processable data that describe digital or non-digital resources. A resource can be anything: an image, an audio file, a video, artefacts in a museum's collection, or any other physical or conceptual object. From a technical perspective, metadata are information objects that are processed by various systems and applications. The heterogeneities of these systems, the divergent semantic and structural properties of the metadata, and also the distinct interpretation contexts of their designers result in incompatible metadata.

In order to exchange metadata among systems or to provide uniform access to metadata objects in a multitude of autonomous and distributed systems, *metadata interoperability* must be established. One possible, well-known, and in practice accepted technique is the definition of *mappings* between incompatible metadata objects. This technique has widely been studied in the database domain proliferating a multitude of mapping solutions that operate for data models of closed-world data management systems, such as the relational model in relational databases or the semi-structured XML data model. For data models that were designed for open, uncontrolled environments, such as RDF/S, effective mapping solutions, which can operate in such an environment, are still an open issue.

We believe that the trend of exposing structured metadata on the Web will continue and even increase in the near future. Especially institutions that host metadata of public-interest, such as libraries, museums or archives, have a strong incentive to share and integrate their metadata sets with those of other institutions (e.g., see [HH05]), be it due to public obligations or because they want to achieve higher visibility. The World Wide Web with its few, simple-to-use standards (URI, HTTP) gives them a stable and proven infrastructure to share and exchange their metadata. With the RDF data model, we have a mechanism to represent metadata in a way that other machines and applications can process and interpret them.

In such a scenario, where institutions use the Web infrastructure for making their metadata accessible, besides the metadata themselves, the corresponding metadata schemes must be published on the Web too, in order to guarantee that the metadata can be interpreted correctly by other machines. Since these metadata schemes can follow different metadata standards (e.g., Dublin Core, MODS, MARC, TV-Anytime, etc.) or even reflect proprietary needs, one must define *mappings* or *crosswalks* between these schemes in order to reconcile the semantic and structural heterogeneities among metadata from different sources. If we consider the digital library domain, we can observe (see [KHS08]) that even within a restricted, to a certain extent controlled domain, institutions use a variety of standards or in-house solutions.

The technologies provided by the Semantic Web to represent schema information, such as RDFS and OWL, only provide limited abilities to express mappings between elements of distinct schemes. One can define subsumption hierarchies for classes and properties (`rdfs:subClassOf`, `rdfs:subPropertyOf`), define property equality (`owl:equivalentProperty`), or define same individuals (`owl:sameAs`), but one cannot represent more complex mappings that occur in real-word systems: schema A could, for instance, define a single property name and assign metadata instances as a comma-separated sequence of lastname and firstname (e.g., `Doe, John`); schema B could represent the same metadata instances using two properties `lastname = Doe` and `firstname = John`. With the currently available mapping primitives provided by RDFS and OWL, one cannot define adequate mapping relationships between these properties. Also the issue of instance transformation, i.e., how to deal with the comma separated name sequence from the perspective of schema B, is still an open issue in the Semantic Web community.

Furthermore, it is still unclear how to process the mappings between two RDFS or OWL metadata schemes at application run-time. At the end, applications must be able to transform metadata information objects from one representation into another in order to enable the exchange of, or the uniform access to metadata. This can be achieved by a transformation engine or directly by a query language that gives structured access to metadata. SPARQL is the query language for the family of Semantic Web technologies. How this language can be used to provide uniform access to data sources in a view-like manner, as it is common in the database domain, is also an open issue. Especially, how to obtain executable SPARQL queries from mapping declarations, which can transparently handle metadata heterogeneities.

Finally, a mapping mechanism also requires some kind of registry where metadata schema and mapping information can be deposited. Such a registry must be accessible for both humans and machines and provide the required information.

In fact, we need to lift the mapping methodologies and concepts that are already established in the database domain and implemented in various commercial mapping solutions to the level of the open, uncontrolled environment of the Web, which uses novel (Semantic Web) technologies to handle metadata and schema definitions. The goal of this thesis is to provide concepts, methodologies, and a prototypical solution to reduce the insufficiencies existing technologies suffer from in the context of establishing interoperability among metadata information objects on the Web.

1.1 Contributions

In this thesis, we propose a Web-based mapping technique for establishing interoperability among metadata on the Web. Opposed to existing commercial solutions and academic prototypes, our approach contributes the following features, which are perceivable for domain experts that utilise our solution:

1.1. Contributions

- *Seamless integration with the Web architecture*: metadata and metadata schemes are exposed on the Web using existing Web standards. Mapping services, which process these mappings and provide uniform access to metadata in distinct sources, are part of the Web too. They are Web-applications accessible via certain URLs.

- *Light-weight solution*: for domain experts, who need to establish interoperability among metadata originating from a set of distinct sources, there is no need to install any heavy-weight mapping suite or enterprise information integration suite. They can integrate our proposed mapping solution as a Web service into their system architecture.

- *An easy-to-use interface*: with a few clicks a domain expert can set up a productive SPARQL access point, which integrates metadata from a set of data sources.

A central approach of this thesis is to consider *metadata mapping* not as a single task but as a cyclic process consisting of four subsequent phases that lead to the goal of providing uniform access to a set of distributed, heterogeneous, and autonomous data sources: first, one must determine mapping relationships among incompatible metadata schemes. Second, one must find a way to represent them in a machine-interpretable way, which requires a mapping model that goes beyond the expressiveness of existing Semantic Web standards. Third, one must translate mappings into executable queries and provide query processors that can deliver the requested metadata. Forth, one requires the means for organising metadata schema definitions and the mappings created among them, which enables the reuse of previously created mapping specifications.

To summarise, the main scientific contributions, which are beyond user-perceivable features, are:

- An extensive elaboration on the subject of *metadata interoperability* and a comparative study of known interoperability techniques, published in [HK08]. We have further analysed and evaluated existing commercial and prototypical mapping solutions, described in [Has08].

- A general methodology for providing uniform access to a set of heterogeneous, distributed, and autonomous metadata sources, published in [Has06]. The practical relevance of that methodology in the digital libraries domain has been presented in [Has07].

- An *abstract mapping model*, which reflects the mapping problem on a generic level and provides the means for reconciling structural and semantic heterogeneities among metadata information objects expressed in graph-based data models. It is independent of any concrete schema definition language and binds the metadata mapping process to the architecture of the World Wide Web by introducing the concept of globally unique URI identifiers.

- A binding of the abstract mapping model to the RDFS schema definition language that allows for the expression of mappings between RDFS schema declarations. Those mappings can then be translated into executable SPARQL queries, which is a necessary requirement in order to achieve uniform query access to metadata in a set of distributed and heterogeneous data sources.

- The OAI2LOD Server, which is a wrapper component that encapsulates data sources that expose metadata via the Open Archives Initiative Protocol for Metadata Harvesting (OAI-PMH). It publishes the contained metadata on the Web and provides SPARQL query access to these metadata. The design and implementation details have been published in [HS08].

Therefore, the focus of this thesis is clearly on building the core components of a Web-based mapping solution. These are the mapping model, which provides the primitives to define mapping specifications for incompatible RDFS metadata schemes, and algorithms for the conversion of mapping specifications into executable SPARQL code. Both are part of a broader metadata integration architecture and a methodology that provide the means and guidelines to set up uniform query interfaces to distinct data sources.

The following areas are out of the scope of this thesis:

- *Schema matching algorithms*: the determination of mapping relationships can be supported by matching mechanisms, which is a separate research area and has been studied intensively throughout the past years. Although in the academia many schema matching approaches and solutions have been developed so far, they have, as we see in this thesis, not yet found widespread adoption in productive environments. Our strategy has been to factor out the schema matching research field and concentrate on other phases in the mapping process. However, we do provide interfaces to integrate such algorithms into our solution.

- *Mapping GUI*: we provide a Web-based user interface, which allows domain experts to set up and configure integrated query endpoints to multiple metadata sources. Developing a GUI for specifying mapping relationships in an interactive way has been out of the scope of this thesis, but is subject of our future work.

- *Fully-Fledged Registry Solution*: we discuss the concept of a Web-based registry for metadata schemes and mappings and also provide a basic but functional implementation. However, since registries are not the main focus of this thesis, we do not elaborate further on that topic.

1.2 Organisation

Chapter 1 provides the basic motivation or the problems addressed in this thesis, identifies the essential contributions, and introduces the outline of this thesis.

Part I, consisting of Chapters 2 and 3, introduces the technical background of this thesis and analyses existing, related work:

1.2. Organisation

In Chapter 2, we present an illustrative example to which we will refer throughout this thesis. Then we analyse the various notions of metadata one can currently find in literature and identify and characterise the main technical building blocks of metadata information objects. Based on that, we define our conception of the term *metadata interoperability* and analyse the various types of heterogeneities that impede metadata information objects from being interoperable. Finally, we analyse and compare existing techniques for establishing metadata interoperability.

Metadata mapping is such a technique and is discussed in Chapter 3. After describing our perception of that technique, we analyse in detail how mapping solutions can support domain experts in reconciling heterogeneities. Based on an extensive literature study, we set up a requirements framework, against which we compare a representative selection of existing mapping solutions.

Part II, consisting of Chapters 4 and 5, describes our overall methodology for establishing uniform access to heterogeneous metadata sources and presents the conceptual design of our mapping approach:

In Chapter 4, we describe our *Web-based metadata integration architecture* and present a methodology that makes heterogeneous data sources accessible via single, uniform query interface. We present the workflow between the domain expert who wants to create an integrated metadata access point and outline the major components in our architecture and briefly describe the technologies they are based on. Finally, we derive the requirements for the mapping part of such a Web-based metadata integration architecture.

The general mapping problem and also the previously derived requirements are reflected in the *abstract mapping model*, presented in Chapter 5. Independent of any metadata schema definition language, we formally describe a model that can represent mappings between metadata schemes. The behavioural aspects of the model also reflect the previously mentioned mapping process.

Part III, consisting of Chapters 6, 7, and 8, describes the implementation of our mapping approach and provides the proof of concept in terms of a qualitative evaluation and an exemplary case study:

In Chapter 6, we bind the abstract mapping model to the RDF Vocabulary Description Language. We describe how existing schema definitions can be lifted to the level of RDFS and how metadata mappings can be defined among them. Further, we describe how such RDFS mapping specifications can be processed in the subsequent mapping phases. This includes the transformation of mapping specifications into SPARQL query templates and their execution. We also present a Web-based metadata registry approach for maintaining mappings and thus for supporting the fourth phase. Finally, we provide the implementation details of our RDFS-enabled, Web-based mapping solution.

In Chapter 7, we present a wrapper component for the OAI-PMH protocol that follows the Linked Data principles [BL06] and can expose OAI-PMH metadata and schema information on the Web.

In Chapter 8, we compare our Web-based metadata mapping solution with other existing mapping solutions. Additionally, as a proof of concept and to demonstrate the feasibility of our approach, we describe a sample case study, which provides uniform SPARQL access to three autonomous metadata repositories, whereas each of them employs a different metadata schema.

We conclude this thesis in Chapter 9 and discuss existing limitations and areas of future work.

Part I

Background and Related Work

Chapter 2

Background

Metadata are machine processable data that describe resources, digital or non-digital. While the availability of metadata, as a key for efficient management of such resources in institutional media repositories (e.g., [SK98]), has been widely recognised and supported in highly standardised ways, *metadata interoperability*, as a prerequisite for uniform access to media objects in *multiple* autonomous and heterogeneous information systems, calls for further investigation. Since this is not given per default, it must first be established by domain experts before uniform access can be achieved.

Regarding the literature from various domains, we can observe that the term *metadata interoperability* has a very broad meaning and entails a variety of problems to be resolved: on a lower technical level, machines must be able to communicate with each other in order to access and exchange metadata. On a higher technical level, one machine must be able to process the metadata information objects received from another. And on a yet higher, semantic level, one must ensure that machines and humans correctly interpret the intended meanings of metadata. Since there exists a wide assortment of possible techniques that aim at establishing metadata interoperability, we believe that it is necessary to analyse the interoperability problem in the context of multimedia metadata and to critically assess available techniques.

In the following sections, we first introduce three illustrative examples we will use throughout this work (Section 2.1). Then, in Section 2.2, we deeply analyse the various notions of metadata one can find in the literature and identify and characterise the main technical building blocks of metadata information objects. Thereafter, in Section 2.3, we focus on *metadata interoperability* and systematically, for each building block, elaborate on the factors that impede interoperability among metadata. In Section 2.4, we give an outline of currently available techniques for achieving metadata interoperability and compare their quality according to their capabilities to resolve certain types of heterogeneities in Section 2.5.

2.1 Illustrative Example

This example involves three autonomous institutions[1]: the BBC, the Austrian National Library, and the National Library of Australia. Each institution offers different types of contents (audio, video, images, documents) about the Olympic Games and uses its own technical infrastructure to maintain the contents and the adjacent metadata. A journalist, for instance, who is preparing a documentary about the history of the Olympic Games might want to electronically access these repositories to obtain historical as well as up-to-date multimedia material about this topic. Even if all the repositories were reachable through a single technical infrastructure, uniform access would still be impossible because, as we will see in the following examples, their metadata are not interoperable.

2.1.1 Institution 1: BBC TV-Anytime Service

The BBC offers an online program information service[2] for its TV and radio channels. Via a SOAP Web Service, clients can request various details about the content including basic program information such as the title or synopsis of a broadcast. The TV-Anytime [ETS06] standard has been chosen for representing program information. Its principal idea is to describe the multimedia content of broadcasts such that a user, or an agent on behalf of the user, can understand what content is available and thus be able to acquire it [McP02]. For representing audio-visual metadata, TV-Anytime encompasses a large number of elements defined by the MPEG-7 [ISO07b] standard.

Figure 2.1 depicts a sample TV-Anytime metadata description about a video showing Ingmar Stenmark's victory in the 1980 Olympic Winter Games in Lake Placid. The video has been created by John Doe, belongs to the genre Sports, and has been annotated with several terms that further describe the video's contents.

2.1.2 Institution 2: Austrian National Library

The Austrian National Library's image archive[3] is the most important source of digitised historical images in Austria and also includes well-catalogued images from past Olympic Games. All the images in the archive are described using a proprietary metadata schema and as many other institutions, the Austrian National Library stores their metadata in a relational database that is accessible via a non-public SQL interface.

Figure 2.2 shows an example description about an image of Willy Bogner who led in the first run of the slalom during the Olympic Games in Squaw Valley back in 1960. In July 2003, the Austrian National Library has digitised the image, originally taken by Lothar Rübelt. Details about the person Willy Bogner are maintained in a so-called authority record that unambiguously identifies him as an entity in

---
[1] Although these institutions exist in the real world, the samples have been adapted to the needs of this work.
[2] BBC TV-Anytime service: http://backstage.bbc.co.uk/feeds/tvradio/doc.html
[3] The Austrian National Library's image archive portal: http://www.bildarchiv.at

2.1. Illustrative Example

```
<TVAMain "...">
  <ProgramDescription>
    <ProgramInformationTable>
      <ProgramInformation programId="crid://bbc.co.uk/123456789">
        <BasicDescription>
          <Title>Lake Placid 1980, Alpine Skiing, I. Stenmark</Title>
          <Synopsis>Ingmar Stenmark's (SWE-Alpine skiing) victory in
            the Giant Slalom in Lake Placid</Synopsis>
          <Genre href="urn:tva:metadata:cs:ContentCS:2004:3.1.1.9">
            <Name>Sports</Name>
          </Genre>
          <CreditsList>
            <CreditsItem role="urn:mpeg:mpeg7:cs:RoleCS:2001:AUTHOR">
              <PersonName>
                <mpeg7:GivenName>John</mpeg7:GivenName>
                <mpeg7:FamilyName>Doe</mpeg7:FamilyName>
              </PersonName>
            </CreditsItem>
          </CreditsList>
          <CreationCoordinates>
            <CreationLocation>us</CreationLocation>
          </CreationCoordinates>
        </BasicDescription>
      </ProgramInformation>
    </ProgramInformationTable>
  </ProgramDescription>
</TVAMain>
```

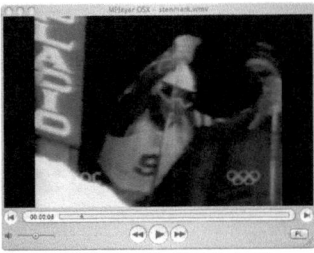

Figure 2.1: TV-Anytime metadata describing a video

order to avoid naming conflicts. Also technical features, such as the MIME-type or the dimension of the image are part of the metadata description.

2.1.3 Institution 3: National Library of Australia

As a result of the Olympics in Sidney in the year 2000, the National Library of Australia[4] now maintains a huge image collection from this event. The Dublin Core Element Set [DC06] has been chosen for representing metadata for these images and all images have been digitised and are now available online.

---
[4]The Australian National Library's Web site: http://www.nla.gov.au/

Chapter 2. Background

PERSON	
ID	120
FIRSTNAME	Willy
LASTNAME	Bogner
BIRTHDAY	23
BIRTHMONTH	01
BIRTHYEAR	1942

IMAGEDATA	
ID	330976
TITLE	Olympic Wintergames 1960 in Squaw Valley
INFO	Willy Bogner in the slalom; minimum time in the first run
AUTHOR	Rübelt, Lothar
CREATION DATE	03-JUL-03
DATE	1960
FK_PERSON	120

IMAGEOBJECT	
ID	517849
INFO	http://www.bildarchivaustria.at/Bildarchiv//302/B1117424T4299954.jpg
MIMETYPE	image/jpeg
IMAGEWIDTH	2333
IMAGEHEIGHT	3147
FK_IMG_DATA	330976

Figure 2.2: Proprietary metadata describing a JPEG image

The metadata are exposed via the Open Archives Protocol for Metadata Harvesting (OAI-PMH)[5], an HTTP-based protocol that allows the retrieval of XML metadata descriptions.

Figure 2.3 shows a picture of marathon runners cross the Sydney Harbour Bridge during the Olympics 2000. The adjacent metadata description gives further details about the photographer, the format of the image and the date when it was taken. Keywords such as Runners (Sports) or Sportsmen and sportswomen further describe the contents.

---

[5] The Australian National Library's OAI-PMH service: http://www.openarchives.org/OAI/openarchivesprotocol.html

2.2. Unveiling the Notion of Metadata 13

```
<OAI-PMH "...">
   ...
   <metadata>
      <oai_dc:dc "...">
         <dc:title>Sydney Olympics 2000, marathon runners cross Sydney
             Harbour Bridge [picture] /</dc:title>
         <dc:creator>Mahony, David (David James)</dc:creator>
         <dc:format>1 photograph : gelatin silver ; image 26.9 x 38.4 cm.
             on sheet 30.5 x 40.3 cm.</dc:format>
         <dc:coverage>New South Wales</dc:coverage>
         <dc:date>2000</dc:date>
         <dc:description>Photograph by David Mahony -- On reverse in pencil.;
             Condition: Good. Group of [marathon] runners feature
             eventual Gold Medal Winner Gezahgne Abero of Ethiopia (No.
             1651) [Sydney, N.S.W., September 2000]</dc:description>
         <dc:subject>Runners (Sports) -- Australia -- Portraits.</dc:subject>
         <dc:subject>Sydney Harbour Bridge (Sydney, N.S.W.)</dc:subject>
         <dc:subject>Olympic Games (27th :, 2000 : Sydney, N.S.W.)</dc:subject>
         <dc:subject>Marathon running -- Australia -- Photographs.</dc:subject>
         <dc:subject>Sportsmen and sportswomen.</dc:subject>
         <dc:type>Image</dc:type>
         <dc:identifier>nla.pic-an22842546</dc:identifier>
         <dc:source>Item held by National Library of Australia</dc:source>
         <dc:rights>You may save or print this image for research and study.</dc:rights>
         <dc:identifier>http://nla.gov.au/nla.pic-an22842546</dc:identifier>
      </oai_dc:dc>
   </metadata>
   ...
</OAI-PMH>
```

Figure 2.3: Dublin Core metadata describing a JPEG image

2.2 Unveiling the Notion of Metadata

In this section we briefly introduce the notion of *metadata*, which is essential in order to fully understand the metadata interoperability problem. Then, in Section 2.2.1, we identify the main building blocks of metadata descriptions. Since metadata interoperability must be established not only on the conceptual but also on the technical level, in Section 2.2.2 we examine how metadata reside or appear in actual information systems.

2.2.1 Metadata Building Blocks

Following Gilliand's definition [Gil05], we conceive metadata as *the sum total of what one can say about any information object at any level of aggregation*, in a machine understandable representation. An information object is *anything that can be addressed and manipulated by a human or a system as a discrete entity*. Defining metadata more abstractly as *any formal schema of resource description, applying to any type of object, digital or non-digital* [NIS04] is also appropriate especially for application scenarios that apply metadata for describing non-digital resources (e.g., persons).

Metadata can be classified according to the functions they are intended to support (descriptive, structural, administrative, rights management, preservation metadata) [NIS04, Joh04], or to its level of semantic abstraction (low-level vs. high-level metadata) (e.g., [WK03]). Low-level technical metadata have less value for end users than high level, semantically rich metadata that describe semantic entities in a narrative world such as objects, agent objects, events, concepts, semantic states, semantic places, and semantic times, together with their attributes and relationships [BZCS01]. Hence, the semantic quality and expressiveness of metadata is essential for effectively retrieving digital objects.

To put it simply, metadata are data that describe some resource. In the examples presented in the previous section, the resources are digital images and videos, hence information objects. The adjacent metadata descriptions mainly consist of high-level, semantically rich descriptive information, such as the name of persons (e.g., Ingmar Stenmark, Willy Bogner) or events (e.g., Sydney Olympics 2000). Only the Austrian National Library provides some low-level technical metadata (mime-type, imagewidth, imageheight).

We can identify the following common characteristics: each description is made up of a set of elements (e.g., `title`, `author`, `subject`) and content values (e.g., `Lake Placid,...`, `Rübelt Lothar`, `Runners`); the elements are defined as part of a metadata schema, which can be standardised, as it is the case with Dublin Core or TV-Anytime, or proprietary; from the fact that two metadata descriptions are expressed in XML and one in terms of relations in a relational database, we can derive that the metadata elements have previously been specified using a certain language. For the case of XML, the language is usually XML Schema [W3C06], for the case of a relational database a schema is expressed in terms of tables using SQL-DDL [ISO03b].

Based on this observation, we can identify three main metadata building blocks: we denote the set of content values in a metadata description as *metadata instance*, the element definitions as *metadata schema*, and the language for defining metadata schemes as *schema definition language*. Figure 2.4 illustrates these three building blocks and their dependencies. In the following we will further focus on each of these building blocks in a reverse order.

Schema Definition Language

An application and domain-specific metadata schema is expressed in a certain schema definition language, whereas each language provides a set of language primitives (e.g., class, attribute, relationship).

2.2. Unveiling the Notion of Metadata

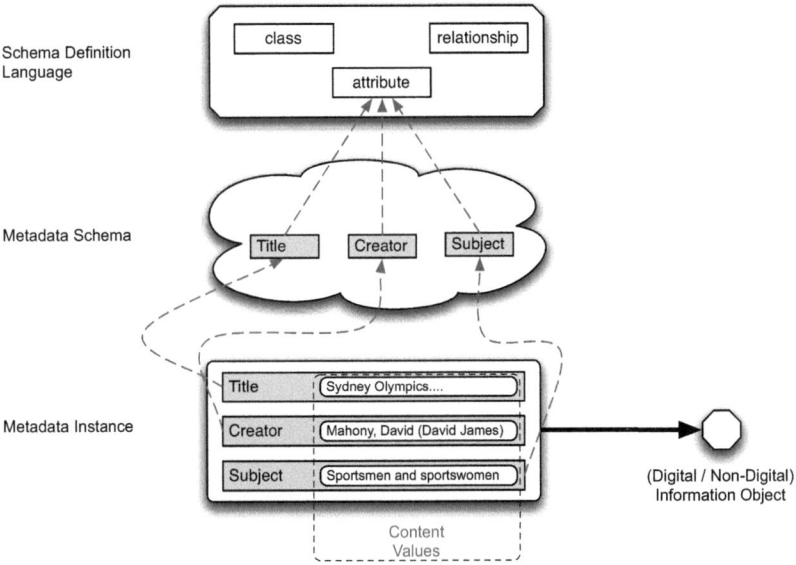

Figure 2.4: Overview of the three metadata building blocks

Because machines must *understand* a language, the primitives are not only syntactic constructs but also have a semantic definition.

The semantic definition of the term *language* already implies[6] that, in order to communicate with each other, there must exist an agreement on the meaning of a language's primitives. This is also the case for schema definition languages: usually there exist language standards or at least some kind of consensus[7]. Sample schema definition languages are XML Schema, SQL-DDL, the RDF Vocabulary Description Language (RDFS) [W3C04a], the Web Ontology Language (OWL) [W3C04c], or the Unified Modeling Language (UML) [OMG07].

Metadata Schema

Another metadata building block are the element definitions, which we denote as metadata schema. A metadata schema is simply a *set of elements* with a *precise semantic definition, optionally connected by some structure* [RB01]. The semantics of a schema is defined by the meanings of its elements. A schema usually defines the names of elements together with their semantics and optionally content rules that define how content values must be formulated (e.g., capitalisation, allowable content values). For the

---
[6]Language: the system of communication used by a particular community or country (The New Oxford American Dictionary)
[7]The W3C consortium for instance does not publish *standards* but *recommendations*.

encoding of the elements and their values, a schema can define syntax rules. If no such rules are defined, a schema is called *syntax independent* [NIS04].

At this point we must mention that the notion *metadata schema*, which originates from the database domain, is often named differently in other contexts or communities. For instance, knowledge workers, librarians or others working in the field of knowledge and information organisation tend to use the term *metadata vocabulary* for what we call metadata schema. These communities tend to regard metadata more from a linguistic rather than a technical point of view. Another very common notion is the term *ontology*, which has its origin[8] in the Artificial Intelligence domain and is defined as *a specification of a conceptualisation* [Gru93]. In its core, an ontology is the same as a schema: a set of elements connected by some structure. Apart from that, Noy and Klein [NK04] have identified several features that distinguish ontologies from schemes in a database sense: the first and probably the most important one is that ontologies are logical systems that define a set of axioms that enable automated reasoning over a set of given facts. Second, ontologies usually have richer data models involving representation primitives such as inverse properties. And third, ontology development is a much more decentralised and collaborative approach than schema development, which opens the potential for reusing existing ontology definitions. As a consequence of these different perceptions, we can also find different names for the languages used for defining metadata elements: *vocabulary definition language* and *ontology definition language* are examples for that.

Despite these different perceptions, we believe that the term *metadata schema* is appropriate for the purpose of this work because it regards metadata interoperability mainly from a technical perspective. Stronger than the term *vocabulary*, it emphasises that metadata elements have a technical grounding in information systems, which is a significant aspect when metadata interoperability should be achieved also on a technical level. Weaker then the term *ontology* it sets the limits for the underlying technical system. It encompasses logical system in the AI sense (e.g., First Order Logic, Description Logics) but also other, in practice more widespread, systems such as relational database schemes or XML schemes. However, in this work the term *metadata schema* does not refer to traditional database schemes only. We rather regard it is a common denominator for all the previously mentioned terms.

Metadata Instance

Continuing with the metadata building blocks, we can identify a third one — the *metadata instance*. A metadata instance holds a set of metadata elements drawn from a metadata schema, and adjacent content values. These element-value combinations form a metadata description about a certain information object. As already mentioned, the rules for creating such metadata instances are imposed by the metadata schema it is related to. If there exists such a relationship, we say that a metadata instance *corresponds* to a schema.

---

[8]The term *ontology* actually originates from Philosophy; in the AI domain it has its technical origin.

2.2.2 The Appearance of Metadata in Information Systems

Metadata are *information objects* that are designed for, persistent in, retrieved from, and exchanged between information systems. The form of appearance of metadata in information systems is defined through information models on various levels. In a typical information system we can identify four such levels: the physical, the logical, the programming/representation, and the conceptual level.

On the lowest level — the *physical level* — metadata are bits and bytes that are represented in memory, written to disks, and transmitted over wires. The system components that are working on this level are mainly concerned with optimising heap allocation, assigning records to file partitions and building indices for efficient retrieval. Thus, the information model on this level comprises concepts like format, files, records, or indices.

The physical level is usually hidden from application developers through the *logical level*. This is the level where database management systems are located. Information models such as the Relational Data Model [Cod70] provide the basis for creating technically precise and complete information models for a certain target domain. A metadata schema is defined using a data definition language and represented through a set of relation schemes. The metadata instances are described as sets of tuples contained in tables. Besides providing the necessary transparency from the underlying physical model, the logical level organises metadata efficiently (e.g., through normalisation) and introduces important features for application developers, such as data consistency, concurrency control, and transactions. However, metadata are scattered in tables that do not directly reflect the application domain[9] and must be aggregated into higher level, conceptual entities when being processed by applications.

On the *programming/representation level*, the constituents of conceptual schema models are manifested or presented in various forms: metadata schemes can be transformed into code of a certain (object-oriented) programming language and reflect the application domain in terms of classes or types while metadata descriptions become run-time objects. Metadata elements and their contents can also be encoded using a certain mark-up language such as XML or be represented on the Web using HTML. This requires metadata descriptions to be adapted to certain programming and document models (e.g., W3C DOM), and metadata schemes to be modelled using the modelling language (e.g., Java syntax, XML Schema, DTD) imposed by the programming/representation technology.

A metadata schema on the *conceptual level* resembles real-world entities with their properties and relationships among entities. The TV-Anytime standard for instance, which is used in the illustrative example in Section 2.1, defines real-world entities such as `Video` or `Creator` and properties such as `GivenName` or `FirstName`. Common languages for creating conceptual models are the Entity-Relationship Model [Che76] or the Unified Modelling Language [OMG07].

---
[9] Also called *domain of discourse* or *universe of discourse*.

Metadata — A Model Perspective

All these levels have in common that the information elements of a metadata schema, i.e., its elements and their relationships, are implemented in terms of a data model. Such a *data model for metadata* — further called metadata *model* — encapsulates the defined elements of a metadata schema, represents their semantics (their meaning) in a formal way, and provides a syntax for serialising metadata descriptions. The semantic interpretation of a metadata model is given through the mapping of the model elements to the corresponding entities in a certain application domain. The syntax of a metadata schema, i.e., the legal elements and rules how and what values can be assigned to elements, is defined using a certain notation, which can be symbolic (e.g., words, formulas), textual (e.g., natural language sentences), or graphical (e.g., diagram).

Schema definition languages occur on each information level and are used for expressing information models. The core of such a language is its meta-model — we call it metadata *meta-model* — which is the machine-internal representation of the language. It reflects the language primitives (abstract syntax) together with a concrete notation (concrete syntax) and semantics. Further it defines and constrains the allowable structure of models. The semantics or interpretation of a language is the mapping of the meta-model's (abstract syntax) elements to the language's primitives. Semantic definitions of models may feature varying degrees of formality, ranging from natural language descriptions to formal languages or mathematics. Especially from an interoperability point of view, rigid and semantic precise definitions enable consistent interpretation across system boundaries [Sei03].

Metadata models and meta-models are arranged on different levels that are orthogonal to the previously mentioned levels of information. On the lowest level we can find metadata (descriptions) that are (valid) instances of a metadata model (e.g., Java classes, UML model, database relations) that reflects the elements of a certain metadata schema. The metadata model itself is a valid instance of a metadata meta-model being part of a certain schema definition language. Due to this abstraction, it is possible to create meta-model representations of metadata (e.g., metadata instances of an UML model can also be represented as instances of the UML meta-model).

The MOF specification [OMG06a] offers a definition for these different levels: *M0* is the lowest level, the level of metadata instances (e.g., Title=Lake Placid 1980, Alpine Skiing, I. Stenmark). *M1* holds the models for a particular application; i.e., metadata schemes (e.g., definition of the field Title) are M1 models. Modelling languages reside on level *M2* — their abstract syntax or meta-model can be considered as *model of a particular modelling system* (e.g., definition of the language primitive *attribute*). On the topmost-level, at *M3*, we can find universal modelling languages in which modelling systems are specified (e.g., core constructs, primitive types). Figure 2.5 illustrates the four levels, their constituents and dependencies.

Regarding these abstraction levels, the remaining question is how the abstract syntax (*meta-meta-model*) of an M3 modelling language is expressed. In general, there are two options for defining a meta-model: either by using a different modelling mechanism (e.g., context-free grammars for programming

2.2. Unveiling the Notion of Metadata

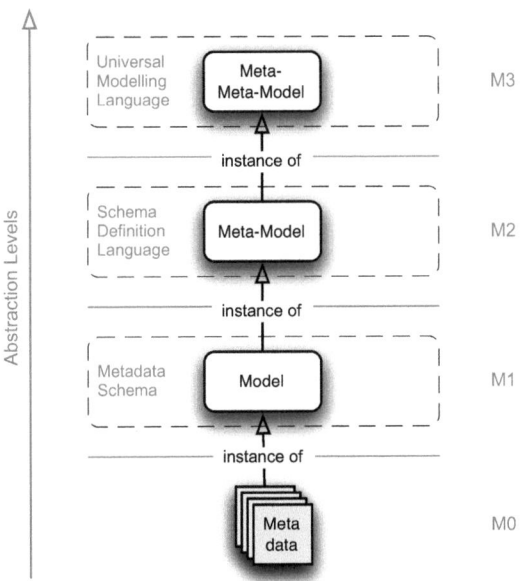

Figure 2.5: Metadata building blocks from a model perspective

languages, formal semantics or an explicit set of axioms and deduction rules for logic-based languages) or by using its own modelling language. In the latter case, the elements of a metamodel are expressed in the same language the metamodel is describing. This is called a *reflexive metamodel* [Sei03] because the elements of a modelling language can be expressed using a (minimal) set of modelling elements. An example for such an approach is the UML metamodel, which is based on the UML Infrastructure Library [OMG06c], which in turn is the minimal reflexive metamodel for UML.

A Selection of Schema Definition Languages

Table 2.1 gives an overview of a selected set of schema definition languages, which can be assigned to the M2 level. For each each language we describe its *concrete syntax*, i.e., how language elements are represented. Further we outline how the *semantics* is defined for each language, assuming that the available options are: natural language, formal semantics (i.e., precise mathematical definitions), reference implementations, and test suites. Finally, we describe the machine-internal representation of a modelling language: its *meta-model* or *abstract syntax*. We outline the meta-model's type (e.g., object-oriented, semantic network-based) and which model construct categories (structural, behavioural) it supports. Further we give an overview of its main model elements, and sketch out if the model is defined reflexively.

		Conceptual					Programming / Representation		Logical		
		UML	ER	Topic Maps	RDF/S	OWL	Java SE 6	XML Schema	SQL-DDL	DL	CL
Abstract Syntax (Meta-Model)	Model Type	Object Oriented	ER-dedicated graph	Semantic Network based / labelled graph	Semantic Network based / labelled graph	Semantic Network based / labelled graph	Object-Oriented	Hierarchical	Relational Model	Logics	Logics
	Model Constructs Categories	Structural & Behavioural	Structural	Structural	Structural	Structural	Structural & Behavioural	Structural	Structural (Behavioural)	Structural	Structural
	Main Model Elements	Class, Composite Structure, Component, Deployment, Activity, Interaction, State Machine, Use Case	Entity Sets, Attributes, Relationships	Topic, Association, Occurrence, TopicMap	Statement, BlankNode, Graph, Property, Literal, Resource, Class, Datatype, Bag, Seq, Alt, List	Ontology, Class, Datatype- & Object-Property, Individual, Restriction	Class, Interface, Field, Method, Annotation, Enum, Package	Data types, Simple Type, Complex Type, Element, Attribute	Relation, Attribute, Schema, Tuple, Domain	Facts, Axioms	Phrases, Terms, Atoms, Sentences,
	Reflexive Definition	Yes (via M3 level)	No	No	Yes	Yes	No	Yes	No	No	No
Concrete Syntax		Graphical Notation	Graphical Notation	XML, HyTime	RDF/XML, N3, N-Triple	RDF/XML, N3, N-Triple	Java Syntax	XML	SQL Syntax	DL Syntax	CLIF, CGIF, XCL
Semantics		Natural language	Formal	Formal	Formal	Formal	Natural language, Reference Implementation	Natural language	Formal	Formal	Formal

Table 2.1: A selection of schema definition languages and their characteristics

The Unified Modeling Language (UML) [OMG07] and the Entity Relationship Model (ER) [Che76] are used for the conceptual modelling of software systems and therefore employ a graphical syntactic notation. Topic Maps [ISO06c], RDFS [W3C04a], and OWL [W3C04c] are conceptual languages that allow the modelling of metadata schemes in terms of semantic networks, which requires that their machine-internal representation is graph-based. Other common features are the fact that their semantics is formally defined and that their syntax is XML based, while RDF also provides other syntaxes such as N3 [BL98] or Triple [SD02].

Java is a representative for the programming part of the programming/representation level. Its syntax and semantics are defined in [GJSB05]; since Java version 6, the Java API also comprises a meta-model [Jav06, BU04] that reflects the structural and behavioral primitives of the Java language. Another modeling language for defining metadata schemes on the presentation level is XML Schema. Its semantics in natural language, as well as its hierarchical meta-model (abstract syntax) are defined in [W3C06].

A prominent representative of languages on the logical level is SQL [ISO03b], or more precisely, the

2.3. Metadata Interoperability   21

SQL Data Definition Language (SQL DDL). Its meta-model is the relational model[10], which is semantically defined through the relational algebra.

For creating knowledge bases, logical languages such as Description Logics (DL) [BCM+03] or Common Logics (CL) [ISO05] can be applied for defining schemes in terms of knowledge graphs. Naturally, their semantics is defined formally; while the syntax of DL is simply symbolic, CL defines the Common Logic Interchange Format (CLIF), the Conceptual Graph Interchange Format (CGIF), and the Extended Common Logic Markup Language (XCL) for the syntactic representation and exchange of CL schema definitions.

2.2.3 Basic Observations

Previously, we have identified three metadata building blocks: metadata instances, metadata schemes, and schema definition languages. When applying a technical view on these blocks, we note that a metadata description is in fact an instance of a metadata model, which in turn is an instance of a metadata meta-model. We can conceive metadata as information objects with three abstraction levels: metadata instances reside on the M0 level, metadata models on the M1 level, and metadata meta-models on the M2 level.

We can summarise this section with two main observations: first, the choice of the schema definition language directly affects the appearance of metadata information objects in an information system. This is because there is a direct technical (instance-of) dependency between metadata instances, metadata schemes, and schema definition languages. Second, although some languages overlap in certain aspects (e.g., graph-based meta-model, support for behavioural modelling constructs), there are exist discrepancies between their abstract and concrete syntax, and in the way their semantics is defined. This implies that an automatic translation between metadata schemes expressed in different modelling languages is a problematic task. For instance, it will require human intervention to find a work-around for translating graph-based to hierarchical tree-like models; a tree is a special kind of a graph, but not vice versa.

2.3 Metadata Interoperability

We have claimed that metadata interoperability is the prerequisite for uniform access to digital media in multiple heterogeneous information systems. Hence, for solutions that aim at establishing uniform access, achieving metadata interoperability is the necessary prerequisite. Before discussing various techniques for achieving interoperability, we first investigate the notion of metadata interoperability in literature and come up with an appropriate definition in Section 2.3.1. Thereafter, in Section 2.3.2, we analyse in detail the various forms of heterogeneities that impede metadata interoperability.

---

[10]In fact, vendors of database management systems employ their own, system-specific, meta-models. But usually they are still based on the relational model.

2.3.1 Uniform Access To Digital Media

In the context of information systems, interoperability literally denotes the *ability of a system to work with or use parts of other systems*[11]. Also in literature we can find similar definitions: for the digital libraries domain Baker et al. [BBB+02] summarise various interoperability viewpoints as *the potential for metadata to cross boundaries between different information contexts*. Other authors from the same domain define interoperability as *being able to exchange metadata between two or more systems without or with minimal loss of information and without any special effort on either system* [NIS04, ALC00] or as *the ability to apply a single query syntax over descriptions expressed in multiple descriptive formats* [HL01].

The notion of interoperability can further be subdivided: for Baker et al. [BBB+02], achieving interoperability is a problem to be resolved on three main levels: the *transport and exchange* level (e.g., protocols), the metadata *representation* level (e.g., syntactic binding, encoding language), and the level of metadata with their *attribute space* (e.g., schema elements) and *value space* (e.g., controlled vocabularies). Based on the perspective of heterogeneities in information systems, Sheth and Larson [SL90] and Ouksel and Sheth [OS99] present four main classes of interoperability concerns: *system interoperability* dealing with system heterogeneities such as incompatible platforms, *syntactic interoperability* dealing with machine-readable aspects of data representation, *structural interoperability* dealing with data structures and data models, and *semantic interoperability*. Tolk [Tol06] proposes another view consisting of six levels: *no interoperability* on the lowest level, *technical interoperability* (communication infrastructure established) on level one, *syntactic interoperability* (common structure to exchange information) on level two, *semantic interoperability* (common information model) on level three, *pragmatic interoperability* (context awareness) on level four, *dynamic interoperability* (ability to comprehend state changes) on level five, and *conceptual interoperability* (fully specified, but implementation independent model) on level six. Miller [Mil00] detaches interoperability from the technical level and introduces, alongside *technical* and *semantic* interoperability, several flavours of interoperability: *political/human*, *inter-community*, *legal*, and *international* interoperability.

Based on its literal meaning, the definitions in literature, and considering the technical characteristics of metadata information objects described in Section 2.2.2, we define metadata interoperability as follows:

Definition 2.1 *Metadata interoperability is a qualitative property of metadata information objects that enables systems and applications to work with or use these objects across system boundaries.*

With this definition we clearly distinguish our conception of metadata interoperability, which is settled on the information level, from system level interoperability issues such as communication infrastructures, hardware or software platform incompatibilities.

---

[11] According to the Merriam-Webster Online Dictionary (http://www.m-w.com/) and the Oxford Online Reference (http://www.oxfordreference.com/)

2.3.2 Heterogeneities impeding Interoperability

The heterogeneities to be eliminated in order to provide interoperability have already been identified in the early ages of database research. A first in-depth analysis has been provided by Sheth and Larson [SL90]. Throughout the years they have been investigated more deeply (e.g., [OS99]), and also regained attention in related domains, such as Artificial Intelligence (e.g., [Wac03, VJBCS97]). In Figure 2.6, we provide a classification of the predominant heterogeneities mentioned in literature from a model-centric perspective. We recall that there is an instance-of relationship between metadata instances, metadata schemes, and schema definition languages, i.e., metadata are instances of metadata models, and metadata models are instances of metadata meta-models. Generalising these relationships, we can distinguish between *model level* and *instance level* heterogeneities as a first dimension for our classification. For the second dimension we differentiate between two classes of heterogeneities: *structural heterogeneity* caused by the distinct structural properties of models and *semantic heterogeneity* occuring because of conflicts in the intended meaning of model elements or content values in distinct interpretation contexts.

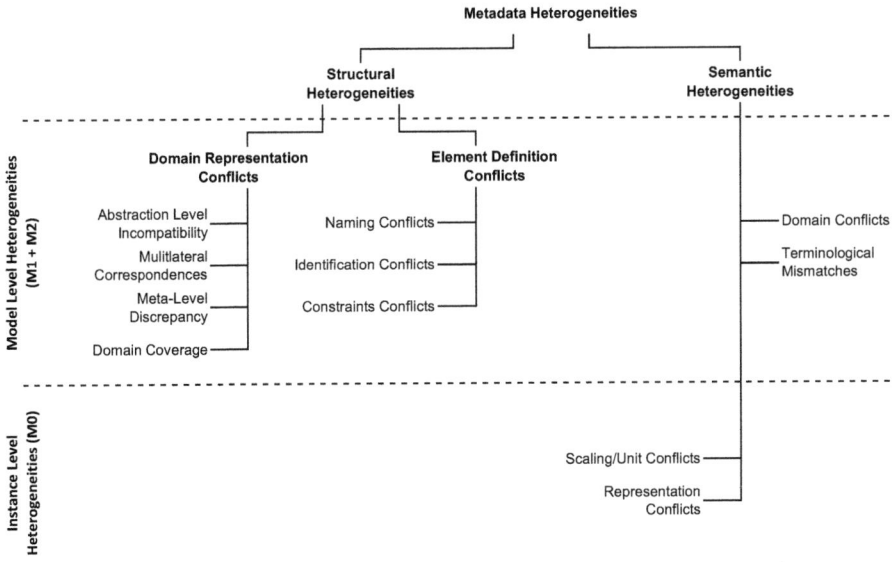

Figure 2.6: Structural and semantic metadata heterogeneities on the model and the instance level

Structural Heterogeneities

Structural heterogeneities on the model level occur because of model incompatibilities. A model mainly consists of its atomic elements (e.g., entities, attributes, relationships) and the combination or arrangement of these elements forming a certain structure for representing a particular domain of interest. That being the case, we can group structural heterogeneities occurring between distinct models into *element definition conflicts*, which are conflicts rooted in the definitions of a model (naming, identification, constraints), and *domain representation conflicts*, which occur because domain experts arrange model elements that reflect the constituents of a certain domain in various ways and detail. In the following we will further analyse these two groups of structural heterogeneities.

Naming Conflicts We denote conflicts that occur because model elements representing the same real-world entity are given different names as naming conflicts. On the level of schema definition languages (M2), distinct meta-models assign different names to language primitives that are used to model the same real-world facts. UML for instance defines the primitive *Class*, while ER uses *EntitySets* to capture the same kind of real-world concepts. Also on the level of metadata schemes (M1), distinct metadata models might assign different names to elements representing the same real world concepts. In the examples presented in Section 2.1, the model elements that represent the image's descriptions are labelled Synopsis in the TV-Anytime, Description in the Dublin Core, and Info in the proprietary schema.

Identification Conflicts A special case of naming conflicts are those dealing with unique identification of model elements. On the M2 level, depending on the language used for defining a model, elements are identifiable either by their name only (e.g., ER, SQL-DDL) or by some (fully) qualified identifier (e.g., XMLS, OWL). Identification conflicts can also arise on the M1 level of metadata schemes. In our example, the TV-Anytime schema comprises model elements that are fully qualified via their namespace. The elements in the proprietary model, i.e., the tables and columns, are identified by their names only.

Constraints Conflicts Element definition conflicts that occur because distinct models provide different possibilities of defining constraints are denoted as constraints conflicts. An example for an M2 constraint is the ability of a schema to import other schema definitions. This is possible in languages such as XML Schema or OWL but not in ER. Incompatible primary keys, conflicting references or domain constraints could lead to the same type of conflict on the M1 level of metadata schemes.

Abstraction Level Incompatibilities Abstraction level incompatibilities belong to the group of domain representation conflicts and turn up when the same real world entities are arranged in different generalisation hierarchies or aggregated differently into model elements. An example for this type of conflict on the M2 level is the ability to define attributes and relationships in various languages: while ER (attribute and relationship) and OWL (datatypeProperty and objectProperty) define primitives for both

2.3. Metadata Interoperability

language features, XML Schema (`attribute`) and Java (`field`) subsume these features under a single primitive. Abstraction level incompatibilities at the M1 level, the level of metadata models, occur for instance when one metadata model aggregates the creator of a digital resource into single entity `creator` as it is the case with Dublin Core, while other models such as TV-Anytime and also MPEG-7 distinguish between `Persons` and `Organisations`, both being a specialisation of the concept `Agent`.

Multilateral Correspondences Another domain representation conflict, which is a direct result of the previously mentioned abstraction level incompatibilities, are multilateral correspondences. On each level, an element in one model can correspond to multiple elements in another model and vice versa. In our example there is such a correspondence between the Dublin Core `creator` element and the TV-Anytime elements `GivenName` and `FamilyName`. This is because in the TV-Anytime metadata description, these elements are used in the context of a `CreditsItem` element that is taking the role of an `author`.

Meta-Level Discrepancy Domain representation conflicts that occur because certain model elements do not have any direct correspondences in another model are subsumed under meta-level discrepancy. This, however, does not necessarily mean that the other model cannot capture the same information about a certain domain. Real-world concepts represented as elements in one model (e.g., author as attribute) could be modelled differently in another model (e.g., author as entity) or even being captured as contents of a model element on the instance level. In our example, the Dublin Core and the proprietary schema store the location of the Olympic Games as content value with the field `Title` while TV-Anytime defines a model element `CreationLocation`, which captures this kind of information. We can distinguish the following kinds of meta-level discrepancies: content-value / attribute, entity / attribute, and content value / entity discrepancy.

Domain Coverage When there exist no correspondences between model elements, we speak of domain coverage conflicts. This happens when real-world concepts reflected in one model are left out in the other model, although both models were designed for the same semantic domain. In our example, the TV-Anytime description does not give any evidence about the image's size while the proprietary one does.

Semantic Heterogeneities

Semantic heterogeneities on the model level are conflicts occurring because of the differences in the semantics of models. We recall that a model's semantics is defined by its semantic domain and the semantic mappings (interpretations) from the domain entities to the model elements. The semantic domain provides the meaning for each model element and can contain language expressions, in the case of schema definition languages, or real-world entities, in the case of metadata models.

Domain Conflicts When domains overlap, subsume, or aggregate others, or when domains are incompatible, we speak of domain conflicts. An example for such a conflicts on the M2 level is the expressiveness of languages; with languages that have a rich domain, i.e., an expressive set of language primitives, we are able to model things that are not expressible with other languages having less powerful primitives. With OWL, for instance, it is possible to express that two classes are equivalent or that one class is the union of two other classes. Other languages such as XML Schema or Java do not have built-in language constructs to indicate such relationships. Obviously, domain conflicts can also occur among metadata models on the M1 level. If one model reflects the domain of electronic billing and another one the domain of multimedia contents, it is unlikely that there are any meaningful correspondences among these models.

Terminological Mismatches Terminological mismatches are another kind of semantic heterogeneity occurring on both model levels: synonym conflicts occur if the same domain concept is mapped to model elements with different names, homonym conflicts exist if different domain concepts are mapped to model elements with the same names.

An example of a homonym conflict on the language level is the polymorphic concept of *overloading* that appears in object-oriented languages like Java. These languages support polymorphic functions whose operands (parameters) can have more than one type. Types can be arranged in a sub-type hierarchy and symbols (e.g., field-names, method-signatures) may be *overloaded*, meaning that the same symbol is used to denote semantically different behaviour [CW85]. In Java, for instance, the *equals* method is usually overwritten and implemented differently for each class, which could lead to unintended behaviour during runtime.

An example for a synonym conflict on the schema level is the usage of distinct terms to denote the same semantic concept. In our example, the proprietary schema uses the term `author` and the Dublin Core schema the term `creator` to represent the person who has created the particular image.

Scaling/Unit Conflicts Semantic heterogeneity occurring on the metadata M0 instance level, when different scaling systems are used to measure content values, are called scaling or unit conflicts. In our examples, the dimensions of the described images are represented in pixels in the proprietary schema and in centimetre in the Dublin Core schema. Even if the images had semantically the same dimension, the content values would be different.

Representation Conflicts Representation conflicts are a result of using different encoding schemes for content values. For instance, two date values, which are semantically the same, could be represented differently in each system (e.g., `date=01.01.2007` or `date=2007/01/01`).

2.4 Techniques for Achieving Metadata Interoperability

Over decades experts working in the field of metadata interoperability have developed methods and solutions to overcome the previously described heterogeneities. The goal of this section is to set up a framework for categorising existing techniques according to their common characteristics.

Metadata interoperability can be achieved by eliminating the structural and semantic heterogeneities at the metadata meta-model (M2), metadata model (M1), and the metadata instance (M0) level. We can identify three principal ways to attain interoperability among models: (i) agreement on a certain metadata model, (ii) introduction of, and agreement on a common meta-model, and (iii) reconciliation of the structural and semantic heterogeneities. Table 2.2 provides an overview of a variety of techniques to achieve metadata interoperability and classifies them according to the three previously mentioned categories. In the following sections we will focus on each of these techniques and discuss their characteristics.

	Model Agreement	Meta-Model Agreement		Model Reconciliation
M2 – Schema Definition Languages		Standardised Language (e.g. OWL, UML, XML Schema)	Metadata Meta-Meta Model (e.g. MOF)	Abstract Metadata Model (e.g. DCMI Abstract Model)	Language Mapping
M1 – Metadata Schemes	Hybrid Metadata System (e.g. MPEG-7, TV-Anytime)	Standardised Metadata Schema (e.g. DC, TEI, MODS)	Global Conceptual Model (e.g. CIDOC-CRM, FRBR)	Metadata Crosswalk, Schema Mapping
			Metadata Framework (e.g. MPEG-21, METS, OAIS)	
			Application Profile (e.g. DC Collection Profile)	
M0 – Metadata			Value Encoding Schema (e.g. ISO-Norms, RFC-Specifications)	Instance Transformation
			Controlled Vocabulary (e.g. LCSH, DCC, MeSH)	
			Authority Record (e.g. LOC Authorities, Deutsche Personennormdatei (PND))	

Table 2.2: A categorisation of metadata interoperability techniques

2.4.1 Model Agreement

Standardisation is a strong form of establishing an agreement by means of consensus building and an intuitive, technically effective and economically well-recognised way to achieve interoperability. It requires accredited institutions (e.g., World Wide Web Consortium (W3C), Object Management Group

(OMG), International Standardisation Organization (ISO), German Institute for Standardization (DIN)) for building consensus, setting a standard, and eventually assuring its uniform implementation. Regarding the building blocks of metadata, standardisation can cover the language level (*standardised language*), the schema level (*standardised metadata schema*), the instance level, or several levels (*hybrid metadata system*).

Standardised Language

In Section 2.2.2, we have already shown a representative selection of various types of schema definition languages ranging from programming languages (e.g., Java), over conceptual modelling (e.g., UML) to logical languages (e.g., Description Logics).

Each schema definition language defines a set of language primitives and, as in natural languages, postulates that multiple parties agree on their semantics. This guarantees interoperability on the level of schema definition languages. Consequently, metadata that are expressed in the same language can be processed by any application that is aware of that language.

Agreement on the M2 level of schema definition languages is typically enforced through various forms of standardisation. Programming languages are often specified by companies (e.g., Java by Sun Inc.) or standardised by standards institutes (e.g., ANSI-C by the American National Standards Institute (ANSI)). Languages designed for data representation and exchange are standardised by international consortia (e.g., W3C, OMG).

Standardised Metadata Schema

If there is an agreement or consensus on a *set of metadata elements* on the M1 level, and this agreement is manifested in a standard, we speak of a standardised metadata schema. In Table 2.3, we present a selection of metadata standards used in various domains. For each standard we indicate its application domain, which requirements or purpose it fulfils, and to which schema definition languages it is bound in order to express a metadata schema also on a technical level. Further we show which standardisation body maintains a standard, the year of initial publication, and the current version together with the year when this version has been released.

Most standardised metadata schemes are designed for a specific domain and a certain purpose. The VRA Core Standard [VRA07], for instance, is tailored to the cultural heritage community and comprises metadata elements for the description of works of visual culture as well as the images that document them. The Dublin Core Metadata Element Set [DC06] is an example for a schema that is broad and generic enough to describe a variety of resources across domains.

Besides Dublin Core and VRA, our selection also comprises the Guidelines for Electronic Text Encoding and Interchange (TEI) [TEI07], a standard mainly used in the humanities and social sciences for representing texts and data about texts in digital form. In the case of TEI, the standardisation body is the consortium that has developed this metadata standard.

2.4. Techniques for Achieving Metadata Interoperability

Name	Application Domain	Purpose	M2 Language Bindings	Standardisation Body	Current Version	Year of Initial Publication
Dublin Core Element Set (DC)	domain independent	description of a wide range of resources	XMLS, RDF/S	ISO/NISO	1.1 (2008)	1998
Visual Resources Association Core (VRA Core)	cultural heritage	description of works of visual culture and images that document them	XMLS	VRA Data Standards Committee	4.0 (2007)	1996
Guidelines for Electronic Text Encoding and Interchange (TEI)	humanities, social sciences, linguistics	representation of texts in digital form	XMLS	Text Encoding Initiative Consortium	P5 (2007)	1990
Learning Objects and Metadata (LOM)	eLearning	description of digital or non-digital learning objects	XMLS, RDF/S	IEEE	1.0 (2002)	1997
Sharable Content Object Reference Model (SCORM)	eLearning	aggregation, description, and sequencing of learning objects	XMLS	Advanced Distributed Learning Initative (ADL)	3rd Edition (2004)	2000
Online Information Exchange (ONIX)	publishing / retail (books and serials)	provision of product information to online retailers	DTD, XMLS	EDItEUR group	release 2.1 (2005)	2000
MARC 21 Format for Bibliographic Data	(digital) libraries	exchange of bibliographic data	XMLS (MARCXML)	Network Development & MARC Standards Office	update no. 7 (2006)	1999
Metadata Object Description Schema (MODS)	digital libraries	subset of MARC fields using language-based tags	XMLS	Network Development & MARC Standards Office	3.2 (2006)	2002
Maschinelles Austauschformat für Bibliotheken (MAB)	(digital) libraries in german speaking countries	exchange of bibliographic data	XMLS (MABxml)	Expertgroup for data formats	2 (2001)	1973
Format for Bibliographic Records (RFC1807)	universities, r&d organisations	description of technical reports	XMLS	Network Working Group	1.0 (revised in 2002)	1995
Geographic Information Metadata (ISO 19115)	geographic information systems (GIS)	documentation of geographic digital resources	XMLS, GML	ISO	1.0 (2003)	2003

Table 2.3: A representative selection of metadata standards

As representatives for the eLearning domain, we have selected the Sharable Content Object Reference Model (SCORM) [ADL07] and the Learning Objects Metadata (LOM) [IEE02] standards. While the first standardises the aggregation and sequencing aspects of learning objects, the latter is mainly concerned with their description. Further, the development of SCORM is driven by the Advanced Distributed

Learning Initiative[12], which embraces several standardisation bodies, including IEEE[13].

The MARC 21 Format for Bibliographic Data [LOC07c], a metadata standard in the libraries domain for the purpose of exchanging bibliographic data, is maintained by the Network Development and MARC standardisation office. MAB and its successor MAB 2 [DNB07a] represent the German counterparts to the family of MARC standards and have been developed by a group of library domain experts. The Metadata Object Description Schema (MODS) [LOC07d] is a metadata standard that defines a subset of the MARC fields using language-based instead of numeric-based tags. RFC1807 [NWG95] is a very old bibliographic metadata standard mainly used in universities and research organisations for describing technical reports.

Online Information Exchange (ONIX) [EDI07] is another metadata standard and is situated at the borderline of bibliographic description and electronic commerce. Its main purpose is to provide product information about books and serials to online retailers. The standard is maintained by an international group of book retailers and vendors, called EDItEUR.

Finally, from the domain of geographic information systems we have selected ISO 19115 [ISO03a], a metadata standard designed for the documentation of geographic digital resources.

The technical implementation of a metadata standard is bound to one or more schema definition languages, which provide the facilities to represent a standard's metadata elements in a machine-readable way. Regarding our selection of metadata standards, we can observe that the majority is bound to XML Schema. Some (e.g., DC and LOM) also provide bindings for RDF/S, and the ISO 19115 standard even defines the Geography Markup Language (GML) [OGC04], which is an extension of the XML grammar.

Hybrid Metadata System

We denote metadata standards that cannot be assigned to a single level but span multiple levels as hybrid metadata systems.

An important representative for a hybrid metadata system is the MPEG-7 [ISO07b] standard. It spans the M2 and M1 levels and defines a set of metadata schemes (MPEG-7 Description Schemes) for creating multimedia metadata descriptions as well as a schema definition language called the MPEG-7 Description Definition Language (DDL), which is an extension of XML Schema. This language provides the solid descriptive foundation for users to create their own metadata schemes, compatible with the MPEG-7 standard [Kos03].

The TV-Anytime standard is a representative for a hybrid metadata system that spans the M1 and M0 levels. On the M1 level, it heavily reuses elements defined by the MPEG-7 standard and tailors them to the requirements of the broadcasting domain. Further it defines a set of classification schemes, which are in fact controlled vocabularies allowing the classification of telecast along various dimensions. Sample dimensions are a telecast's content (e.g., news, arts, religion/philosophies), its formal structure

---

[12] Advanced Distributed Learning Initiative: http://www.adlnet.gov/
[13] Institute of Electrical and Electronics Engineers (IEEE): http://www.ieee.org/

2.4. Techniques for Achieving Metadata Interoperability 31

(e.g., magazine, cartoon, show), or even its atmosphere (e.g., breathtaking, happy, humorous, innovative). The terms listed in the classification schemes are possible content values within metadata descriptions and can therefore be used as content values in M0-level metadata instances.

Instance Level Agreement

If several parties agree on a set of possible content values for M0 level metadata descriptions, we denote this as instance level agreement. In the real world, we can find various forms of agreements or standards on the instance level.

One frequently occurring form are *controlled vocabularies* such as the Library of Congress Subject Headings (LCSH) [LOC07b], the Dewey Decimal Classification System (DDC) [OCL07], or the Medical Subject Headings (MeSH) [NLM07]. The main goal of a controlled vocabulary is to support search and retrieval of resources by indexing them with terms taken from a vocabulary that has been designed by domain experts who posses expertise in the subject area. The complexity of a controlled vocabulary can range from a simple list of terms, over a hierarchical arrangement of terms (taxonomy), to systems that defined terms and the semantic relationships between them (thesaurus).

Authority control is another form of instance level agreement and very similar to controlled vocabularies. The goal is to disambiguate identical entities by linking the content values of metadata descriptions to uniquely identifiable authority records maintained and shared by a central authority. In the library domain, authority control is commonly used to relate potentially distinct names of one and the same person with a single uniquely identifiable entity. The Library of Congress Authorities [LOC07a] or the German Personennormdatei (PND) [DNB07b] are examples for centrally maintained directories of person names.

A *value encoding schema* is a form of instance level agreement, which defines exactly how to encode a certain type of content value. The ISO 8601 [ISO04] standard, for example, provides encoding rules for dates and times; the ISO 3166 [ISO06b] standard defines how to represent country names and their subdivisions. This kind of standardisation guarantees that machines can correctly interpret non-textual content values, such as dates and times, or abbreviated textual values representing some entity, such as country codes.

In theory, if all metadata in all information systems within a certain integration context were instances of a single standardised metadata schema expressed in a single schema definition language, and if also all content values used within the metadata instances were taken from a single controlled vocabulary, all the structural and semantic heterogeneities mentioned in Figure 2.6 would be resolved, at least technically.

2.4.2 Meta-Model Agreement

In real-world environments, we can observe that institutions often do not adhere to standards. Attempts to find an agreement for a standard often results in semantically weak minimum consensus schemes (e.g., the Dublin Core Element Set) or models with extensive and complex semantic domains (e.g., the CIDOC

Conceptual Reference Model (CRM) [ISO06a]). Often it is not practicable for institutions to agree on a certain model or apply an existing standard because they already have their proprietary solutions in place. In such a case, one possibility for achieving interoperability is not to agree on a model but on a common meta-model. For all existing proprietary models in place, instance-of relationships from a model to the common meta-model are established. Through this relationship, the elements of the proprietary models can then be manipulated as if they were elements of the meta-model. Therefore, meta-model agreement implicitly enables interoperability by creating correspondences between proprietary models via a common meta-model.

Metadata Meta-Meta Model

An example for such an approach on the M2 level of schema definition languages is the OMG Meta-Object Facility (MOF), which is a *universal modelling language in which modelling systems can be specified* [OMG06a]. It solves language mismatches by introducing the M3 level and by superimposing a metadata meta-meta model containing a set of elements for modelling language primitives. If the model elements of M2 schema definition languages are aligned with the elements of the M3 MOF model, it is possible to express metadata in terms of the more general MOF model.

Kensche et al. [KQCJ07] propose another model that serves as an M3 abstraction for particular metamodels on the M2 level. They relate certain metamodels (e.g., EER, OWL) with a generic meta-metamodel through generalisation and introduce *roles* to decorate M3 level elements with M2 specific properties that must be preserved.

Abstract Metadata Model

The specification of an abstract metadata model is another way of achieving interoperability. Such a model resides on the M2 level of schema definition languages and serves as a technical reference for the implementation of metadata schemes in information systems. If there is an agreement on such a meta-model in all information systems and all metadata schemes are expressed in terms of the elements provided by this model, the metadata information objects are interoperable at least from a structural point of view because they are technically represented in the same way. The DCMI Abstract Model [PNNJ05] is an example for an abstract metadata model. In a similar manner as RDF/S, it defines an information model for representing Dublin Core metadata in a machine-processable way.

Global Conceptual Model

Introducing a global conceptual model is a way of achieving interoperability on the M1 level of metadata schemes. All information systems to be integrated must align their metadata model elements with the more general elements defined in the global model, which formalises the notions in a certain domain and defines the concepts that appear in a certain integration context.

2.4. Techniques for Achieving Metadata Interoperability 33

The CIDOC CRM is an example for such a model being designed for the Cultural Heritage domain. It defines 81 entities and 132 properties, most of them on a very abstract level (e.g., physical thing, section definition). Another example for a global conceptual model is the Functional Requirements for Bibliographic Records (FRBR) [IFL97] model, which has been defined by the International Federation of Library Associations and Institutions. With its four key entities (work, expression, manifestation, item) it represents a generalised view of the bibliographic universe, independent of any cataloguing standard or implementation [Til04]. The Suggested Upper Merged Ontology (SUMO)[14] is also a global model that *will promote data interoperability, information search and retrieval, automated inferencing, and natural language processing* [NP01]. It defines high-level concepts such as object, continuousObject, process, or quantity. Another example for a global model approach is the Descriptive Ontology for Linguistic and Cognitive Engineering (DOLCE) [Won03].

Metadata Framework

A metadata framework *can be considered as a skeleton upon which various objects are integrated for a given solution* [CZ06] and is another way of achieving interoperability on the M1 level of metadata schemes. It typically provides a data model consisting of a set of abstract terms, and a description of the syntax and semantics of each model element. Again, the idea is to integrate existing metadata by aligning their model elements to a set of elements defined by the metadata framework. Examples for metadata frameworks are the MPEG-21 Multimedia Framework [ISO07a], the Metadata Encoding and Transmission Standard (METS) [LOC07e], or the Open Archival Information System (OAIS) [CCS02].

Application Profile

An application profile [HP00, BDH+01] is a special kind of model agreement. On the one hand, it is a schema consisting of data elements drawn from one or more standardised schemes, optimised for a particular application domain, whereas its focus is on the reuse of existing, standardised model elements. On the other hand, from a technical point of view, an application profile is a metadata model, which is an extension of a set of agreed upon meta-models.

Application profiles are created by application developers who declare how to apply standardised schema elements in a certain application context. Within an application profile one cannot create new model elements that do not exist elsewhere. If this is required, a new metadata schema containing these elements, must be created and maintained. Refinement of standard elements definitions is allowed. Developers can set the permitted range of values (e.g., special date formats, particular formats for personal names) and narrow or specify the semantic definition of the metadata elements. Application profiles are created with the intent of reuse and are tailored for specific purposes or certain user communities.

Example application profiles are the Dublin Core Collections Application Profile [DC07] for describing collections of physical or digital resources, the Eprints Application Profile [AJP07] for describing

---
[14]The Suggested Upper Merged Ontology: http://ontology.teknowledge.com/

scholarly publications held in institutional repositories, or the application profiles[15] that were created when METS was introduced in several digital libraries. An application profile created for the domain of annotations is described in [SHJK08].

2.4.3 Model Reconciliation

Often, especially in settings where the incentives for an agreement on standards are weak, neither model nor meta-model agreement are suitable interoperability techniques. The digital libraries domain, for instance, is such a domain: there is no central authority that can impose a metadata standard on all digital libraries. Such settings require other means for reconciling heterogeneities among models.

Language Mapping

If metadata schemes are expressed in different schema definition languages, mappings on the language level are required to transform the instances, i.e., the M1 level metadata models, from one linguistic representation to another. Because of the substantial structural and semantic discrepancies among schema definition languages (see Section 2.2.2), translation from one language into another can cause loss of valuable semantic information. Nevertheless, in literature we can find many approaches that focus on mappings between OWL and XML Schema [LF04], OWL and the Relational Model [MHS07], XML Schema and the Relational Model [ACL+07], Object Oriented Languages (e.g., UML, Java) and OWL [GDDD04], etc.

Schema Mapping

If an agreement on a certain model is not possible, schema mapping is an alternative to deal with heterogeneities among metadata schemes. In the digital libraries domain, *metadata crosswalks* have evolved as a special kind of schema mappings. A crosswalk is *a mapping of the elements, semantics, and syntax from one metadata schema to another* [NIS04]. The goal of crosswalks is to provide the ability to make elements defined in one metadata standard available to communities using related metadata standards. A complete or fully specified crosswalk consists of the semantic mapping between model elements and a metadata instance transformation specification [PL98]. In practice, however, crosswalks often define only the semantic mapping on the M1 level and leave the problem of instance transformation to the application developers.

Instance Transformation

In the context of mappings, instance transformation is the approach for achieving interoperability on the metadata instance level, when there is no agreement on value encoding schemes or other standardisation

---

[15]A list of METS application profiles is available at http://www.loc.gov/standards/mets/mets-registered-profiles.html

mechanisms. Instance transformations are functions that operate on the content values and perform a specified operation, such as the concatenation of the values of two fields (e.g., `GivenName=John`, `FamilyName=Doe`) into a single field (e.g., `Creator=John Doe`).

2.5 On the Quality of Interoperability Techniques

In this section, we focus on the quality of the previously mentioned interoperability techniques and analyse to what extent a certain technique can deal with the various kinds of heterogeneities discussed in Section 2.3.2.

For two reasons we restrict ourselves on techniques that enforce interoperability on the metadata model (M1) and instance level (M0): first, as we have generalised in Section 2.2.2, we can apply an abstract view on models on various levels and distinguish between model and instance level heterogeneities. This is because at the core of both, the schema definition language and the metadata schema, are in fact models. Therefore, we can analyse their potential of dealing with heterogeneities between models and their instances. The second reason is that in practice one can assume that all metadata can be transformed into a uniform language representation.

For determining the quality of an interoperability technique, we have analysed whether it can resolve a specific heterogeneity type. Table 2.4 summarises the results of this analysis: one dimension shows the various interoperability techniques, the other the heterogeneities grouped by their types. The dotted line separates the model (M1) and the instance level (M0) for both, techniques and heterogeneity types. The greyed areas represent the groups of heterogeneities described in Section 2.3.2.

2.5.1 Model Agreement Techniques

Model agreement techniques are an effective means for achieving interoperability. If all proprietary systems adapt their existing information systems in a way that their models fit into a hybrid metadata system, a standardised metadata schema, or an application profile, most heterogeneity problems can be resolved.

A fixed and semantically well defined set of given metadata elements resolves naming-, identification-, and constraints conflicts. Neither occur abstraction level incompatibilities, multilateral correspondences or meta-level discrepancies if there exists only one agreed-upon metadata model. If all involved parties use the same model, it cannot occur that some concepts are not available in a model, which implies that model agreement techniques also resolve domain coverage conflicts. Further, a standardised or agreed-upon schema or application profile can also resolve domain conflicts by fixing the semantic domain (e.g., application profile for the domain of videos or audio material).

The remaining semantic heterogeneity conflicts on the instance level (scaling/unit and representation conflicts) can also be resolved: through the combination of constraints on the model level and agreement on the instance level (value encoding, controlled vocabulary, authority record) it is possible to narrow

Chapter 2. Background

	M1 Level Interoperability Techniques						M0 Level Interoperability Techniques			
	Hybrid Metadata System (e.g. MPEG-7, TV-Anytime)	Standardised Metadata Schema (e.g. DC, TEI, MODS)	Global Conceptual Model (e.g. CIDOC-CRM, FRBR)	Metadata Framework (e.g. MPEG-21, METS, OAIS)	Application Profile (e.g. DC Collection Profile)	Metadata Crosswalk, Schema Mapping	Value Encoding Schema (e.g. ISO-Norms, RFC-Specifications)	Controlled Vocabulary (e.g. LCSH, DCC, MeSH)	Authority Record (e.g. LOC Authorities, Deutsche Personennormdatei (PND))	Instance Transformation
M1 Level Heterogeneities										
Naming Conflicts	■	■	■	■	■	■	□	□	□	□
Identification Conflicts	■	■	■	■	■	■	□	□	□	□
Constraints Conflicts	■	■	□	□	■	■	□	□	□	□
Abstraction Level Incompatibility	■	■	□	□	■	■	□	□	□	□
Mulitlateral Correspondences	■	■	□	□	■	■	□	□	□	□
Meta-Level Discrepancy	■	■	□	□	■	■	□	□	□	□
Domain Coverage	■	■	□	□	■	■	□	□	□	□
Domain Conflicts	■	■	■	□	■	■	□	□	□	□
Terminological Mismatches	■	■	■	■	■	■	□	□	□	□
M0 Level Heterogeneities										
Scaling/Unit Conflicts	■	□	□	□	□	□	■	■	■	■
Representation Conflicts	■	□	□	□	□	□	■	■	■	■

Table 2.4: The quality of various interoperability techniques

the domain of possible content values within a metadata description to a fixed set of values. Hybrid metadata systems, such as TV-Anytime, also span the M0 level by defining fixed classification schemes and therefore also provide interoperability on the instance level.

2.5.2 Meta-model Agreement Techniques

Meta-model agreement techniques such as global conceptual models or metadata frameworks are less powerful than model agreement techniques. Rather than agreeing on a certain model, their approach is to impose a meta-model and use generalisation relationships (e.g., `sub-class` or `sub-property`) to relate the elements of existing proprietary models to the elements of the common meta-model.

2.5. On the Quality of Interoperability Techniques

These alignment possibilities are very restricted: neither can they deal with instance level heterogeneities, nor can they handle structural heterogeneities. Figure 2.7 illustrates that problem based on the example presented in Section 2.1. It shows the TV-Anytime and the Dublin Core elements for representing the name of a person who has created a certain resource. The TV-Anytime model defines two separated fields GivenName and FamilyName, while the Dublin Core model defines only a single field Creator to capture the same information. A global conceptual model containing the elements Person and Name has been introduced to bridge this structural heterogeneity conflict. We can see that global conceptual models cannot deal with basic heterogeneity conflicts such as multilateral correspondences. It is not possible to relate the elements GivenName and FamilyName with the element Name in a way that machines can process their instance content values appropriately.

Other types of heterogeneities, which are not resolvable for meta-model agreement techniques, are meta-level discrepancies (e.g., Name modelled as entity instead of an attribute) and domain coverage conflicts. Concepts available in the global model may simply not be explicitly available in the proprietary models. The heterogeneities that can be resolved are abstraction level incompatibilities and, in the case of global conceptual models, domain conflicts if the models' domains are not completely incompatible. Unlike global conceptual models, metadata frameworks are domain independent and cannot resolve domain conflicts by imposing a certain domain. As we can see in the example, both interoperability approaches could resolve terminological mismatches by aligning terminologically conflicting elements to a common element in the global model (e.g., Creator sub-property Name).

In general, the problems with global conceptual models are manifold: first, it is hard to find a model that covers all possible ontological requirements of all systems in an integration context. Second, also the generic nature and complexity of global models can lead to varying interpretations and inconsistent alignments between the global conceptual models and the metadata schemes in place. Third, conceptual models (e.g., the CIDOC CRM) often lack of any technical specifications with the result that they are implemented differently in distinct systems. Meanwhile the belief on a success of global conceptual model approaches is decreasing: Wache [Wac03] asserts that *no global model can be defined in such a way that it fulfils all conceptual requirements of all possible information systems that are integrated in a certain domain*. Halevy et al. [HIST05] argue that *in large scale environments global models, which should enable interoperability, actually become the bottleneck in the process of achieving interoperability*. For a more detailed discussion of the problems encountered with global conceptual models, especially with the CIDOC CRM, we refer to [NH07].

2.5.3 Model Reconciliation Techniques

Schema mapping (metadata crosswalks) is powerful enough to produce the same interoperability quality as model agreement techniques. Provided that the underlying mapping mechanism is strong enough, schema mapping can deal with all kind of heterogeneities on the schema level such as different element names, different ways of identifying these elements, incompatible constraints definitions and all

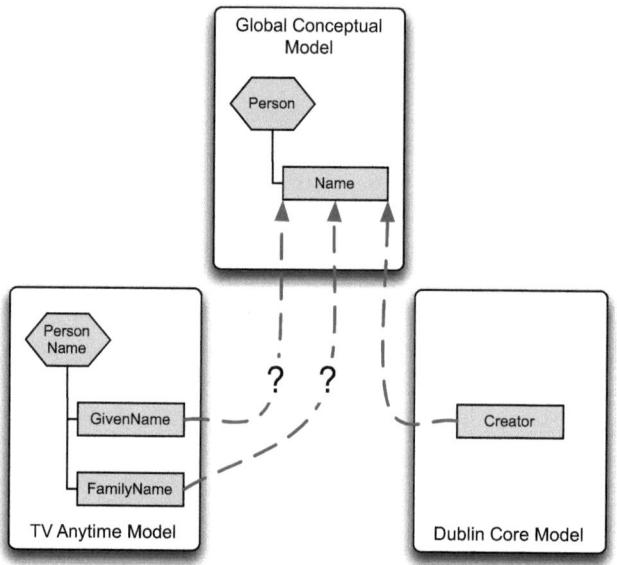

Figure 2.7: Example for achieving interoperability via a global conceptual model

the remaining conflicts ranging from abstraction level incompatibilities to terminological mismatches. In combination with instance transformation, it can also resolve semantic heterogeneities on the instance level, i.e., scaling/unit and representation conflicts.

2.5.4 Observations on the Quality of Interoperability Techniques

Regarding our analysis, we can observe that there exist various options for providing interoperability among heterogeneous metadata information objects. Each option has its special qualities and can be seen as complementary building block for achieving metadata interoperability. Standardised metadata schemes alone, for instance, cannot deal with instance level heterogeneities. Therefore they must be combined with value encoding schemes, controlled vocabularies, or authority records in order to address also the instance level. The same is the case for schema mappings or crosswalks; they operate only on the schema level and must be combined with instance transformation techniques to achieve maximum interoperability. Meta-model agreement techniques such as global conceptual models or metadata frameworks have the disadvantage that they provide only a restricted set of alignment relationships (sub-class, sub-property). Furthermore, they can hardly be combined with instance level interoperability techniques.

If we also consider the technical implementation effort that arises for each of the previously presented techniques — small effort for model agreement, large effort for model reconciliation — it turns out that model agreement or standardisation, both on the schema and the instance level, should be the prime choice. However, often this is not possible, because information systems are already in place or institutions do not have sufficient incentive to follow a certain standard. In such scenarios, the more labour intensive, but equally effective approach of metadata mapping, i.e., schema mapping in combination with instance transformation, is an appropriate way for achieving interoperability.

2.6 Summary

As we can clearly see from the discussions in this chapter, metadata interoperability affects all technical levels of metadata: the M2 level of schema definition languages, the M1 level of metadata schemes, and the M0 level of metadata instances. For achieving metadata interoperability, several types of structural and semantic heterogeneities must be resolved on each level. We distinguish between three categories of interoperability techniques: agreement on a certain model, agreement on a certain meta-model, and model reconciliation.

From our analysis, we can observe that model agreement techniques, such as hybrid metadata systems and standardised metadata schemes, as well as model reconciliation techniques cover large parts of possible heterogeneities, if they are combined with appropriate techniques on the instance level: metadata standards should be applied in combination with value encoding schemes, controlled vocabularies, or authority records. Metadata mapping should also consider M0 level heterogeneities and support instance transformation.

Global conceptual models and metadata frameworks provide only restricted means for relating source model elements with those of a global model and do not consider the instance level. Therefore, one outcome of our analysis is that these techniques are less powerful than metadata standardisation or mapping. Comparing standardisation and mapping, the clear disadvantage of mapping is its technical complexity. However, in open environments having no central standardisation authority, metadata mapping is the remaining, more complex but equally powerful technique.

The Web is such an open environment. It already exposes a multitude of autonomous, incompatible media repositories and it is unlikely that there will ever exist a single agreed-upon metadata schema. Like [FHM05], we also believe that in future, many institutions and organisations relying on a large number of diverse, interrelated media sources will make use of the Web architecture to access available repositories. Since, also in the Web context, the metadata information objects exposed by these repositories are not compatible by default, it requires novel mapping techniques that build upon the Web infrastructure and are powerful enough to deal with the heterogeneities we outlined in this chapter.

Chapter 3
Metadata Mapping

In the previous chapter, we have defined *metadata* as information objects that describe resources. Example resources are digital images, videos, or other multimedia content objects but also non-digital objects such as artefacts in museums or books in libraries. The nature of metadata information objects, i.e., their structure and the meaning of their elements (e.g., author, description, etc.), largely depends on the metadata creator's design choices as well as on the characteristics of the repository they reside in (e.g., relational database, flat files). For establishing uniform access to multiple autonomous metadata repositories, one needs to deal with the distinct characteristics of the information objects stored therein. Hence, one must establish *metadata interoperability* and find an appropriate technique to deal with various kinds of heterogeneities.

In this chapter, we analyse *metadata mapping*, a technique that allows domain experts to reconcile the various heterogeneities that impede metadata information objects from being interoperable. First we precisely describe our perception of metadata mapping and analyse in detail how mapping solutions can support domain experts in mapping metadata (see Section 3.1). Then, in Section 3.2, we set up an evaluation framework by conducting an requirements analysis based on state-of-the-art mapping literature. In Section 3.3, we present and categorise a representative selection of mapping solutions, which is then, in Section 3.4, evaluated against the evaluation framework.

3.1 What is Metadata Mapping?

From all previously mentioned interoperability techniques, those classified as model reconciliation techniques are the most complex ones. Since heterogeneities can occur on all tree levels, it is necessary to specify mappings for each level: language mappings for the M2 level, schema mappings for the M1 level, and instance transformations for the M0 level. Before a mapping on a certain level can be defined, the heterogeneities on the level above must be reconciled, i.e., one must deal with M2 language differences before specifying M1 schema mappings.

Previously, in Section 2.2.2, we have already outlined the characteristics of a representative set of schema definition languages and pointed out the divergence in their abstract and concrete syntax. Because of that, metadata mapping does not deal with heterogeneities on the language level (M2) but assumes that all metadata information objects are expressed in the same schema definition language. This can be achieved by transforming metadata information objects from one language representation into another, which could also entail loss of semantics

Here we further elaborate on *metadata mapping*, a technique that subsumes *schema mapping* and *instance transformation* as described in Section 2.4.3. Before discussing its technical details, we define the scope of this technique as follows:

Definition 3.1 *Given two metadata schemes, both settled in the same domain of discourse and expressed in the same schema definition language, we define metadata mapping as a specification that relates their model elements in a way that their schematic structures and semantic interpretation is respected on the metadata model and on the metadata instance level.*

From a model perspective, a metadata mapping defines structural and semantic relationships between model elements on the schema level and between content values on the instance level. To represent such relationships, any mapping mechanism requires a set of mapping elements with a well-defined syntax and semantics. From this perspective, we can regard not only metadata schemes but also a mapping between metadata schemes as being a model. Bernstein et al. [BHP00] as well as Madhavan et al. [MBDH02] have proposed such a perspective. Furthermore, we can denote the total of all mapping relationships contained in a mapping model as *mapping specification*.

Technical Details

From a technical perspective a metadata mapping can formally be defined as follows:

Definition 3.2 *A metadata mapping is defined between a source schema $S^s \in S$ and a target schema $S^t \in S$, each consisting of a set of schema elements, $e^s \in S^s$ and $e^t \in S^t$ respectively, which are optionally connected by some structure. A mapping $M \in \mathcal{M}$ is a directional relationship between a set of elements $e_i^s \in S^s$ and a set of elements $e_j^t \in S^t$, where each mapping relationship is represented as a* mapping element $m \in M$. *The semantics of each mapping relationship is described by a* mapping expression $p \in P$. *The cardinality of a mapping element m is determined by the number of incoming and outgoing relationships from and to the schema elements. To support heterogeneity reconciliation on the instance level, a mapping element carries an appropriate* instance transformation function $f \in F$.

Figure 3.1 illustrates the main elements of a metadata mapping specification. Typically, the cardinality of a single mapping element is either 1:1, 1:n, or n:1, meaning that an element from a source schema is related with one or many elements from the target schema and vice versa. In theory, m:n mappings would also be possible, but in practice they rarely occur because one can model that kind of element correspondence using multiple 1:n or n:1 relationships.

3.1. What is Metadata Mapping?

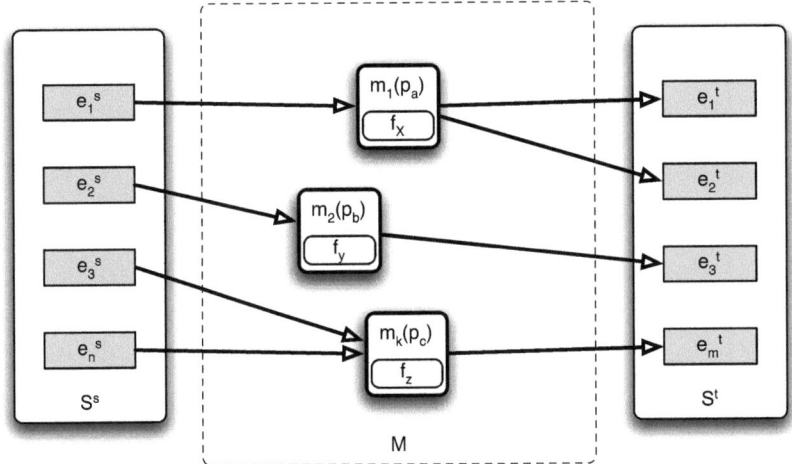

Figure 3.1: The main elements of a metadata mapping specification

A mapping expression p defines the semantics of a mapping element, i.e., it describes how the interpretations of the model elements, denoted as $I(e_i^s)$ and $I(e_j^t)$, are related. In its simplest form, such an expression could be *unknown*, stating that two elements are related, without giving any evidence how. A more complex example are mapping expressions that indicate the confidence of a mapping relationship according to a specified metrics, as described in [MIKS00]. One can distinguish between the following types of mapping expressions (e.g., [SPD92]):

- exclude ($I(e_i^s) \cap I(e_j^t) = \emptyset$): the interpretations of two schema elements have distinct meanings. In the example presented in Section 2.2, the interpretations of the elements rights in the Dublin Core and birthday in the proprietary schema exclude each other.

- equivalent ($I(e_i^s) \equiv I(e_j^t)$): the interpretations of two, possibly lexically different schema elements are equivalent. The elements author in the proprietary and the element creator in the Dublin Core schema are examples for such a relationship.

- include ($I(e_i^s) \subseteq I(e_j^t) \vee I(e_j^t) \subseteq I(e_i^s)$): the interpretation of one schema element contains the interpretation of another element. In the context of our example, the interpretation of the Dublin Core element creator includes the interpretations of the TV-Anytime elements GivenName and FamilyName because these elements describe a person in the role of an author.

- overlap ($I(e_i^s) \cap I(e_j^t) \neq \emptyset \wedge I(e_i^s) \nsubseteq I(e_j^t) \wedge I(e_j^t) \nsubseteq I(e_i^s)$): the interpretations of two schema elements overlap but do not include each other. The elements description, synopsis, and info are examples for elements with overlapping interpretations. A description element usually provides similar information as a synopsis or info element, but in a more comprehensive form.

Instance transformation functions are the mechanism to cope with the structural and semantic heterogeneities on the instance level. If, for instance, two models (e.g., the TV-Anytime and the DC illustrative samples) are incompatible due to a multilateral correspondences conflict (e.g., GivenName and FamilyName in the source model and Creator in the target model), this can be resolved by relating the elements through a mapping relationship and assigning an instance transformation function concat, which concatenates the data values of the respective fields and returns the appropriate result. Figure 3.2 illustrates the role of mapping expressions and instance transformation functions in metadata mappings.

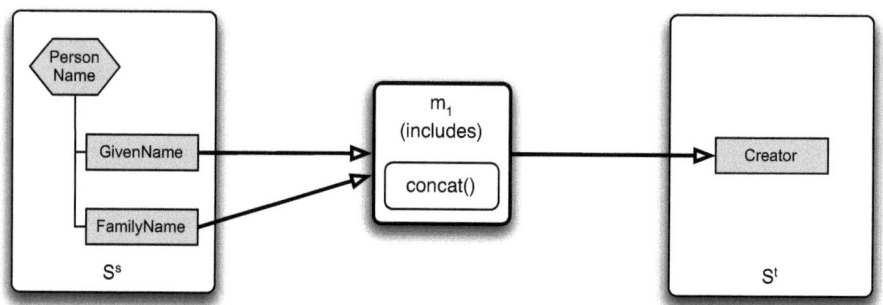

Figure 3.2: Achieving metadata interoperability through instance transformation

Mapping Phases

Besides being a mechanism for capturing the semantic and structural relationships between the elements of distinct models, metadata mapping is also a process consisting of a cyclic sequence of phases. As illustrated in Figure 3.3, we can identify four such phases: (i) mapping discovery, (ii) mapping representation, (iii) mapping execution, and (iv) mapping maintenance.

The reason for the cyclic arrangement of the mapping phases is the fact that mapping maintenance is also the key for discovering new mappings from existing ones. If for instance, there is a mapping between schema A and schema B and another mapping between schema B and schema C, and all this information is available in a registry, the system could derive an additional mapping between schema A and C, based on their transitive relationship.

Mapping discovery is concerned with finding semantic and structural relationships between the elements of two schemes and reconciling the heterogeneities on both the schema and the instance level. Deep domain knowledge is required to understand the semantics of the elements of the source and target schemes in order to relate their elements on the schema and the instance level. Rahm and Bern-

3.2. Requirements Framework

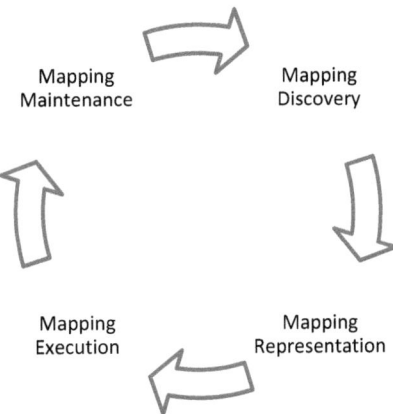

Figure 3.3: The four major phases in the metadata mapping cycle

stein [RB01] as well as Kalfoglou and Schorlemmer [KS03] describe a variety of mapping discovery techniques that operate on both levels.

Mapping representation is the second phase of the mapping process and denotes the formal declaration of the mapping relationships between two metadata schemes. Noy and Musen [Noy04] identifies three types of formalisms for representing mappings: (i) representing them as instances of a defined mapping model, (ii) defining bridging axioms or rules to represent transformations, and (iii) using views to define mappings between a source and a target schema.

Mapping execution is the phase for executing mapping specifications at run-time. Mappings can be used for various interoperability-dependent tasks such as metadata transformation, answering queries over a set of metadata sources, or creating software stubs that encapsulate the mappings and provide transparent access to the underlying metadata source. Halevy [Hal01] gives an overview of view-based mapping approaches.

Mapping maintenance is the last step in an iteration of the metadata mapping phases. Usually, a registry provides the necessary maintenance functionality and keeps track of available metadata schemes and mappings between them. This information allows systems to deal with issues like versioning (e.g., [NM04]), which is required whenever there are changes in the source or target schema of a certain mapping.

3.2 Requirements Framework

In the subsequent presentation, we focus on a discussion of requirements for metadata mapping solutions. This discussion provides the understanding needed to form the basis for the evaluation framework we use for our mapping tool analysis later in this chapter.

We have organised the requirements into general requirements for mapping tools (Section 3.2.1) and requirements for each of the previously mentioned phases in the mapping process: mapping discovery (Section 3.2.2), mapping representation (Section 3.2.3), mapping execution (Section 3.2.4), and mapping maintenance (Section 3.2.5). Finally, in Section 3.2.6, we summarise the requirements in terms of an evaluation framework for comparing existing mapping solutions.

3.2.1 General Requirements

Turning metadata mapping into practice requires the implementation of a mapping component, which is usually part of a larger metadata integration architecture. Like any other piece of software, an integration architecture has some general requirements. First, it should fulfil some architectural properties common to any metadata integration architecture. Second, it should be able to lift and normalise metadata represented in various schema definition languages to a common level; otherwise, if language mismatches are not resolved, metadata mapping is hardly possible. Third, and this is essential for creating mappings, it should provide a graphical user interface that supports domain experts in creating mappings.

Architecture Design

The ultimate goal of any metadata interoperability technique is to achieve uniform access to metadata and digital media objects stored in multiple autonomous media repositories. Like other interoperability techniques, metadata mapping is just a prerequisite for achieving this goal. Therefore, the ultimate goal and the general requirement for any metadata integration architecture is *uniform accessibility* of metadata via a single interface. This requirement can be fulfilled by providing a query interface for a certain query language or by exposing a well-defined Application Programming Interface (API) for accessing the metadata.

Another basic requirement for an integration architecture is *modularity*. For each data source involved in an integration scenario, one has to implement an adapter. Also the mappings and particularly the processing of the mappings must be embedded into a software component. An additional data source joining an integration scenario, should not affect the adapters of other data sources. Also the (re-)specification of mappings should not affect the implementation of software components; this should rather be a configuration task.

Domenig and Dittrich [DD99] give an overview of possible integration architectures. A very well known architecture for a modular integration approach are Mediated Query Systems, which have been proposed by Wiederhold [Wie92]. They consist of two types of software modules: mediators and wrappers. Each data source is encapsulated by a wrapper, which is an application specifically designed for each kind of data source. Its task is to accept queries from a mediator and to answer them on the basis of the underlying data source's technology. Mediators are modules that accept user queries formulated

3.2. Requirements Framework

over a user-selected target (mediation) schema and reformulate them into sub-queries according to previously defined metadata mappings. Then they disperse them to the local sources where they are executed, collect and combine the results and present them to the user in a certain format. Other architectural designs, especially Peer-to-Peer data management systems (e.g., Piazza [HIMT03], P-Grid [Abe01], Edutella [NWQ+02], Hyperion [RGKG+05]), abstain from central mediators and mediation schemes and define point-to-point mappings directly between the models of the involved data sources (e.g., GridVine [ACMHvP04]). However, as Halevy et al. observe in [HIMT03], from a formal mapping perspective, there is little difference between these two kinds of mappings.

Lifting and Normalisation

As already mentioned in Section 3.1, metadata mapping postulates that all metadata information objects are expressed in the same schema definition language. This means, that all metadata models are internally represented as instances of the same metadata meta-model. Therefore, *lifting and normalisation* of metadata expressed in distinct languages to a common representation is another general requirement. A practical example from typical data integration scenarios, is the mapping of relational database schemes to XML Schema.

The LIFT tool which is part of the MAFRA ontology mapping framework [MMSV02] is an example for a component that fulfils this requirement. It provides means to lift DTDs, XML Schemes, and relational databases to a common structural ontology level.

Graphical User Interface

Metadata mapping cannot be fully automated and will always depend on interactions with domain experts. Usually it is not the technicians who define semantic relationships between schema elements, but expert users such as librarians, curators, or knowledge workers. Technicians are concerned with the technical implementation of mappings. Based on the semantic relationships, they reconcile structural heterogeneities among schemes and concentrate on the implementation of instance transformation functionality. For both aspects, the domain expert view, and the technician view, a mapping solution should provide a *graphical user interface (GUI)* to support the domain experts as well as the technicians in their mapping tasks. Especially the domain expert view must follow an intuitive design and guide the users' attention to the relevant places, especially when large metadata schemes need to be mapped.

Robertson et al. [RCC05] present several advanced visualisation methods for larger schemes. Following and highlighting existing links when a model element is selected is one of the proposed techniques, auto-scrolling during typing and an incremental search mechanism are other examples.

Another useful design strategy is to separate between schema and data view, as it is implemented in Clio [MHH+01, HHH+05]. The schema view represents the main perspective for mapping definition. To get further information on a schema element's semantics, the user can switch to the data view and retrieve sample data for that element.

The majority of mapping solutions is implemented as stand-alone desktop applications. However, recently they have also begun to emerge on the Web, Yahoo Pipes [Yah07] being the prime example for this category. Via a simple, intuitive Web-interface users can aggregate XML data and define mappings between model elements. Provided that a Web-based mapping solution is simple enough, this category of mapping solutions can attract a large number of users, lead to collaborative mapping efforts, and give insights on the different semantic perceptions of model elements.

3.2.2 Mapping Discovery Requirements

The first metadata mapping step is to determine the relationships between a source and a target schema. In the literature, mapping discovery is also denoted as *matching*, *mapping*, and especially in combination with ontologies, *alignment*. Although finding the matching elements is an intellectual task, which is mainly carried out by humans, there are automated approaches to support users in mapping discovery. When many users are involved in determining the right mappings, building consensus on the defined mappings is essential.

Matching / Alignment Support

The larger metadata schemes are, the more difficult it is to find the set of potential mappings between schema elements. Fully automatic schema matching is considered to be an AI-complete problem, that is, as hard as reproducing human intelligence [BMPQ04]. Although this problem is not yet solvable, there are many (semi-)automatic techniques that can support the user in matching tasks. Hence, a mapping solution should provide some mechanism for the automated resolution of semantic correspondences between the elements of heterogeneous metadata schemes; we call this requirement *alignment support*[1].

The term *alignment* frequently occurs in the context of *ontology alignment* and is used interchangeably with the term *ontology mapping*, wherefore Kafoglou and Schorlemmer [KS03] provide a survey of automatic and semi-automatic techniques. Rahm and Bernstein [RB01] provide a survey of approaches in the database domain, Shvaiko and Euzenat [SE05] analyse both schema and ontology mappings, and Doan and Halevy [DH05] analyse mapping discovery solutions from a data integration perspective. Most of the approaches cited in these surveys are based on heuristic algorithms comparing the lexical and structural features of models (e.g., PROMPT [NM03]), or employ machine learning techniques to find mappings (e.g., GLUE [DMDH02]). Some approaches operate either on the schema level (e.g., Cupid [MBR01]) or only on the instance level (e.g., SemInt [LC00]), recent developments (e.g., COMA++ [ADMR05]) include both levels in order to automatically discover mappings between models.

---

[1]On the Web, there are two sites that provide up-to-date information on the research topic of ontology alignment: the Ontology Alignment Source (http://www.atl.lmco.com/projects/ontology/) and OntologyMatching.org (http://www.ontologymatching.org/)

3.2. Requirements Framework

Consensus Building

When metadata schemes are developed independent from each other, their structural and semantic properties are likely to be different, which leads to the heterogeneities we have discussed earlier in Section 2.3. This is also the case when two schemes are mapped. As their semantic interpretation, also the mappings between two metadata schemes are always bound to a certain context. A mapping created by person A is not necessarily true for person B. Therefore, *consensus building* is a principal requirement for any integration scenario. The prerequisite for consensus building is a precise definition and documentation of the semantics of the schemes to be mapped. If only one person is involved in establishing the mappings, no tool support is required for consensus building. Larger scenarios involving several persons and extensive metadata schemes to be mapped will benefit from tool support for consensus building.

Zhdanova and Shvaiko [ZS06] propose a public, community-driven approach for mapping discovery where end users, knowledge engineers, and developer communities take part in the process of establishing mappings. The resulting mappings are handled as *subjective alignments*, hence as mappings that are customised to a certain user, a community, or application requirements. From already existing mappings, and the information about users, communities, groups, and social networks, the system can determine valuable information for mapping discovery. For instance, if several users have mapped their user-defined schemes to the same target schema, the system can leverage past experience and propose mappings for new mapping tasks.

Another approach that supports consensus building is the ESP game, proposed by von Ahn and Dabbish [vAD04]. Although being developed for another purpose, which is the labelling of online images, it demonstrates how a game like approach can motivate people to build a consensus on the semantics online resources. If we consider metadata schemes and mappings as being online resources, such game-like approaches could open the door for novel consensus building techniques.

3.2.3 Mapping Representation Requirements

After metadata mappings have been discovered, they must be represented in a machine read- and interpretable way. A semantically well-defined formalism ensures that mappings can actually be processed in the subsequent mapping phases. Since the decision whether a metadata mapping is semantically correct, depends on the context, the formalism must provide means for context representation. Finally, the properties of a metadata mapping largely depends on the schema definition language used for describing metadata schemes. Therefore, a mapping formalism should be flexible in its *language bindings*.

Mapping Formalism

For reconciling heterogeneities by means of metadata mapping, one needs to formally declare mapping relationships between the elements of two metadata schemes. A set of such relationships is denoted as *mapping specification*. A mapping formalism builds the basis for mapping specifications. It provides a machine read- and interpretable language for creating mappings and, as it is the case with schema definition languages, a concrete and an abstract syntax. The concrete syntax (e.g. a serialisation in XML or the graphical illustration of a mapping element) allows the serialisation, registration, and exchange of mapping specifications and also enables human readability. The abstract syntax, i.e., the meta-model of mapping specifications, represents a semantically well-defined corpus for mapping specifications and ensures the correct interpretation of mappings across machines and system boundaries.

The *strength* of a mapping formalism denotes its ability to express those relationships that are required to reconcile the various kinds of heterogeneities, mentioned in Section 2.3.2. We have distinguished between two levels (model and instance level) and two main heterogeneity categories: structural and semantic heterogeneities. In combination with instance transformation, metadata mapping can reconcile a broad range of heterogeneities: naming, identification, and constraints conflicts as well as abstraction level incompatibilities, multilateral correspondences, domain coverage conflicts, terminological mismatches and meta-level discrepancies can be resolved through mappings on the schema level. Instance transformation, if it is an integral part of a mapping formalism, can resolve the remaining semantic heterogeneity conflicts on the instance level.

In the literature we can find many approaches that support mappings among metadata schemes. Unfortunately, most of them do not consider the whole heterogeneity spectrum but focus mainly on schema level mappings and disregard the instance level. Observer [MIKS00], for instance, only allows the specification of *synonym*, *homonym*, *overlap*, *disjoint*, and *overlap* relationships between entities of metadata schemes. Xiao and Cruz [XC06] have defined a mapping language for P2P systems, which provides one-to-one mapping relationships such as *equivalent*, *broader*, *narrower*, *union*, and *intersection* between schemes. Even less expressive is GridVine [ACMHvP04], which relies on the very restricted set of built-in OWL mapping primitives (e.g., `owl:equivalentProperty`). Although these kind of mappings suffice for human interpretation, the question remains how machines should interpret them in order to provide uniform access to the sources. They need exact information about relationships between concepts and precise processing instructions for dealing with the instances or data originating from heterogeneous sources.

The MAFRA ontology mapping framework [MMSV02] is an example for a system that covers the whole heterogeneity spectrum through the definition of *semantic bridges*. Piazza [HIMT03] is a representative for the family of integration systems that uses queries (views) as representation mechanism for mappings. This approach is well known from the domain of relational databases and is, depending on the expressiveness of the query language, also suitable for other technologies (e.g., XML, XQuery).

Mapping Context

Like metadata schema definitions, also metadata mappings are formal declarative specifications that are subject of interpretation. More specifically, metadata mappings define how heterogeneity conflicts, if they are detected, should be resolved. The problem is that even within a single metadata integration

3.2. Requirements Framework

scenario, data sources as well as the mappings created between their metadata schemes and instances may embody different assumptions on how information should be interpreted. If, for instance, a schema A is mapped to two schemes B and C, which differ in their semantic domain, an element of A could be interpreted differently in relation with elements of B than it is interpreted in relation with elements of C. If mappings are created across integration scenarios, the importance of context grows. Therefore, a mapping formalism should provide support for specifying the *mapping context*, i.e., the setting in which the interpretation of a metadata mapping is semantically correct.

COIN [GBMS99] has been one of the early information integration system that has explicitly incorporated context into mapping definitions. With the *context interchange framework*, it provides a formal, logical specification for modelling metadata models, axioms for identifying correspondences between model elements, and context axioms, that permit the specification of named contexts and therefore the definition of alternative interpretations of information objects. Based on this work, Wache [Wac03] has provided an integration formalism that supports not only the representation of context but also the transformation of information objects between contexts to enable cross-context reconciliation of semantic heterogeneities.

Language Binding

As described in Section 2.2.2, metadata information objects are instances of metadata models that can be expressed in various schema definition languages. A metadata scheme for describing books, for instance, can be, depending on an application's requirements, expressed as Java or XML Schema model. Therefore, if mappings between schemes are established, the resulting mapping is always bound to a certain language.

Expressing and representing mappings requires a formalism that can either be language independent or bound to a certain schema definition language. The advantages of a language independent or generic approach are its applicability for other schema definition languages. The main disadvantage is the increased complexity and additional development effort: if a mapping tool follows a language-independent approach, i.e., if it is open to any schema definition language, a generic metadata meta-meta model as well as language-specific extensions must be defined. However, we believe that *flexibility* in the language binding is necessary to support the variety of existing schema definition languages and for being open to future developments.

With the Ontology Definition Metamodel Specification (ODM) [OMG06b], the Object Management Group (OMG) has released a set of metadata meta-models that reflect the abstract syntax of RDF, OWL, Common Logic (CL), and Topic Maps. In addition, mappings between these models are provided and expressed in the MOF QVT Relations Language [OMG05]. The goal of the ODM approach is to support interoperability between MOF-based modelling tools independent of the schema definition language they support.

MAFRA [MMSV02], a mapping framework that enables the transformation of instances of source ontologies into instances of target ontologies is an example for a language dependent approach that expresses mappings as instances of a meta-ontology expressed in DAML-OIL [W3C01]. We can find language-dependent bridging axioms in ontology languages such as OWL, which provide language primitives to define relationships (e.g., equivalent, sameAs) between ontology concepts. RuleML [The06] is an effort to develop a rule language that is independent of any schema definition language. Semex [CDH+05] is an example for a system that formulates mappings between schemes in terms of queries. In other words, the elements of one schema model are defined as a query over the elements of another schema model.

3.2.4 Mapping Execution Requirements

We have defined the mappings. Now What? With this question, Noy [Noy04] points out that the definition and representation of mappings is the necessary precondition but not the goal in itself. The ultimate goal of metadata mapping is to achieve uniform access to metadata in multiple autonomous information systems.

In the mapping execution phase, mappings are used to reformulate queries over one schema into queries over another schema, to calculate query plans, to optimise queries, and to generate stubs or wrappers to data sources.

Query Reformulation

Users of an integrated and interoperable system environment should have the possibility to formulate queries over a user-selected target metadata schema and receive results from a set of integrated data sources, each potentially employing a different source metadata schema. Hence, the integration system must convert the queries formulated over the user-selected schema into queries over the data sources' metadata schemes. Metadata mappings are the technical specifications that serve as input for this process, which is commonly referred to as *query reformulation*.

If we regard metadata mappings as definitions that describe how to construct the elements of a target schema from the elements in a source schema, they fulfil the same functionality as views. Previously, we have already mentioned that using views is a common formalism for representing mappings in the context of relational databases. Hence, if mapping specifications are not available in terms of views per se, as it is the case in systems such as Piazza [HIMT03], they can be transformed into such a representation. In principle, there are two ways of representing mappings using views: (i) the data sources, i.e., their schema elements, are described as queries (views) over the user-selected schema — this is referred to as *Local as View (LaV)* — or (ii) the user-selected schema is described as a set of views over the data sources — this is known as *Global as View (GaV)*. In the first case, query reformulation means rewriting the queries similar to rewriting a query using a view [Hal01]. In the second case, reformulation works analogously to view unfolding in traditional relational database systems.

Rajaraman et al. [RSU95] follow an approach similar to view-based query reformulation and use

3.2. Requirements Framework

a global query language to define *query templates* consisting of a head and a body clause. The head contains a predicate denoting the view, arguments for the predicate, and binding patterns that indicate, which arguments of the predicate are expected to be bound and which are free. The body contains a program that produces the query result.

Query Plan

For efficiently accessing integrated data sources, the system must calculate a query plan and optimise query reformulation. Usually, the main goal of a query plan is to reduce the execution time of queries on the data sources. There are two main tuning possibilities to achieve that: first, by avoiding redundant queries, i.e., queries that return a subset of results of a previously executed query. This is also known as *query containment* [MLF00] and is a metric that can be calculated prior to query execution. Second, query time can be reduced by analysing the *capabilities* [PGH96] of the involved data sources. The capabilities of a data source depend on its physical properties such as network connection speed, average response time, but also on logical properties, such as the availability of data in a data source[2]. Another optimisation goal that can be achieved by a query plan is the *minimisation of response time*. This reduces the time it takes until the first query response is returned from a data source, which is important especially in distributed environments, such as P2P systems.

Calculating query plans and optimisation techniques are well studied in the domain of traditional database systems. Jarke and Koch [JK84] provide a survey of available techniques. Tatarinov and Halevy [TH04] propose optimisation techniques for Peer-to-Peer Data Management Systems and describe an algorithm for calculating XQuery query containment and optimisation algorithms for pruning of redundant queries and for minimising the required query reformulations.

Integration Component Generation

In order to enable a data source to be integrated with other sources, all the previously mentioned requirements must be packed into data source specific integration components. If a mapping solution follows a federated architecture, such components are typically *mediators* or *wrappers*.

Semi-automatic mechanism, which support users in setting up these components, can avoid a purely manual implementation for each data source. Although it will always be necessary to perform certain source-specific adoptions, at least some generic aspects (e.g., query reformulation) can be realised automatically. Such a feature could, for instance, be embedded in a mapping tool and allow the generation of source code skeletons based on mapping specifications.

TSIMMIS [CGMH+94] is one of the early data integration systems that automatically generates mediator as well as wrapper components based on high level configurations. Another approach, which is also relevant for capability-based optimisation, is to transform the mapping specifications into *templates*,

---

[2]Even if a certain entity is represented in a data source's metadata schema, this doesn't guarantee that the instance data are available.

which represent the possible queries a mediator can ask. Wrapper Generators [UWGM02] can be applied to create a table holding the various query patterns contained in the templates; since it is not realistic to create a template for each possible form of a query, the wrapper must include a mechanism which works with query containment.

3.2.5 Mapping Maintenance Requirements

Mapping maintenance is necessary to keep track to available metadata schemes and mappings between them. This enables domain experts to reuse already existing schemes and mappings, which in turn contributes to greater metadata interoperability. Furthermore, as discussed in Section 3.1, mapping maintenance provides valuable input for subsequent mapping discover phase.

Metadata registries play a central role in the maintenance phase. They provide means for registering mapping specifications together with the metadata schemes involved in an integration scenario and can offer advanced functionality based on the pool of available mappings and schemes: they can verify mapping specifications by detecting potential conflicts with other mappings, propose existing mappings for specific or similar metadata schemes, or infer potential, not yet explicitly expressed mapping relationships.

Mapping Verification

Although the *truth* of a mapping always depends on its interpretation in a certain context (e.g., the one of the mapping creator), it is possible to detect potential conflicts with other already existing metadata mappings. Although it is difficult to resolve such conflicts automatically, it is at least possible to provide some kind of notification mechanism. In general, mapping verification can improve the quality of mappings and could also contribute to building consensus on mappings in the context of a certain application domain.

In Clio [MHH+01, HHH+05], mappings are verified by proposing alternative mappings to the user. They see example instance data and how they would appear under the current mapping. This should illustrate a given mapping and the perhaps subtle differences between other mappings.

Mapping Reusability

Mappings can potentially be reused for future integration tasks. A metadata registry can analyse the relationships between existing schemes and mappings and use heuristics to identify similarities. On that basis, the system can, for instance, propose possible mappings to domain experts. Especially with a growing number of schemes and mappings, registries play an important role for mapping reusability.

3.3. Mapping Solutions

Mapping Inference

Based on existing mapping relationships, a mapping registry could also infer not yet explicitly available mappings. Suppose we have three metadata schemes A, B, and C. If there is a mapping between the elements of A and B, and B and C, it is possible to exploit these transitive relationships and explicitly derive a proposal for a mapping relationship from A to C. In another setting, if for instance some elements of B are *subclasses*, or *subproperties* of elements of A, and there exist mapping relationships between the elements of A and C, the system could automatically or semi-automatically infer mapping relationships between the elements of B and C.

GridVine [ACMHvP04] and Piazza [HIMT03], both belonging to the domain of Peer-to-Peer data management infrastructures, are systems that perform that kind of transitive mapping inference: each node in the system has mappings to a small set of other nodes and when a query is posed over a node, it transitively follows the nodes that are connected by semantic mappings (*chaining mappings*).

3.2.6 Requirements Summary

As a summary of the discussions in the previous sections, Table 3.1 outlines the requirements that are, in our conception, the essential ingredients for building mapping solutions. We do not consider them as obligatory features, which must be fulfilled by any mapping solution, but rather as complementary building blocks, some of which are more essential than others.

Through the arrangement of the requirements along the four phases of the metadata mapping cycle, we want to emphasise the importance of considering metadata mapping as a process rather than a single step. Mapping discovery, for instance, is not enough to achieve the goal of uniform accessibility. It requires a formalism that can capture the various heterogeneity aspects and a mechanism for executing mapping specifications. Also having some kind of mapping registry gains great importance when the number of data sources and metadata schemes to be integrated grows.

Different from many other approaches in the field of metadata mapping, we discuss mapping discovery only superficially: we only distinguish between solutions that support users in discovering mapping relationships and those that do not. For further details on this topic we refer to the surveys of Rahm and Bernstein [RB01] as well as Kalfoglou and Schorlemmer [KS03]. The main focus of our analysis lies on the mapping process as whole and especially on the strength and expressiveness of the underlying mapping formalism.

3.3 Mapping Solutions

Mapping solutions are the means to establish metadata interoperability in integration scenarios where *mapping* has been chosen as being the appropriate technique. We can regard them as technical manifestation of the previously mentioned mapping phases (discovery, representation, execution, maintenance)

	Requirement	Description
General	Uniform Accessibility	Provide access to a set of (distributed) metadata sources via a single access point
	Modularity	Adding additional sources and mappings without affecting/changing existing system components
	Lifting & Normalisation	Flexible means to convert metadata expressed in distinct schema definition languages to a common metadata meta-model
	Mapping GUI	A graphical user interface supporting domain experts and technicians in creating mappings
Mapping Discovery	Schema Matching / Alignment Support	(Semi-)automatic support for determining mappings; either on the schema level, the instance level, or on both levels
	Consensus Building Features	Providing features that support users in building consensus on conflicting mappings
Mapping Representation	Model-Level Structural Heterogeneity Reconciliation	The ability to represent and reconcile structural heterogeneities on the model level
	Model-Level Semantic Heterogeneity Reconciliation	The ability to represent and reconcile semantic heterogeneities on the model level
	Instance-Level Semantic Heterogeneity Reconciliation	The ability to represent and reconcile semantic heterogeneities on the instance level
	Context Representation	The ability to capture context of interpretation of a metadata mapping
	Flexible Language Binding	A generic, language independent mapping formalism that can easily be bound to a certain schema definition language
Mapping Execution	Query Reformulation	Reformulate queries over a user selected schema into queries over the target schema representation according to mapping definitions
	Query Plan / Optimisation	Algorithmic support for minimising the query execution / response time
	Integration Component Generation	(Semi-)automatic generation of data-source specific integration components (mediators, wrappers, adapters, etc.)
Mapping Maintenance	Mapping Verification	Detection of potential conflicts with other mappings
	Mapping Reusability	System support for reusing existing mapping definitions
	Mapping Inference	Infer not yet explicitly expressed mapping relationships from existing mapping specifications

Table 3.1: Requirements framework for the evaluation of metadata mapping solutions

— though it depends on the mapping solution how and to what extent it supports a certain phase.

There exists a multitude of mapping solutions with varying mapping capabilities, different stages of stability and distinct underlying business models. In this section, we introduce a categorisation for a

3.3. Mapping Solutions

representative while not complete selection of mapping solutions. It includes tools from major software vendors that are active in the domain of data integration, such as BEA, IBM, Sybase, Microsoft, Cape Clear, Altova, and Data Direct, as well as frequently cited research projects, and novel Web-based solutions such as Yahoo Pipes. The focus of our evaluation is on solutions and tools; theoretical mapping approaches lacking an at least prototypical implementation are therefore not part of this evaluation. After an initial categorisation of mapping solutions in Section 3.3.1, we will describe each category of mapping solutions in detail in Sections 3.3.2 to 3.3.5 and conclude with preliminary observations in Section 3.3.6.

3.3.1 A Categorisation of Mapping Solutions

For a coarse-grained categorisation of mapping solutions, we investigate their architectural properties, which are a direct result of the application domain they were designed for. In industrial, large scale environments metadata mapping solutions are an integral part of *Enterprise Information Integration (EII)* and *Enterprise Application Integration (EAI)* suites. EII and EAI systems are usually extensive and heavyweight software suites, where mapping is usually only a small subset of the supported features. Besides that, we have also identified the category *mapping tools*, which embraces lightweight standalone tools designed for the sole purpose of mapping. The category *other solutions* contains all mapping tools that cannot be assigned to any of the previously mentioned categories, such as XML editors or modelling tools that may also provide mapping support for certain kinds of schema definition languages, or Web applications.

For each solution we describe what type of software it is (commercial, research prototype) and to which solution category it belongs (EII suite, EAI suite, mapping tool, other). Furthermore, we analyse for what kind of schema definition languages a solution provides mapping capabilities and which software platforms are supported. Additionally, we briefly sketch which mapping phases are covered by a certain mapping solution.

3.3.2 Enterprise Information Integration (EII) Suites

EII subsumes industrial solutions dealing with the problem of data integration. Generally, they aim at (i) identifying data sources, (ii) building virtual schemes, and (iii) reformulating queries over a virtual schema into queries over multiple data source specific schemes. EII systems provide real-time information by integrating heterogeneous data sources on demand without moving or replicating them [HAB+05]. In such solutions, mappings are generally represented as views and executed through a query rewriting mechanism. To what extent mapping discovery and maintenance is supported depends on the solution.

BEA Liquid Data 8.1

BEA Liquid Data for WebLogic [BEA07] is an Enterprise Information Integration suite that allows to establish a real-time unified view over heterogeneous data sources such as relational databases, XML data, flat files (e.g., CSV-files), and third party application data. It leverages XML standards throughout the mapping phases and also delivers query results structured in XML. Liquid Data is available for all major software platforms.

While not supporting the discovery phase of the mapping process, BEA Liquid Data offers a view-based approach for the mapping representation phase: all supported schema definition languages are lifted to the level of XML Schema. The mappings between source and target schemes are expressed in XQuery. For executing mappings, BEA provides the Liquid Data Server for deploying mapping specifications and a distributed query processor for translating queries according to the mappings. To a certain extent, BEA Liquid Data also supports the mapping maintenance phase: schemes as well as mappings between schemes are stored in the Liquid Data Repository, which enables the reuse of mappings.

Sybase Data Integration Suite — Avaki Studio / Server 7.0

The Sybase Data Integration Suite [Syb07], with its components Avaki Studio and Avaki Server 7.0, is a data federation solution which provides standardised access to distributed heterogeneous data through a single layer. It supports the integration of the same types of data sources as BEA Liquid data, but follows a mapping approach based on the relational model. Both Avaki Studio and Server are available for all major software platforms.

Mappings are created using the Avaki Studio application — support during the mapping discovery phase is not provided. For mapping representation Avaki defines a mapping model based on the relational model. One or more input sources, a single result element, and a set of operators which can be arranged sequentially to combine or transform data from one or more input sources, are the main constituents of that mapping model. For the mapping execution phase, the mapping models are deployed as data services exposing SQL-DDL (view) schema definitions. All data services and mapping models are registered and maintained in a data catalogue.

3.3.3 Enterprise Application Integration (EAI) Suites

EAI systems deal with the problem of integrating applications through business processes. They are well known in the context of *Service Oriented Architectures (SOA)* where they connect and integrate loosely coupled, distributed software components usually by using Web Services in order to fulfil a certain business task (e.g., booking a flight). Since the applications involved in a business process expose metadata corresponding to various, incompatible schemes, also EAI systems require mapping techniques for resolving these discrepancies.

Different than EII systems, which can query a set of heterogeneous sources via a virtual unified target schema, the focus of EAI systems is on the exchange of data residing at multiple sites. Hence, during the execution phase, mappings do not serve as input for query reformulation but for transforming data from a source into a target schema.

3.3. Mapping Solutions

Microsoft Biztalk 2006

Microsoft BizTalk Mapper [Mic07] is part of the BizTalk Server Enterprise Application Integration Suite and allows to create and edit mappings in order to translate or transform messages within business processes from one format into another. Since BizTalk is a pure EAI suite and XML has evolved as the de-facto standard for structuring messages within business processes, mapping is supported among XML schema definitions. Like the whole BizTalk suite, also the mapper is available only for Microsoft Windows 2003 and XP platforms.

The mapping discovery phase is supported by the Microsoft BizTalk Mapper, meaning that expert users get technical assistance in determining mapping relationships. Schemes as well as mappings are represented in a BizTalk-specific mapping model and are transformed to XSL style-sheets during the mapping executing phase. For maintaining mappings, BizTalk relies on a simple WebDav repository where mappings can be published and reused in other integration tasks.

Cape Clear Studio and Server 7

The Cape Clear EAI suite [Cap07] comprises two main products: the Cape Clear Server and the Cape Clear Studio. The former provides the environment for deploying business processes and Web Service components. The latter is a design tool for creating Web Services and BPEL processes. Data Transformation Web Services are a special kind of service: they permit the integration of non-XML data sources that represent data as structured text (e.g., CSV, EDI, SWIFT). However, they must first be lifted to the level of XML Schema in order to be mappable with other message formats within a business process. Cape Clear Studio and Server are both Java applications — the Studio is an Eclipse Rich Client Application — and therefore run on all major software platforms.

Cape Clear Studio does not support mapping discovery. Mappings must be defined manually between XML Schema definitions using the Cape Clear Studio XSLT mapper. This implies that mappings are represented as XSL style-sheets. For the execution of mappings at run-time, a Data Transformation Service can be deployed on the Cape Clear Server and be incorporated into any business process. So far the mapping maintenance phase is not supported because there is no possibility to publish or share the created mappings.

IBM WebSphere Integration Developer 6.0.2

IBM's contribution to the market of EAI suites is the WebSphere platform, an environment for deploying reusable business processes on a Service Oriented Architecture (SOA) foundation. The IBM WebSphere Integration Developer [IBM07], a tool for modelling business processes, also has mapping capabilities. Since *business objects* are the WebSphere internal representation of application data, the Integration Developer supports mappings among instances of that proprietary model. Additionally it also supports the development of mediation services, which are services that intercept and modify messages passed between existing services within a business process. For this kind of service, the Integration Developer provides XML Schema mapping capabilities. As the whole WebSphere EAI suite, also the IBM WebSphere Integration Developer is available for all major software platforms.

Although the extent is minimal, we can categorise the IBM WebSphere Integration Developer as solution that supports the mapping discovery phase: it can automatically create mapping relationships among attributes having the same lexical name. Mappings are represented either in a proprietary model (business object maps) when they are created between business objects, or as XSL style-sheet when XML Schema definitions are mapped. They can be deployed as software modules on a WebSphere Process Server or a WebSphere Enterprise Service Bus. Mapping maintenance is not supported.

3.3.4 Mapping Tools

Different from EAI and EII suites, where mapping solutions are only part of a broader application infrastructure, mapping tools are lightweight standalone systems created for the sole purpose of mapping. The market for this category of mapping solutions is still sparsely populated; Altova with its products MapForce [Alt07a] and SchemaAgent [Alt07b] turned out to be the only well-known commercial representative.

Altova MapForce and SchemaAgent 2008

At the time of this writing, Altova MapForce in combination with Altova SchemaAgent is the most powerful mapping solution on the market. MapForce supports mapping between any combination of SQL-DDL definitions in relational databases, XML Schema and DTD declarations, and flat files formats such as CSV or EDI. These tools are currently available only for Microsoft Windows platforms.

MapForce assists the user during the mapping discovery phase by automatically matching child elements of already mapped elements. In contrast to any other mapping solution mentioned so far, MapForce allows the definition of mappings among several kinds of schema definition languages (XML Schema, SQL-DDL, etc.); this implies that internally, MapForce relies on a generic representation for these kind of schemes and also for the mapping between them. For the mapping execution phase, it provides the possibility to generate code from these proprietary mapping representations; a mapping specification can be compiled into XSLT code, XQuery, Java, C++, and C#. The mapping maintenance phase has been completely outsourced to Altova SchemaAgent, which is another standalone product that works in combination with Altova MapForce. Besides capabilities for registering schemes and mappings, it provides graphical means to view and analyse dependencies between them.

COMA++

The COMA++ [ADMR05] research prototype, an extension of COMA [DR02], is a generic schema mapping tool. It supports the user in the mapping discovery phase by matching schemes expressed in

3.3. Mapping Solutions

SQL-DDL, XML Schema, XML Data Record (XDR), or OWL. The tool is written in Java and is therefore platform-independent.

The focus of COMA++ is on the mapping discovery phase; it allows the combination of a variety of matching algorithms in order to find appropriate mappings between schemes. Internally, the schemes are uniformly represented as directed graphs, i.e., also the mappings are represented in a proprietary format. Currently, COMA++ does not support the mapping execution phase, neither for query rewriting nor for transforming models from one schema to another. For the mapping maintenance phase, COMA++ provides a repository component which centrally stores schemes, matching results, and mappings between schemes. An outstanding feature in this phase is the ability to derive new mappings from previously determined matching results.

Clio

Clio [MHH+01, HHH+05] is an IBM research prototype for creating and executing mappings among schemes expressed in SQL-DDL or XML Schema. It is implemented in Java and therefore platform independent.

For the mapping discovery phase, Clio relies on a semi-automatic tableaux-based algorithm which calculates all the possibilities in which schema elements relate to each other and prompts the user to select the semantically correct relationship. Internally, mappings are represented as an abstract query graph which can be serialised into specific languages such as XQuery, XSLT, and SQL/XML. The execution of queries in the mapping execution phase is left to the user. Clio does not provide any mapping maintenance support.

3.3.5 Other Solutions

Mapping support may also be a feature of solutions that do not belong to one of the above mentioned categories. In the following, we briefly discuss tools and applications offering mapping capabilities.

Stylusstudio 2007 / DataDirect XML Converters

Stylusstudio [Dat07] is an XML Integrated Development Environment (IDE) that supports mappings among schemes expressed in SQL-DDL, XML instance documents, XML schemes, DTDs, and EDI documents. In combination with DataDirect XML Converters, it allows the conversion of any legacy data format into XML. At the moment, Stylusstudio is available for Windows platforms only.

The mapping discovery phase is not supported by Stylusstudio. For representing mappings, Stylusstudio relies on standardised XML technologies and compiles mapping relationships drawn on the user interface directly into XSLT or XQuery; hence it does not define a proprietary mapping model. Executing the XQuery code on a certain data source or transforming XML documents using the resulting

XSL style-sheet is left to the user. With Stylussstudio it is currently not possible to deploy mapping services covering the mapping execution phase. The mapping maintenance phase is also unsupported.

TopBraid Composer

TopBraid Composer [Top07], which is the commercial extension of the Protégé OWL editor[3], is a Semantic Web ontology development platform which also supports the creation of mappings between ontologies. The tool has been implemented in Java, using the Eclipse Rich Client Platform and therefore runs on any Java-enabled software platform.

In version 2.3.0, TopBraid does not support the mapping discovery and maintenance phases. However, it is possible to create mappings between ontologies, which can be compiled either into SPARQL query construct statements or into SWRL[4] rules. Support for the mapping execution phase is currently not provided.

Yahoo Pipes

Yahoo Pipes [Yah07] has introduced a novel facet into the metadata mapping domain. Through a Web application, users can aggregate data from various sources such as XML feeds, online CSV files, or other online applications (e.g., Flickr, Google and Yahoo search results) and deploy new data services (mashups) that provide uniform access to these sources. This also includes mapping between the various source formats — a task which is supported by Yahoo Pipes by an intuitive, easy-to-use online interface. Since all Yahoo Pipes features are part of a Web application, this mapping solution can run in an ordinary Web browser on any platform.

Mapping discovery is the only phase not supported by Yahoo Pipes; users have to identify the semantic and structural correspondences on their own. For representing metadata (e.g., XML tags of feeds), Yahoo Pipes relies on a very simple hierarchical model consisting of elements and sub-elements only. Thus, it does not regard any schema definitions, which might not even exist for certain data sources, but concentrates on the instance level. Users can create mappings between elements without being confronted with complex schema definitions. For representing the mappings between the data elements, Yahoo Pipes employs its own proprietary model which defines a collection of modules for assembling data transformation pipes. The fact that Yahoo Pipes also supports the mapping execution phase becomes obvious when creating a pipe: during the modelling process, each mapping module automatically executes itself and presents the resulting instance data to the user. Each pipe created is stored and optionally published on Yahoo Pipes — the maintenance phase is therefore supported. Other users can copy existing pipes and adapt them to their needs or include the resulting instance data of an existing pipe as data source in their own pipe. These features enable even non-expert users to collaboratively assemble pipes and create mappings in a trial-and-error manner.

---

[3]Protégé OWL editor: http://protege.stanford.edu/overview/protege-owl.html
[4]Semantic Web Rule Language (SWRL): http://www.w3.org/Submission/SWRL/

3.3. Mapping Solutions

3.3.6 Preliminary Observations

In Table 3.2 we have summarised the features of the previously discussed mapping solutions. Before we perform an in-depth analysis of each mapping solution in respect to the supported mapping phases, we conclude this section with some preliminary observations:

		General Properties			Mapping Phases Support			
		License Type	Schema Definition Language Support	Supported Platforms	Discovery	Representation	Execution	Maintenance
EII Suites	BEA Liquid Data 8.1	Commercial	XML Schema	HP-UX, MS Windows 2000/XP, Red Hat Linux, Sun Solaris, IBM AIX	☐	■	■	■
EII Suites	Sybase Data Integration Suite - Avaki (Studio/Server) 7.0	Commercial	Proprietary	Red Hat/Suse Linux, Windows 2003/XP, Sun Solaris, IBM AIX	☐	■	■	■
EAI Suites	Microsoft BizTalk Server 2006	Commercial	XML Schema	Windows 2003/XP	■	■	■	■
EAI Suites	Cape Clear 7 (Studio/Server)	Commercial	XML Schema	Red Hat Linux, Sun Solaris, Windows 2003/XP	☐	■	■	☐
EAI Suites	IBM WebSphere Integration Developer	Commercial	Proprietary, XML Schema	Red Hat/Suse Linux, Windows 2000/2003/XP	■	■	■	☐
Mapping Tools	Altova MapForce / SchemaAgent	Commercial	Proprietary	Windows 2000/2003/XP/Vista	■	■	■	■
Mapping Tools	COMA++	Research	Proprietary	Java	■	■	☐	■
Mapping Tools	Clio	Research	Proprietary	Java	■	■	☐	☐
Other Solutions	StylusStudio / DataDirect XML Converters	Research	XML Schema	Windows Platforms	☐	■	☐	☐
Other Solutions	TopBraid Composer	Commercial	OWL	Java	☐	■	☐	☐
Other Solutions	Yahoo Pipes	Commercial	XML	Windows 2000/XP	☐	■	■	■

■ Supported
☐ Not Supported

Table 3.2: Metadata mapping solutions — categorisation and overview

First, only Altova MapForce in combination with Altova SchemaAgent as well as Microsoft BizTalk

Server support all four mapping phases. Other tools lack at least one phase. Especially mapping discovery, an issue which has gained much attention in scientific literature, has not yet found its implementation in commercial mapping solutions — and if at all, then only to a minor, rather trivial extent such as the comparison of schema element names.

The second observation is that many solutions use their own proprietary models for representing schemes and mappings among them. Additionally, we notice that there is a strong support for XML technologies (XML Schema and DTD) and the relational model (SQL-DDL); support for other technologies is rather minor.

Third, we can observe that most mapping solutions support the mapping execution phase by compiling mapping specifications into executable code (e.g., XSLT, XQuery) and providing the possibility to deploy this code as an executable service.

Our last observation is that the majority of mapping solutions support the mapping maintenance phase, but in a varying degree: in Microsoft BizTalk, for instance, users can publish their mappings in a web-accessible WebDav repository that does not provide any further sophisticated functions. Altova's SchemaAgent, COMA++, and Yahoo Pipes mark the opposite end of the spectrum and provide an extensive set of maintenance functionality.

3.4 Analysis of Mapping Solutions

After we have set up the evaluation framework in Section 3.2 and presented a representative selection of mapping solutions in Section 3.3, we now analyse these solutions according to the imposed requirements.

In the previous section, where we briefly introduced the mapping solutions, we already outlined which mapping phases a solution supports. Here we analyse in detail how and to what extent a solution supports the requirements of a certain mapping phase.

3.4.1 General Requirements

In the evaluation framework, this category contains all requirements that must be supported by any mapping solution but cannot be assigned to any of the four mapping phases.

Uniform Accessibility

Uniform accessibility denotes the possibility of deploying a single access point to a set of heterogeneous sources from previously defined metadata mappings. A single access point could be a query interface or a service that provides transparent access the metadata provided by other services.

By their nature, Enterprise Information Integration (EII) Suites fulfil exactly that requirement. BEA Liquid Data, for example, provides the means to create data views over a set of data sources that can

3.4. Analysis of Mapping Solutions

then be queried in a uniform manner using XQuery. Also the Sybase Data Integration Suite allows the deployment of a unified data layer.

Different from EII Suites, the mapping solutions categorised as Enterprise Application Integration Suites (Microsoft BizTalk Server, Cape Clear, and IBM Websphere Integration Developer), do not provide uniform access via a single query interface but rather allow transparent access to data from incompatible data sources through deployed business processes. In Service Oriented Architectures, a business process typically exposes the aggregated and converted data via a Web Service interface.

Among the *pure* metadata mapping tools we cannot find any solution that supports uniform accessibility. Although it is possible to deploy mappings with Altova MapForce in terms of services that provide integrated access to a single source, this is not possible for multiple sources. COMA++ does not support mapping execution at all and therefore cannot provide uniform access. Clio has the facilities to convert mappings into queries or transformation style-sheets without considering query execution.

From the group of non-categorised solutions, StylusStudio enables the deployment of so called XML Pipelines[5]. An XML Pipeline allows to aggregate metadata from a set of XML sources and define various processing steps to transform them into a single format exposed by a single endpoint. StylusStudio therefore supports uniform accessibility. Yahoo Pipes acts in a similar manner, with the difference that all pipelines may be created and shared on the Web. TopBraid Composer does provide means to deploy a uniform access interface for various sources.

Modularity

Assuming that a mapping solution already provides access to a set of data sources, often the need arises to add additional or remove already integrated data sources without changing any existing implementations. Depending on the modularity of a mapping solution's architecture, this requirement can optionally be supported. Obviously this is only relevant for solutions that do fulfil the previous requirement and provide uniform access to multiple sources.

When using EII Suites such as BEA Liquid Data or the Sybase Data Integration Suite, removing or adding metadata sources requires the redefinition and redeployment of previously created views. We regard this task as a minor modification of an integration definition rather than a change in the implementation and therefore categorise EII Suites as mapping solutions that support modularity.

With EAI Suites the required effort is similar: BizTalk Server, Cape Clear Server, and the IBM WebSphere Server require the redefinition and redeployment of existing business processes and service orchestrations whenever new sources are added. Therefore they partially fulfil the modularity requirement.

Mapping solutions that follow a pipe-line approach for providing uniform access to metadata sources (StylusStudio, Yahoo Pipes) are highly modular: data sources can be included into an integration scenario by defining an additional input source for a pipe and the corresponding mappings; a task, which can be

---

[5] XMLPipelineDefinitionLanguage:http://www.w3.org/TR/xml-pipeline/

performed without redeploying previously defined pipe components.

Flexibility in Lifting and Normalisation

Lifting and Normalisation denotes the ability to lift metadata expressed in distinct schema definition languages to a common metadata meta-model. As already mentioned in Section 3.1, it is commonly agreed that this is a pre-condition for metadata mapping. Therefore mapping solutions should provide the flexibility to lift metadata of any kind to that common meta-model.

All analysed Enterprise Information Integration as well as all Enterprise Application Integration Suites fulfil this requirement. BEA Liquid Data can lift any data available in relational databases (RDB), XML files, delimited files, Web Services, and third party applications (e.g., Siebel, SAP) to the level of XML Schema. The Sybase Data Integration Suite offers so called *data services* to transform data available in specific source formats to its internal, proprietary representation. Microsoft BizTalk and IBM WebSphere both provide extensible and customisable adapter frameworks[6] for lifting external data to their internal representation. Also CapeClear provides a fixed set of data transformers for common formats such as SOAP, CSV, structured text (e.g., EDI, SWIFT), or Excel spread-sheets.

Since Altova MapForce supports mapping between any combination of SQL-DDL, XML Schema, Flat Files, and EDI messages, internally it must have the facilities to lift these meta-models to a common representation. However, it is not possible to extend MapForce with adapters for custom data formats. Although not providing the flexibility to lift any proprietary format, COMA++ and Clio can both lift SQL-DDL and XML Schema definitions to their internal representation. COMA++ also supports lifting of OWL ontologies and XML Data Records (XDR).

The DataDirect XML Converters give StylusStudio the flexibility to lift practically any format to the level of XML Schema, which is its internal meta-model. DataDirect already contains a large number of converters for widely-used formats and gives users the means to easily build their own converters. TopBraid supports the lifting of a fixed set of other meta-models (e.g., UML) to the level of OWL. The same is the case for Yahoo Pipes which provides data sources adapters for XML, RDF, JSON, iCal, and CSV files.

Mapping GUI

Metadata mapping is a complex task, both for domain experts and technicians. Therefore any mapping solution must support these user groups by providing a Graphical User Interface (GUI).

Since all analysed solutions fulfil this requirement, its importance becomes obvious. The EII Suites provide graphical means for building data views (BEA Data View Builder, Sybase Avaki Studio), and the EAI Suites provide orchestration design tools (BizTalk Orchestration Designer, Cape Clear Studio, WebSphere Integration Developer). Also all other solutions offer graphical means for creating mapping

---

[6]Microsoft BizTalk Adapter Framework and IBM WebSphere Integration Framework

3.4. Analysis of Mapping Solutions

specifications. Compared to all other solutions, Yahoo Pipes provides an outstanding and easy to use Web-based mapping GUI.

3.4.2 Mapping Discovery Requirements

This category of the evaluation framework lists the common requirements that occur during the first mapping phase, which is mapping discovery. From the previous section we already know that this phase is supported only by a few tools.

Schema Matching / Alignment Support

The Schema Matching or Alignment requirement denotes the ability to (semi-)automatically support users in determining metadata mappings.

Among the commercial solutions, IBM WebSphere Integration Developer supports the user in creating mappings by automatically aligning model elements with the same lexical representation. This could be the case, if, for instance, two attributes in two distinct schemas have the same label (e.g., Person). Altova MapForce extends this feature and automatically aligns lexical equivalent child elements (e.g., firstName) of already mapped elements. Since this kind of mapping support is trivial, these solutions support the schema matching requirement only partly.

Microsoft BizTalk, or more specifically the BizTalk-Mapper, offers advanced schema matching capabilities and therefore supports this requirement. Besides having the capability of matching schema elements based on their lexical names, it can also *autolink* elements based on their structure (e.g., their sub-elements).

COMA++ and Clio are research prototypes whose main feature is in fact schema matching. While the Clio matching algorithm operates only on the schema level, COMA++ uses a composite approach to combine different schema and instance level matching algorithms.

Consensus Building Features

A mapping solution offering consensus building features supports users or user communities in building consensus on conflicting mappings.

From all solutions under investigation, only Yahoo Pipes partly supports this requirement. It has built-in user and community management features, which are an important prerequisite for building consensus. Further it is built upon Web technology, which lowers the entry barriers for building communities. For existing mappings, Yahoo Pipes offers search and browsing as well as ranking features. Mappings can be cloned and reused for other integration tasks; we can assume that cloning demands at least a minimal degree of agreement and consensus on a certain mapping.

3.4.3 Mapping Representation Requirements

By their nature, all mapping solutions require a formalism for representing mappings. As we have seen in Figure 3.2 in the previous section, this is indeed the case for all solutions under consideration. At this point we will analyse the strength and expressiveness of each formalism, i.e., its ability to capture the various kinds of heterogeneities and interoperability conflicts.

Model-Level Structural Heterogeneity Reconciliation

Structural conflicts on the model level fall into two categories: *element definition conflicts* occur because the elements of distinct models might have assigned different names, identifiers, or conflicting constraints. *Domain representation conflicts* arise because domain experts reflect the constituents of a domain in different generalisation hierarchies, using a different number and different types of elements. While element definition conflicts are easily resolvable by renaming elements, dealing with domain representation conflicts is a more complex task. They can be reconciled by providing the ability to relate, for instance, a general entity in one model with more concrete entities in another model.

All EII Suites under investigation can resolve element definition conflicts and relate elements with different names, identifiers, or data type constraints. BEA Liquid Data can also resolve a majority of domain representation conflicts. Although not directly reflected in the Data View Builder GUI, one can create XQuery expressions to relate a source element to multiple target elements. Further it is possible to deal with different generalisation hierarchies and relate concrete with more general model elements by defining conditions that filter out relevant data values. By providing a rich set of operators, Sybase Avaki Studio can also resolve these heterogeneity conflicts.

Among the EAI Suites, Microsoft BizTalk and Cape Clear Studio both rely on the power of XSLT to transform objects from a source schema to a target schema. The creation of XSL style-sheets is supported by mapping GUIs, which in both cases do not reflect the full power of XSLT. In Biz Talk Mapper, for instance, it is not possible to manually create 1:n mapping relationships between model elements. However, when manipulating the XSL style-sheets directly, all element definition and domain representation conflicts can be resolved. The IBM WebSphere Integration Developer does not rely on standardised technologies such as XQuery or XSLT, but allows the definition of so called *business maps* among business objects. Using a predefined set of *transform type* objects, domain experts can relate different model structures and resolve structural heterogeneities.

Altova provides a powerful mapping model for reconciling any structural heterogeneity and can transform such representations into XSLT or XQuery. Clio does not provide these capabilities on the GUI, but also relies on XQuery and can therefore represent the required mapping information. COMA++ is a schema matching tool with the primary intent to discover mappings but has limitations in representing mapping relationships between an entity and one or more attributes.

Stylusstudio also relies on XQuery and can therefore deal with any structural heterogeneity. Top-Braid Composer uses SPARQL, or more specifically, the SPARQL CONSTRUCT statement, which like

3.4. Analysis of Mapping Solutions 69

XQuery gives the freedom to design and construct any target model from a set of source models. Finally, also Yahoo Pipes can indirectly represent structural mappings through its operators.

Model-Level Semantic Heterogeneity Reconciliation

The two main classes of semantic conflicts on the model-level are *domain conflicts* (e.g., semantically overlapping, subsuming, or incompatible model elements) and *terminological mismatches* (e.g., synonyms and homonyms). A mapping formalism should provide means to define the type of heterogeneity between two model elements (e.g., element X and element Y semantically overlap, element X and element Y are synonyms) and the ability to reconcile that conflict, if possible.

From the category of EII Suites, all solutions provide means to resolve domain conflicts and terminological mismatches, if the domains of the mapped schemes are not incompatible (e.g., billing and gardening). However, it is possible, for instance, to map semantically subsuming elements (e.g., author and person) by filtering and transforming instances according to specific conditions (e.g., authors = persons that have written books). Sybase Avaki provides a library of operators and expressions, BEA Liquid Data the expressiveness of XQuery to perform that task. However, none of them provides the means to explicitly define the type of heterogeneity (e.g., *subsume*, *overlap*, *synonym*, etc.), which is remarkable because many scientific approaches in literature concentrate on this kind of semantic representation (see Section 3.2.3).

EAI Suites support semantic heterogeneity reconciliation on the model level in a similar way as EII Suites and do not offer means to represent the semantics of mapping relationships. Microsoft BizTalk provides an extensible set of functions that fulfil the same task as operators in the above mentioned EII Suites. WebSphere relies on the definition of *maps* that describe a series of transformation steps, which defines how to transform source into target business objects. Since each map is in fact Java code, one can utilise the full expressiveness of a programming language for the semantic reconciliation of incompatible model elements.

For Altova our analysis bears the same results as for EII and EAI Suites: semantic reconciliation is possible through a set of operators but there is no mechanism to represent the nature of a mapping relationship. Clio does not provide such operators or functions (sort, join, rename) in its mapping model and therefore does not have any advanced capabilities for resolving semantic heterogeneities, if we disregard the fact that one could manually edit the XQuery interpretation of the mapping generated by Clio. The same is the case for COMA++ — it has no reconciliation operators and does not offer means to represent the semantics of a mapping relationship.

Stylusstudio utilises the full power of XQuery and its functions for heterogeneity reconciliation; TopBraid represents mappings in SPARQL which also uses the set of XQuery function primitives for reconciling semantic heterogeneities on the model level. Yahoo Pipes is not extensible with respect to its operators but provides a fixed set, which is sufficient to deal with semantically conflicting model elements.

Instance-Level Semantic Heterogeneity Reconciliation

Instance transformation is the means for reconciling semantic heterogeneities on the instance level. It specifies how an instance value can be transformed from one representation into another. A transformation is usually implemented in terms of functions, which can define simple operations such as data type conversion (e.g., string to integer) but also more complex tasks such as converting scales (e.g., weight:pound to weight:kg). For complex transformation tasks, a mapping formalism should support the implementation of custom, domain-specific functions.

BEA Liquid Data provides a set of standard functions for creating data views and is also extensible by creating custom functions to perform specialised tasks. The same is the case for the Sybase Data Integration Suite.

Also the EAI Suites provide such means: Microsoft BizTalk and Cape Clear rely on XSLT which in fact is a fully functional language for implementing a broad range of transformation scenarios. IBM WebSphere does not rely on standard technologies but allows to implement custom transform types for converting data values within business objects from one representation to another.

Altova offers a variety of standard functions for transforming data and also allows the implementation and registration of custom functions. Clio implicitly supports this feature by relying on XQuery but does not provide the necessary means on the GUI level. COMA++ does not have any data transformation capabilities.

Also Stylusstudio and TopBraid Composer support instance level reconciliation of semantic heterogeneities. The former allows the definition of user-defined XQuery functions. The latter relies on SPARQL which also uses the XQuery function set. Yahoo Pipes currently provides only a fixed set of functions that cover a wide, but not extensible spectrum of possible transformations.

Context Representation

Since the semantic correctness of mappings depends on the *mapping context*, i.e., the setting in which a mapping has been created, a mapping formalism should be able to capture such information.

A very simple and limited form of context representation is to capture user information, i.e., the username of the domain expert that has created a mapping. From all mapping solutions under consideration, only Yahoo Pipes binds established mappings to a certain user. More suitable support to represent the context of mappings is not provided by any other representative mapping solution under investigation.

Flexible Language Binding

If a mapping solution relies on a generic formalism, it is open for mappings between schemes expressed in a variety of schema definition languages. The drawback of such an approach is the increased complexity and additional implementation effort for each single language to be supported. As already illustrated in Figure 3.2, some solutions have mapping capabilities for specific languages (e.g., XML Schema, OWL)

3.4. Analysis of Mapping Solutions

while others rely on proprietary meta-models.

Solutions bound to a specific language do not have the flexibility to map metadata expressed in other languages without lifting them to a common representation. BEA Liquid Data, all EAI Suites, Stylusstudio, and also Yahoo Pipes are bound to XML Schema or XML respectively and therefore cannot be considered as having a flexible language binding. This is also the case for TopBraid composer, which is bound to OWL.

Sybase Avaki relies on a proprietary model and has specific bindings for other types of models. Also Altova MapForce, Clio and COMA++ rely on a generic approach and have bindings for languages such as XML, OWL, or SQL-DDL.

3.4.4 Mapping Execution Requirements

In this section, we analyse to what extent the analysed mapping solutions fulfil common requirements that occur when mappings are executed during run-time.

Query Reformulation

Mapping solutions that are part of *virtually integrated* systems, hence systems that leave the data in their data sources without replicating them to a central store, require a mechanism that reformulates queries according to a mapping definition. A common way to implement such a mechanism is to work with views, i.e., the user selected target schema is described as a set of views over the data sources.

Regarding our representative selection of mapping solutions, we can further divide them into two categories: those that use mappings to generate views, and those that use them to transform metadata from one representation to another. Only the Enterprise Information Integration (EII) Suites fall into the first category: in BEA Liquid Data, the domain experts create views over a set of data sources using XQuery. Sybase Avaki follows a hybrid approach: it supports the definition of so called *view models*, which are sequences of operations that combine or transform data from one or more sources. Other solutions, such as Altova MapForce or Stylussstudio, allow to generate XQuery code from mapping definitions, but do not provide means to execute these queries. Therefore we consider them not to support query reformulation in the mapping execution phase.

Query Plan / Optimiser

Obviously, only metadata solutions that provide capabilities for query reformulation, can offer means for optimising query access to data sources.

BEA Liquid Data offers a variety of features for query optimisation. First it allows to view query plans and to analyse the execution times for each part of a query. Users can either rely on a built-in optimiser or perform manual optimisation by, for instance, changing the order of the data sources to be queried or by giving optimisation hints that override the default behaviour of the optimiser. Sybase Avaki does not provide any query optimisation features but relies on a built-in caching service, which stores (temporary) query results for a definable time span.

Integration Component Generation

A mapping solution should provide at least some semi-automatic means to compile mapping specifications into executable integration components, such as data source adapters, stubs, wrappers, or mediators.

With BEA Liquid Data one can deploy mapping specifications on the Liquid Data Server, while Sybase Avaki allows the deployment of mapping models as data services. On Microsoft BizTalk Server and all other EAI Suites under investigation, mapping specifications are deployed as part of executable business processes. Altova MapForce provides the possibility to generate executable Java or C# source code from a mapping specification and also in Yahoo Pipes users can deploy and execute their pipes.

3.4.5 Mapping Maintenance Requirements

The mapping maintenance phase is usually supported by a kind of *mapping registry*, which stores information about available schemes and mappings between schemes.

Mapping Verification

If schemes and the mappings between schemes used in a certain integration context are available, an automated mechanism could detect conflicting mapping specifications.

None of the mapping solutions under investigation provides such a fully automatic mechanism. Only Clio and Altova SchemaAgent partly support this requirement: Clio verifies mappings by presenting alternative mappings to the user during the mapping discovery phase. SchemaAgent provides a GUI that allows users to browse available schemes and already established mappings between those schemes.

Mapping Reusability

Reusing existing schema definitions is a very simple way of achieving interoperability; the same is the case with schema mappings. If there is already a mapping specification that reconciles the heterogeneities among two schemes, and the mapping could also fit for other integration scenarios, one should reuse and possibly modify that mapping.

As soon as mappings are available in a mapping repository, they can be discovered and reused in other scenarios. Additional repository features, for instance searching and browsing mappings, could even improve the reuse potential. However, only Altova SchemaAgent and Yahoo Pipes provide such advanced functionality. In SchemaAgent users can browse existing schemes and mappings and Yahoo Pipes provides a faceted search interface that guides users through the bulk of already created pipes. All other solutions offer rather unsophisticated repository features such as storing mapping specifications in a central WebDAV repository.

Mapping Inference

Deriving new mapping relationships from existing ones currently seems to be an invariably scientific topic because it has not yet been implemented in any of the commercial products or research prototypes we have analysed in this section.

3.4.6 Analysis Results

Regarding the results of our analysis, summarised in Table 3.3, from a high level perspective, we can make the following observations:

Most mapping solutions fulfil the general requirements we have set up for our analysis; heavyweight EII and EAI Suites fulfil them better than standalone mapping tools. This is because the latter are designed solely for the task of mapping and produce mappings that can be deployed in other systems. Heavyweight suites cover the whole spectrum from creating mappings to providing uniform access to data sources.

The mapping discovery phase is weakly supported, which leads us to the conclusion that the field of automatic schema matching, which has extensively been studied in literature, is still not mature enough for being deployed in practice. Only the category of research prototypes includes sophisticated schema matching support; if a commercial solution supports this phase, then only in a very unsophisticated way, such as comparing the lexical representation of model elements.

Mapping representation is well supported: almost all solutions provide the means to reconcile heterogeneities among schemes and their instances. However, none of them puts an emphasis on the semantic nature of a mapping relationship. Furthermore, none of them has strong means to represent a mapping context. Most mapping solutions rely on a single, specific schema language (e.g., XML Schema), which implies that these tools must support lifting and normalisation in order to provide support for metadata expressed in other schema definition languages.

The mapping execution phase is very weakly supported. From the analysed EII Suites, only BEA Liquid Data executes queries, reformulates them according to previously defined mappings and optimises the queries using a tailorable query optimisation algorithm. EAI Suites do not provide such means but rely on the deployment of business processes, which also transform data from one format into another using pre-defined mappings. In a similar way, in Yahoo Pipes, mappings are an integral part of pipe definitions, which can be deployed and executed on the Web.

The potential of mapping maintenance has not yet been considered by most mapping solutions. Only Altova SchemaAgent can be regarded as a suitable and useful schema and mapping repository, which enables (manual) mapping verification and reuse. Due to its Web-based nature Yahoo Pipes, implicitly enables mapping maintenance. Users can search existing pipes, i.e., also existing mappings, for specific sources, and tailor them to their specific needs. This leads to high reusability of existing mappings and thereby to higher interoperability.

		EII Suites		EAI Suites			Mapping Tools			Other Solutions		
		BEA Liquid Data 8.1	Sybase Data Integration Suite - Avaki (Studio/Server) 7.0	Microsoft BizTalk Server 2006	Cape Clear 7 (Studio/Server)	IBM WebSphere Integration Developer	Altova MapForce / SchemaAgent	COMA++	Clio	StylusStudio / DataDirect XML Converters	TopBraid Composer	Yahoo Pipes
General	Uniform Accessibility	■	■	■	■	■	□	□	□	■	□	■
	Modularity	■	■	■	■	■	□	□	□	■	□	■
	Lifting & Normalisation	□	□	■	■	■	□	□	□	■	□	□
	Mapping GUI	■	■	■	■	■	■	■	■	■	■	■
Mapping Discovery	Schema Matching / Alignment Support	□	□	■	□	◘	◘	■	■	□	□	□
	Consensus Building Features	□	□	□	□	□	□	□	□	□	□	◘
Mapping Representation	Model-Level Structural Heterogeneity Reconciliation	■	■	■	■	■	■	◘	■	■	■	■
	Model-Level Semantic Heterogeneity Reconciliation	◘	◘	◘	◘	◘	□	□	□	◘	◘	◘
	Instance-Level Semantic Heterogeneity Reconciliation	■	■	■	■	■	■	■	■	■	■	◘
	Context Representation	□	□	□	□	□	□	□	□	□	□	◘
	Flexible Language Binding	□	■	□	□	□	■	■	■	□	□	□
Mapping Execution	Query Reformulation	■	◘	□	□	□	□	□	□	□	□	□
	Query Plan / Optimisation	■	□	□	□	□	□	□	□	□	□	□
	Integration Component Generation	■	■	■	■	■	■	□	□	■	■	■
Mapping Maintenance	Mapping Verification	□	□	□	□	□	◘	□	◘	□	□	□
	Mapping Reusability	□	□	□	□	□	■	□	□	□	□	■
	Mapping Inference	□	□	□	□	□	□	□	□	□	□	□

■ Supported   □ Not Supported   ◘ Partly Supported

Table 3.3: Metadata mapping solutions evaluation summary

3.5 Summary

In this chapter we have analysed the characteristics of a representative set of metadata mapping solutions against an evaluation framework derived from the state-of-the-art literature. In contrast to other surveys,

3.5. Summary

we have conceived metadata mapping as being a cyclic sequence of phases rather than a single task (e.g., mapping discovery). We believe that this viewpoint is essential for domain experts who want to employ these solution also in real-world scenarios.

One outcome of this study is that many solutions concentrate only on a specific mapping task: research prototypes concentrate mainly on mapping discovery and disregard how these mappings could be executed in a real-world system. Commercial solutions, in contrast, have a completely different focus: they support the mapping representation and execution phases, and disregard the discovery phase. Both research and commercial solutions have in common, that the support for mapping maintenance is rather weak.

So far, the majority of mapping solutions operates in closed environments on the basis of metadata available in structured data sources. Yahoo Pipes is the only Web-based solution that allows users — also non-experts — to create and share mapping specifications (pipes), which integrate metadata from several sources, on the Web.

Part II

Methodology and Concepts

Chapter 4

Towards A Web-based Metadata Integration Architecture

After having presented the technical background and the related work in the previous chapters, we now introduce the main contribution of this thesis: a Web-based metadata integration architecture that conceives the data sources to be integrated as Web services that are accessible by their URLs via the HTTP protocol. Without forcing domain experts to adopt a pre-defined schema, as it is the case in global-ontology approaches, we want to give them the possibility to query multiple autonomous and distributed metadata services by formulating SPARQL queries over a selected target metadata schema.

In Section 4.1, we first analyse the goals to be achieved by such an architecture. Thereafter, in Section 4.2, we give a high-level overview of the principal metadata architecture, discuss a set of technical properties that influence our design, describe the technical components involved, and briefly motivate the technology choices for our implementation. Then, in Section 4.3, we describe how domain experts can utilise these components to realise a certain metadata integration scenario. Finally, in Section 4.4, we define the functional requirements for the mapping model we will focus on in the subsequent chapters.

4.1 Goals

From an institutions' perspective there is often a strong need to keep in place already existing systems and the metadata stored therein. Due to technical reasons but also because of legal issues (e.g., digital rights management) many institutions are not able to export their metadata into a central data store or adjust their systems to requirements coming from external systems. So rather than *materialising* metadata from various sources into a central data store, we need to provide a *virtual integrated system* that builds on top of existing architectures and integrates metadata on demand. In the following we describe the major high-level goals to be achieved by such a system. Although most of them originate from the well-known problems of data integration [SL90], we believe that it is worth to investigate them further from the perspective of metadata integration.

4.1.1 Any Kind of Data, any Type of Data Source

A given system may store highly structured metadata in a relational database, maintain semi-structured metadata descriptions like XML or HTML documents, or even store completely unstructured metadata, such as files on the file system. In case that two data sources maintain structured metadata, the applied data models might still differ in their usage of constraints. Depending on the data model's structural properties, data sources are accessible through different interfaces including Web browsers, structural query languages (e.g., SQL), unstructured queries (e.g., Google-like full-text search), or domain specific interfaces such as metadata exchange protocols (e.g., OAI-PMH[1], Z.39.50[2]).

Since our goal is to build a metadata integration framework that can be used by higher level applications to access metadata from various sources, providing a full-text search interface is insufficient. We rather need to offer a more expressive, structured query language.

4.1.2 Reconciliation of Heterogeneous Metadata

Metadata schemes define the semantics of metadata. Many institutions use standardised schemes (e.g., TV-Anytime [ETS06], Dublin Core [DC06], MARC-21 [LOC07c]), others apply their own proprietary schemes, which are tailored to their specific needs. The complexity of metadata schemes ranges from flat element lists (e.g., Dublin Core) to complex ontologies (e.g., CIDOC-CRM [ISO06a] or FRBR [IFL97]). As soon as there is more than one metadata schema involved it is likely that semantic conflicts occur. The common approach to deal with this issue is to specify *metadata mappings* between schema elements. In the digital library domain such mappings are called *crosswalks* and are already available at least for some standardised schemes[3].

Client applications usually formulate their queries over a certain target metadata schema[4] and expect the results to be returned according to that schema. If for instance an application provides a query interface for the Dublin Core Element Set, the queries are formulated using the DC elements (e.g., return all books with `dc:creator` XY) and also the expected results should contain DC elements. It is the task of the integration system and its built-in mapping mechanism to translate between queries formulated over a chosen target schema into queries over other source-specific schemes.

4.1.3 Location Transparency

The metadata themselves should not be replicated or moved into a centralised storage system but must remain within the institutions that host the metadata. For a client that queries multiple systems in order to retrieve metadata that match a certain query-criterion, the location of the involved data sources should be

---
[1] The Open Archives Initiative Protocol for Metadata Harvesting (OAI-PMH), http://www.openarchives.org/oai
[2] Z.39.50 Gateway: http://www.loc.gov/z3950/gateway.html
[3] A list of mappings (crosswalks) between various metadata formats: http://www.ukoln.ac.uk/metadata/interoperability/
[4] In other contexts, the *target metadata schema* is also called *mediation schema* or *global schema*.

transparent. Therefore, we must build components that establish this transparency and hide the technical details of the involved data sources from the requesting client application. As a technical prerequisite, we assume that each institution is connected to the World Wide Web and has the possibility to serve its metadata using common Web technologies.

Transparent access to decentralised data sources requires *discovering* and *retrieving* metadata from relevant sources without client intervention. Since factors like connection speed or the technical capabilities of a data source can affect query response time of the integration system, these aspects should be taken into account when formulating a query plan. They are, however, out of the scope of this work.

4.2 Architecture Overview

In this section, we discuss the technical properties of our metadata integration architecture. Thereafter, we present its main technical components and the standards we will use for its implementation.

4.2.1 Technical Considerations

The field of metadata integration has been widely studied in the past and today there exists a variety of established standard architectures we have to consider in our design. Furthermore, we are facing an open distributed environment in which well-known principles from the closed-world database do not hold anymore. In the following we will elaborate on these issues and furthermore discuss, why metadata updatability is out of the scope of this thesis.

The Spectrum of Metadata Integration Architectures

The purpose of any integration systems is to give users or applications the ability to query information of different kind from different sources and to return the results in a uniform way. Figure 4.1 illustrates a taxonomy of known architectures for querying heterogeneous data and describes what kind of data can be integrated by a certain architecture type; Universal Database Management Systems, for instance, can integrate native structured data, while (Meta)search-Engines are designed for unstructured native data.

We can distinguish between two main classes of integration systems: *materialised* and *virtual integrated* systems.

In materialised systems, metadata are integrated a priori into a central data store. Data warehouses are an example for the materialised approach: they provide a central data store that gets populated once and retrieves updates via periodic data imports. The central store defines a so called *star-schema*, which has been designed bottom-up for a certain purpose (e.g., business reporting, data analysis) and integrates the elements of the data source specific schemes. The advantage of materialised systems is the query response time, which can be as low as in traditional database systems. The drawbacks are the lacking

Chapter 4. Towards A Web-based Metadata Integration Architecture

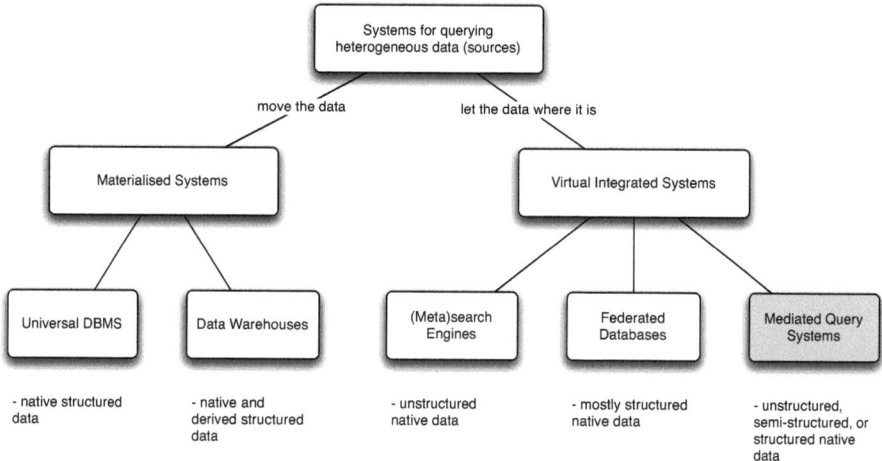

Figure 4.1: A taxonomy of known architectures for querying heterogeneous data [DD99]

up-to-dateness of the integrated metadata, which depends on the update frequency, and the redundancy of metadata.

Virtual integrated systems integrate metadata on demand from decentralised data stores. Queries are executed in a decentralised manner and the integration system must translate and forward the queries to the right data sources. The query translation process relies on previously defined schema mappings, which makes this approach more difficult to implement. The advantage of a virtual integrated system is that the data sources remain autonomous, that only those metadata required for answering queries are transmitted and that those metadata are always up to date. On the other hand, the involved data sources must always be available, and the query response times heavily depend on the quality of the network connection.

In the previous section we have already outlined our motivation for following the principles of virtual integrated systems: the involved institutions want to keep their metadata in their own data stores. Furthermore, the intent of our architecture is to provide access to up-to-date metadata from a large amount of data sources for search and discovery purposes. Metadata analysis or other query latency time critical tasks are out of the scope of this thesis.

Regarding the various types of virtual integrated systems presented in Figure 4.1, our architectural choice clearly falls on *mediated query systems*, since they support any kind of metadata: unstructured, semi-structured, and structured metadata. A mediated query system supports a virtual view over the integrated data sources and does not store any data itself. It obtains the relevant data from the sources and uses the answers from the sources to answer user queries. Levy [Lev99] summarises the problems mediated query systems aim to solve as follows:

4.2. Architecture Overview

- Data sources can contain closely related and overlapping metadata.

- The systems where metadata are stored have different query capabilities and expose distinct interfaces.

- Metadata is stored in multiple data models and corresponds to various incompatible schemes.

The Open-World-Assumption and its Implications

Database systems are based on the so called *closed-world-assumption*, which states that what is not explicitly known to be true, is false. It is assumed that the available knowledge base is complete and that a system has full control over the available information. A variety of techniques, which contribute to the high performance and efficiency of today's database systems, are based on the closed world assumption: integrity constraints, data validation mechanisms, query optimisation algorithms, etc.

In metadata integration scenarios, which follow a virtual integrated approach, the closed-world assumption does not hold anymore. It is replaced by the so called *open-world-assumption*, which states that what is not explicitly known to be true, is unknown. It assumes that no single observer has a complete knowledge base or control over the available information.

We can identify several implications caused by open-world-assumption:

- The maintainers of the data sources decide which metadata to expose. Therefore, it cannot be guaranteed that the results returned to the user or requesting application are complete.

- Validation, as it is known from database systems, is possible only to a limited extent within the boundaries of the open-world-assumption. It might even be out of place because it is not possible to determine if a given metadata set violates the constraints of a superimposed schema.

- Query optimisation requires different techniques than those known from the database domain. We cannot estimate the cost of a query using a complete, source-spanning data dictionary but must rely on other methods such as query containment and capability-based optimisation.

Metadata Updatability

An issue that is closely related to the closed- and open-world-assumptions, is the updatability of integrated metadata.

Even in controlled database environments, where the contained data are known to be complete, supporting updates through mappings is still a critical, only partially resolved issue. Since mappings in databases are typically realised as views, this issue is also known as the *view update problem* and has first been investigated by Dayal and Bernstein [DB78]. They observed that finding a unique update translation even for very simple views is rarely possible due to the intrinsic under-specification of the update behaviour by a view, i.e., a view that maps a source to a target schema does not necessarily define the corresponding mapping relationship for the opposite direction. Consequently, today's commercial database systems provide only limited support for updatable views.

What is difficult to achieve in close-world systems is hardly possible in uncontrolled, open-world environments: virtual integrated systems, especially those based on mediated query systems, generally do not support metadata updatability and provide read-only access to the metadata they integrate from various sources. Since our metadata integration approach will follow such an architecture, we will give users and applications the possibility to retrieve metadata via a structured query language but abstain from providing write access or update functionality.

4.2.2 Components

Our integration architecture comprises two main components, which are typical for a mediated query system: *wrappers* and *mediators*. Additionally, we employ an *integration registry* that is aware of available components and their technical as well as semantic query capabilities. All components in our integration architecture expose their functionality on the Web via dereferencable URIs. Thus, we can already achieve a certain degree of technical interoperability by building our metadata integration architecture on-top of the Web Architecture.

In Figure 4.2, we illustrate the main architectural components of our architecture using an example that involves two metadata sources: one (source A) that maintains its metadata in a relational database and another one (source B) that stores metadata descriptions in some XML-based format. Both data sources are encapsulated by *wrapper* components, which expose the semantics of the provided metadata in terms of a *source schema* (S_A and S_B), and provide a uniform query interface for requesting applications. The *mediator* also provides a query interface, exposes a target schema S_T, and maintains mappings (M_{AT} and M_{BT}) between the two source schemes and the target schema. The *integration registry* maintains references to all involved architectural components as well as to all schemes and mapping specifications.

Wrappers

Wrappers encapsulate local data sources and provide query access to the metadata stored therein. They accept queries formulated in a certain query language and return the matching metadata in a unified format. The semantics of metadata is expressed and exposed in terms of a *source schema* and it is the wrapper's task to translate between the source schema and native data descriptions (e.g., RDBMS tables, XML files, flat-file structures).

The purpose of wrapper components is to lift the involved data sources to a common technical level, which is necessary to overcome the technical heterogeneities between the involved data sources. This requires that:

- Each wrapper exposes its metadata using a common data model.

4.2. Architecture Overview

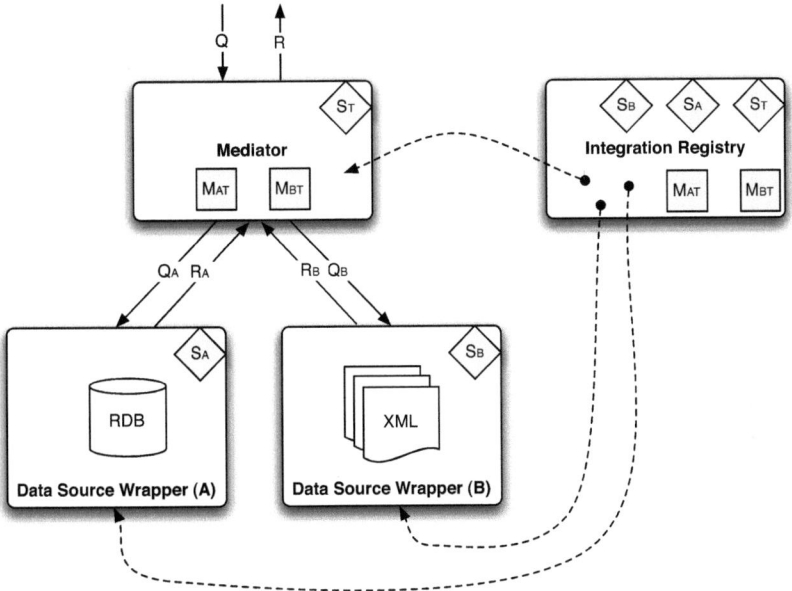

Figure 4.2: Components of a mediator-wrapper architecture

- Each wrapper describes its source schema using a common schema definition language.
- Each wrapper provides an interface that accepts queries expressed in a common query language.

Since we want to provide a Web-based metadata integration architecture that conceives the data sources to be integrated as Web services, the applied data model, schema definition language, and query language should also be Web-enabled, i.e., they should incorporate common Web standards and protocols such as HTTP and URI.

Mediators

Mediators accept queries from the application layer, unfold them into sub-queries, disperse them to local data sources where they are executed, and finally combine and present the results to the client application. A mediator defines a *target schema* that is exposed to the client and can be used for formulating structured queries. The process of unfolding queries relies heavily on previously defined *mapping specifications* between the target and the source schemes, which are exposed by the wrappers. Mapping specifications are part of more extensive *integration specifications*, which contain all the information required for the query unfolding process. Integration specifications contain all the information for setting up a mediator component instance; the mediator itself is a generic component.

In principle, mediators have to fulfil the same technical requirements as wrappers: they must operate on the same data model, schema definition language, and query language as wrappers. Additionally, they must be able to process mapping specifications, which are based on the data models and schema definition languages that are used by wrappers and mediators.

Integration Registry

Each artefact that is part of the integration architecture (e.g., wrappers, source schemes, mediators, target schemes, mappings) is registered with the integration registry. By introducing such a registry we ensure that data sources can be discovered and enforce a certain community aspect in metadata integration: we allow institutions or organisations, which elaborate an integration scenario, to publish their integration- and mapping-specifications. Other institutions can reuse these specifications and the integration registry could derive additional operational mappings from existing ones.

Integration specifications describe the technical details of a wrapped data source: its access parameters (e.g., URL), the source schema it exposes (e.g., Dublin Core), and also other technical information (e.g., average response time; data statistics) required by the mediator for unfolding queries. A central aspect each integration specification must cover is the information about structural and semantic mismatches between source and target schemes. We denote this kind of information *mapping specification*; it contains the mapping relationships among the elements of the source and the mediator's target schemes.

Furthermore, it is likely that two data sources, even if they expose the same schema, do not contain the same contents, which results in queries that cannot be answered by all data sources. Hence, during mapping execution time, the mediator needs a mechanism to determine if a certain wrapper is relevant to a query. For our metadata integration architecture, we follow the approach of parameterised views [PV99] and compile mapping specifications into a *capability description*, which contains a set of *query templates*, each defining how to rewrite the conditions of a query over the target schema into conditions over the source schema. A query transformer, which is part of the mediator, takes the capability description and unfolds the original query by substituting its conditions. In this way, templates reflect the operational mappings as well as the set of possible queries and the mediator can handle semantic mismatches and determine if a data source is relevant to a query. Further details on the generation of query templates as part of capability descriptions will be given in the subsequent chapters.

4.2.3 Standards-based Metadata Integration

As we have seen in the previous section, building a mediated metadata integration system requires a common schema definition language, a common data model and a query language that operates on this data model. We believe that the usage of standards in integration scenarios is a major step forward towards interoperability, at least on a technical level. Therefore we have decided to rely on the *Resource Description Framework (RDF)* [W3C04b], the *RDF Vocabulary Description Language (RDFS)* [W3C04a], and the *SPARQL Query Language for RDF* [W3C08].

The main design goal of RDF is to provide a framework for representing metadata about arbitrary resources in a way so that machines can exchange and *understand* the meanings. Another often unfamiliar aspect of RDF is that it has been designed for metadata integration and aggregation[5] purposes: the RDF data model is a directed labelled graph, which is simple and yet powerful enough to allow the description of metadata of any kind originating from various heterogeneous sources [PGMW95].

RDFS is a language for describing ontologies and schematic descriptions in a machine-processable way. It provides the constructs and the expressiveness to describe the semantics of data. Although it was originally not intended to be used for data integration, we can benefit from its popularity, which is reflected in the availability of various RDFS-specific tools. One can, for instance, resort to existing RDF APIs (e.g., Jena[6], RDF databases (e.g., OpenLink Virtuoso[7], Oracle RDF[8]), and also already existing wrapper components (e.g., D2RQ [BS04]).

SPARQL is a query language that operates on the RDF data model and can be used to express queries across diverse data sources. Given that wrappers can translate between RDF and native data models, we can use this query language for accessing the data sources in an integrated fashion. Therefore, in our architecture, each wrapper and mediator exposes a SPARQL query interface in terms of a Web Service definition.

4.3 Metadata Integration Workflow

In the following, we describe the interaction between a client, which can be a domain expert or an application, and our propose metadata integration architecture. We assume that the client requires search functionality on multiple institutions based on the Dublin Core metadata schema and that one wrapper encapsulates a relational database containing proprietary ONB metadata, while the other exposes BBC TV-Anytime metadata that is natively stored in an XML data source. Figure 4.3 illustrates[9] the interactions between the client and the proposed metadata integration architecture as well as the workflow within the system.

1. Each wrapper component that exposes metadata from a certain data source is registered at the integration registry. It publishes a basic profile, which is a human readable description, an interface description and the wrapper's source schema. In our example, the published profiles points to the proprietary ONB (S_A) and the TV-Anytime schema (S_B).

---

[5]The W3C RDF Data Access Working Group is working on this issue, has defined data access use cases and has released a W3C recommendation for the SPARQL query language in January 2008
[6]The Jena Semantic Web Framework: http://jena.sourceforge.net/)
[7]Virtuoso RDF DB: http://virtuoso.openlinksw.com/wiki/main/Main/VOSRDF
[8]Oracle Spatial RDF: http://www.oracle.com/technology/tech/semantic_technologies/index.html
[9]In this illustration, we have omitted the reference pointers between the registry and the mediator and wrapper components. The numbers in the figure correspond to the numbering in the following description.

Chapter 4. Towards A Web-based Metadata Integration Architecture

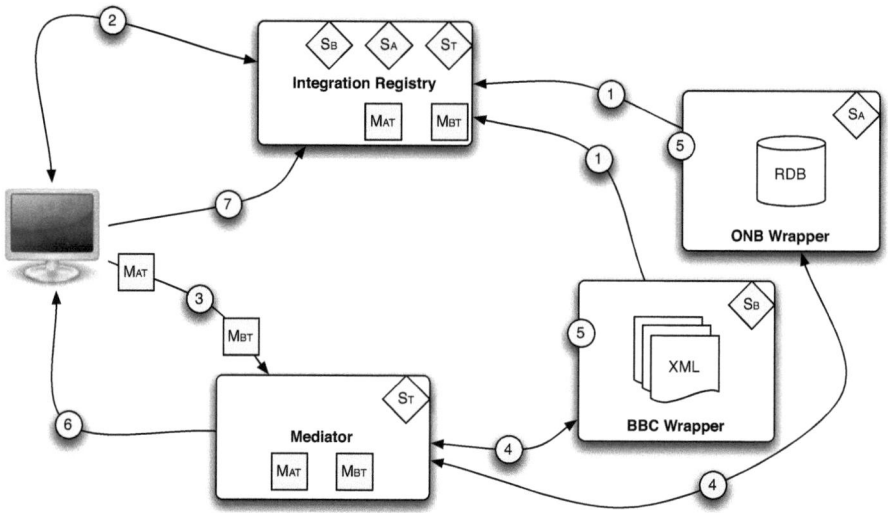

Figure 4.3: Metadata integration workflow

2. A client who wants to query multiple autonomous sources using a specific target schema S_T (in our case Dublin Core) contacts the integration registry and checks if there are existing integration and mapping specifications available for the wrappers to be integrated. If this is not the case for a certain wrapper, the domain expert must create one (M_{AT} and M_{BT}).

3. The client application uses the integration specification to set up the generic mediator component, expresses a query over a previously selected target metadata schema and executes it at the mediator.

4. The mediator component rewrites the query over the target schema into queries over the source schemes, which requires that the operational mappings between the target (Dublin core) and the source schemes (TV-Anytime, ONB) are available in terms of mapping specifications. Based on that, the mediator unfolds the original query into rewritten sub queries and forwards them to the wrappers.

5. The wrappers receive the queries from the mediator and answers them from the data available in the encapsulated data source. For the relational data source, the corresponding wrapper must translate the mediator's query into a native SQL query; for the XML data source, XQuery could provide the necessary native access.

6. The mediator collects the query results that are returned from the wrappers, combines them and returns them to the client in a uniform way.

7. For reusability purposes, the client may publish the integration specification in the integration registry.

4.4 Functional Requirements

Earlier, in Section 3.1, we have defined metadata mapping as being a cyclic process consisting of four subsequent phases: *discovery*, *representation*, *execution*, and *maintenance*. Given the metadata integration architecture presented in the previous section, we now discuss and identify the functional requirements, denoted as **FR**, we have to consider for each of these phases in the conceptual design and the implementation of our mapping model we will focus on in subsequent chapters.

4.4.1 Mapping Discovery

The first mapping phase is *mapping discovery*. It is concerned with determining semantic mapping relationships among incompatible metadata schemes and usually supported by automated matching tools. Although the development of such tools is out of the scope of this work, we at least want to consider the requirements that enable mapping discovery in an open, Web-based environment.

Enabling Collaborative, Intellectual Mapping

Finding another automatic or semi-automatic mapping discovery algorithm is out of the scope of this work. Much research has already been conducted in that area and found its implementation in various scientific prototypes, but, as we have discussed in Section 3.4, not so much in commercial mapping solutions.

In the context of this thesis, we take one step back and rely on human intellect as the primary source for determining mapping relationships. Mappings designed by domain experts are collected and build the basis for proposing suitable mappings to other domain experts that need to create mappings in a similar context. A critical mass of domain experts in a certain domain can produce a pool of mapping specifications, which can then serve as input or blue-print for other domain experts. A mapping mechanism can support this by considering the following functional requirements:

- **FR 1:** Mapping specification must be *sharable*. The technical barriers for accessing metadata schemes and mappings must be as low as possible.

- **FR 2:** Mapping specifications must be *readable* for humans and machines. Domain experts must be able to read and comprehend mappings created by others and also applications must be able to process and interpret them correctly.

- **FR 3:** Mapping specifications must be *reusable:* to a large extent, the Web consists of Web pages that have been created by simply copying and pasting and then adapting them to changing needs.

In a similar manner, this should also be possible for mapping specifications; a mapping mechanism should give domain experts the possibility to take (copy) mappings created by others and adapt (paste) them to their specific needs.

At an advanced stage, we can introduce automatic mapping algorithms that operate on the pool of available, manually crafted mapping specifications. They could, for instance, exploit transitive mapping relationships among distinct schemes and derive additional mapping specifications from existing ones. In the context of this work, however, this is a long-term goal and therefore out of the scope.

Bottom Up Mapping Approach

Schemes that need to be mapped are often extensive and contain a large amount of schema elements, which is a factor that makes metadata mapping an extremely complex task. This is where automatic discovery algorithms can support domain experts in finding mapping relationships. Most algorithms (see Section 3.2.2) take complete source and target schemes as input and try to determine mapping relationships among all their elements.

It is a fact that domain experts often need to integrate only a subset of the metadata available in a data source. Therefore they also need to consider only a subset of all available schema elements. A digital library repository, for instance, which maintains metadata about digital images, might also store other institution-specific data that are irrelevant for a certain integration context. We assume that domain experts concentrate on the metadata relevant for their context and only need to create mappings for a subset of all schema elements. Over time, when additional metadata are selected from a source, the number of mapped schema elements can increase.

Our mapping mechanism must support such a bottom up mapping approach as follows:

- **FR 4:** If we allow domain experts to map only a selected set of elements of a certain schema, then a mapping solution must support *element-based identification*, i.e., the elements must have unique identifiers that can be referenced from outside a schema.

- **FR 5:** Mapping specification must provide at least basic means for representing the *mapping context*. Distinct domain experts are likely to map different schemes differently, whereas each mapping is true in a domain expert's interpretation context but can be false in another expert's context.

4.4.2 Mapping Representation

Closed-world, stand-alone mapping solutions can employ their own format for storing and serialising mapping specifications because there is no need to exchange them with other applications. In an open, Web-based environment, the mapping specifications become part of the Web and are accessible by any client that supports the Web protocols. A mapping representation mechanism that exposes mappings on the Web must consider that and publish mappings in an appropriate format.

4.4. Functional Requirements

Webify **Mappings**

The Web has become the primary medium for sharing and accessing information available in distributed locations. From the previous requirements, we already know that our mapping mechanism must support some of the features Web technology already provides (e.g., sharing, reusable contents). Therefore, it makes sense to seamlessly integrate the whole mapping mechanism with the Web Architecture [JW04]. By following the principles of *Linked Data*, we also guarantee that mappings are published in a human- and machine-readable form and that they are easily accessible by simply dereferencing URIs. These principles, adapted to the context of this thesis, are [BL06]:

- **FR 6:** All schemes, schema elements, and mapping specifications must have URIs as names.
- **FR 7:** They must have HTTP URIs so that people can look up those names.
- **FR 8:** When someone (e.g., a domain expert) or something (e.g., an application) looks up a URI, we must provide *useful* information, i.e., interpretable data for humans and machines
- **FR 9:** We must include links to other URIs, so that they can discover more things, i.e., other schemes, mappings, SPARQL endpoints, etc.

For the design of our mapping model, which provides the primitives to represent mappings among metadata models, this implies that all metadata models and their elements, as well as all elementary mapping building blocks must have URIs assigned. The responses returned when dereferencing URIs must deliver a result appropriate for the requesting client. *Content Negotiation*[10], a built-in HTTP feature, is a suitable mechanism for delivering various representations of the same resource when dereferencing an HTTP URI.

Generic Mapping Model — Flexible Language Binding

A mapping model must provide the primitives a domain expert requires to reconcile the semantic and structural heterogeneities on the metadata model and instance level. This calls for a model that allows the definition of mapping relationships between schema elements and also considers the metadata instance level.

One can either define a separate model for each schema definition language or follow a generic approach that provides mapping primitives on an abstract level. The advantage of the generic approach is the possibility to extend the model in order to provide mapping support for a variety of languages. The clear disadvantage is the increased complexity and additional design effort compared to language-specific mapping models. Although we will mainly focus on mappings between RDFS schemes, we follow the generic approach in order to provide future extensibility. Therefore further functional requirements to provide are:

---

[10]A detailed specification for *content negotiation* is available at: http://www.ietf.org/rfc/rfc2295.txt

- **FR 10:** A generic mapping model that captures all the necessary constituents for expressing mappings: the source and target schemes to be mapped with all their elements, the instance metadata descriptions, and the mapping relationships among schema elements together with their instance transformation functions. Since such a model must in fact be able to represent metadata models as well as mappings among them, we denote it as *abstract mapping model*.

- **FR 11:** The abstract mapping model must be flexible enough to support bindings to concrete M2 schema definition languages.

4.4.3 Mapping Execution

After mappings have been specified in terms of mapping specifications, we need to translate them into a machine-interpretable and executable form, whereas that form largely depends on the applied language binding. When mappings are generated between XML metadata schemes, one must be able to generate either XSL stylesheets for transforming metadata from one representation to another; or XQuery code, which allows to query XML data sources in a view-like manner. For mappings among RDF metadata, one must be able to generate SPARQL CONSTRUCT queries that retrieve metadata from an RDF source and return them, also in a view-like manner, in the representation required by the requesting agent.

In a second step, a mapping mechanism must provide the means to execute mappings at run-time. If mappings are translated into executable queries, one must provide mediation endpoints that accept these queries and return the results from the integrated data sources. In a Web-based mapping environment, such an endpoint is usually realised as a Web application that is accessible via a URI and provides the necessary query processing capabilities.

We can summarise the mapping execution requirements as follows:

- **FR 12:** It must be possible to translate mapping specifications into language-specific queries or transformation stylesheets.

- **FR 13:** The results of such a translation must be executable by Web-based mediation endpoints.

4.4.4 Mapping Maintenance

A mapping registry supports interoperability efforts by enabling the reuse of existing metadata models and mappings. Its basic task is to provide access to all models and mappings submitted by domain experts. The Web can fulfil the functional requirements of a mapping registry. It can organise all mapping-relevant information within a certain URI space and deliver models as well mapping elements whenever their URIs are dereferenced.

Since metadata mappings represent valuable information for both humans and machines, a mapping registry must be able to deliver registry information in various formats. Humans typically use Web browsers to view information represented in (X)HTML, machines require machine-processable formats such as RDF. Thus, the mapping registry must be able to provide both.

We can define the following functional requirements for the mapping maintenance phase:

- **FR 14:** We must provide a Web-accessible mapping registry that maintains references to known mapping specifications and corresponding metadata schemes.

- **FR 15:** The information exposed by the mapping registry must be provided in a human- and machine readable format.

4.5 Summary

In this chapter, we have first defined the high-level goals our Web-based metadata integration must achieve. After a discussion on important technical properties of our architecture, such as the adherence to the open-world-assumption or the non-updatability of metadata, we have described its main technical components and the technologies we will apply for realising them. In order to illustrate the interactions between the domain expert and the proposed metadata integration architecture as well as the internal processing steps, we have described the metadata integration workflow our architecture follows. As a result of this chapter and as input for the subsequent chapters we have defined a set of functional requirements, which we must consider in the design and the implementation of our Web-based metadata integration architecture.

The outstanding difference between the proposed metadata integration architecture and existing mapping solutions lies in its Web-focus. We do not provide another heavy-weight standalone mapping suite, which can reconcile heterogeneities among closed-world systems (e.g., RDBMS), but build an open, light-weight mapping solution that integrates with the architecture of the World Wide Web.

Chapter 5

Abstract Mapping Model

In the previous chapter, we have presented the principle properties of our Web-based metadata integration approach and derived a set of mapping-related requirements that influence the design of our mapping solution. Here we elaborate on the mapping model that builds the core of the mapping mechanism we provide in order to deal with structural and semantic metadata heterogeneities. It defines the machine-internal representation — the *abstract syntax* — of the primitives we provide for expressing mapping relationships between distinct, incompatible schemes. The extent to which heterogeneities can be resolved largely depends on the expressiveness of the supported language primitives. If, for instance, a mapping model does not provide instance transformation functions, instance-level heterogeneities such as terminological mismatches or scaling/unit conflicts cannot be resolved.

In this chapter, we define and specify an *abstract mapping model* that is independent of any schema definition language and provides the basis for language-specific extensions. After outlining our overall approach in Section 5.1, we formally describe the generic metadata model for representing the source and target metadata schemes to be mapped in Section 5.2 and provide a formal specification in Section 5.3. Thereafter, in Section 5.4, we extend the generic metadata model with mapping capabilities and provide a formal specification for the *abstract mapping model*. Finally, in Section 5.5, we describe the behavioural aspects of the abstract model in order to reflect the four mapping phases described in Section 3.1.

5.1 A Generic Mapping Approach

We can identify two main requirements an abstract mapping model must cover:

1. It must provide the primitives for expressing mapping relationships between the source and target schemes to be mapped.

2. It must be possible to *hook* these mapping relationships to schema elements expressed in a certain schema definition language

There are two possibilities to reach these requirements: either one builds an abstract mapping model on-top of the abstract syntax of a specific schema definition language (e.g., XMLS, RDF/S, SQL-DDL) and thus extends a certain language with mapping capabilities, or one follows a generic approach, meaning that on an abstract level, the mapping model is capable of representing mappings between the elements of a generic data model. With language-specific extensions it is possible to provide language-specific mapping primitives.

In our approach, we follow a generic approach and define an abstract mapping model that is generic in the sense that it embraces the common elements required for mapping any kind of metadata schema. For mapping schemes expressed in a certain schema definition language, it requires extensions that go along with language-specific characteristics. In RDF/S or OWL, for instance, properties are handled as first class objects and can be defined outside the scope of a class. This is not possible when expressing metadata using the relational model, which requires the correspondences of properties, called attributes, always to be expressed within the scope of a relation. Language specific extensions of the generic mapping model can take these issues into account. Figure 5.1 illustrates the relationship between the generic mapping model and the language specific extensions.

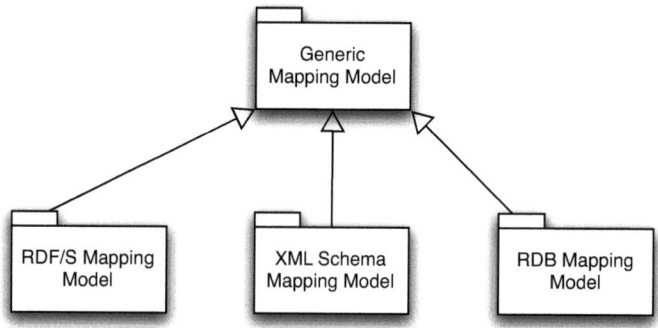

Figure 5.1: The generic mapping model with language-specific extensions

5.2 Representing Source and Target Metadata

Graph database models [AG08] are the predominant formalism for representing metadata in integration contexts. A graph is a data structure, consisting of a collection of vertices (nodes) and edges that connect pairs of vertices. Especially directed graphs with labelled edges, i.e., *directed labelled graphs*, have found their application in the area of data integration, as for instance the semi-structured data model [Abi97]. A directed labelled graph G is a triple $G =< V, E, L >$, where V is a set of distinguishable vertices, E the set of edges, and L the set of distinguishable labels that are assigned to the edges.

5.2. Representing Source and Target Metadata

Data models such as RDF/S are based on graph data models by their nature. Since the hierarchical tree model can be considered as specialisation of a graph, also XML, a semi-structural data model organised in a hierarchical fashion, can be mapped to a graph. Also the prevalent relational model can, as [Cyg05] shows, be mapped to a graph structure.

Our approach of representing metadata information objects follows the already well-established principles of using directed labelled graphs as data model. For covering the metadata building blocks on each abstraction level (see Section 2.2.2), we introduce a *multi-layered, directed-labelled graph model*, where the model on each abstraction level is represented in terms of a graph G. The elements of a graph on a certain level are instances of the graph-elements residing one layer above. This can be expressed by associating the corresponding graph elements using a special edge, having the label *type*. Regarding metadata information objects, we can identify three types of graphs:

- The *language graph* represents the abstract syntax of a schema definition language. In other words, the language graph represents the elements and the structure of the metadata meta-model.

- The *schema graph* constitutes the elements and the structure of a metadata schema, thus the metadata model. These elements are instances of the elements defined in the language graph.

- The *instance graph* contains the elements and content values forming a metadata instance description. They are instances of the elements defined in the schema graph.

In Figure 5.2, we sketch an excerpt of the illustrative metadata description presented in Section 2.1 and arrange its building blocks using a multi-layer directed labelled graph approach:

The instance graph contains a distinguishable vertex (&1) representing an instance of a `PersonName`, which is connected via two directed labelled edges (`FamilyName`, `GivenName`) with two vertices (Doe and John respectively) containing instance values. To distinguish between the two kinds of vertices, we denote each distinguishable vertex as `Resource Node` and a vertex containing a value as `Literal Node`. The resource nodes and labelled edges in the instance graph are connected to the model graph via type relationships. The literal nodes have `datatype` relationships to datatypes defined in the model or language graph.

The model graph defines the metadata schema elements: `PersonName`, `FamilyName`, `GivenName`, `String`. Assuming that the structure and semantics of the schema graph is expressed in XML Schema, the labels of the edges connecting these elements and building up the schema structure are defined by the XML Schema abstract syntax or component model [W3C06]. The `xs:type` relationship within the model graph is XML Schema-specific and assigns simple type, complex type, or data type definitions to elements. The dotted *type* relationships have also instance-of semantics and connect the elements in the model graph with those in the language graph.

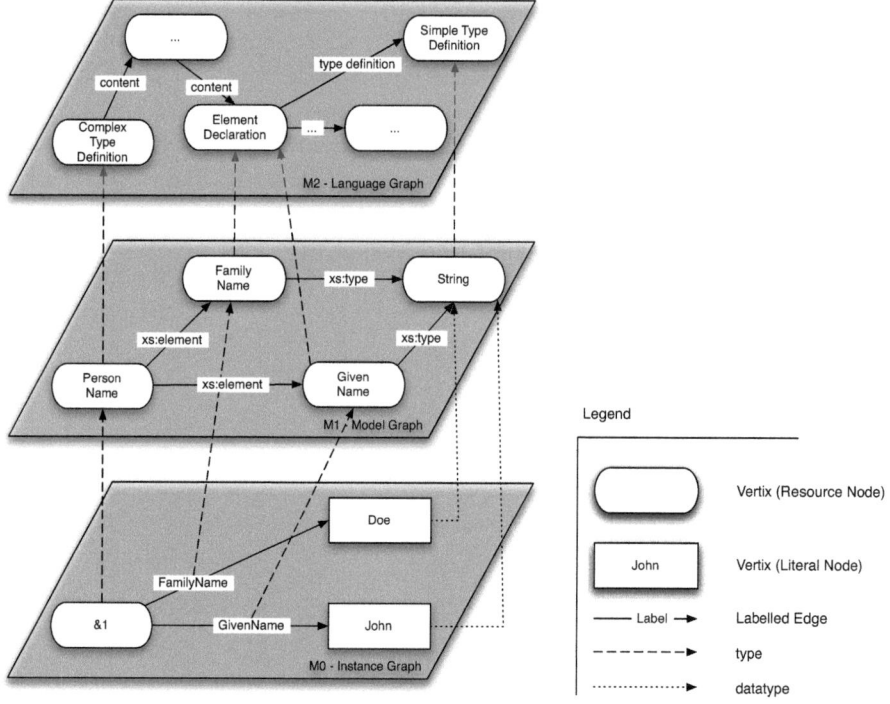

Figure 5.2: XML metadata represented as three layered, directed labelled-graph

5.3 Generic Graph Model Specification

When following a generic mapping approach, we require two types of data models: one for representing the metadata schemes to be mapped, and another one for reflecting the abstract mapping model. Our goal is to build both types of data models on a common core data model that resembles the structure of a directed labelled graph.

Figure 5.3 illustrates the main components of that model from a static perspective in UML notation. For the model elements we adopted the naming conventions used in the RDF abstract syntax, which is also based on a graph data model. An RDF graph is a collection of triples, each consisting of a subject, a predicate, and an object [W3C04e].

A `Graph` is uniquely identified by a Uniform Resource Identifier (URI) and contains an unordered set of triples. Each `Triple` represents two nodes within a graph, connected by a directed, labelled edge. The direction of an edge is given by the order of the nodes within a triple: the `subject` association references an edge's origin node, the `object` association its target node. The label of an edge is a

5.3. Generic Graph Model Specification

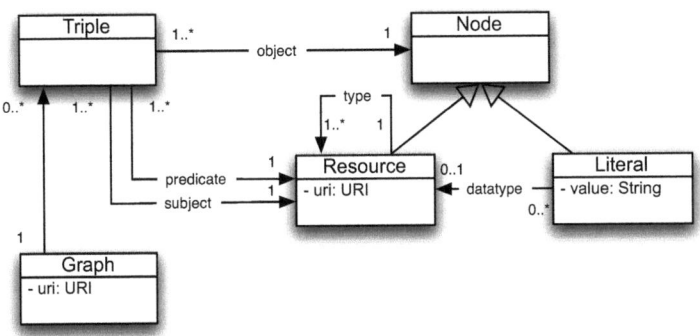

Figure 5.3: The generic data model from a static perspective

resource, referenced by the `predicate` association. We distinguish between various kinds of Nodes: Resource nodes are identified by URIs, which makes them distinguishable and machine-interpretable. Literal nodes represent human-readable labels. Within a triple, only resources can serve as subject, which makes them describable by further triples. This is not the case for literals, which can only be the object of a triple. Triple predicates, i.e., labels of edges, are also identified by resources and therefore distinguishable by their URIs. Each resource within a graph has one or many type associations, which refer to the defining resource residing one abstraction level above the respective graph. For each literal zero or one data type, which is a resource uniquely identified by a URI, can be defined. If no datatype is assigned, the default data type `xsd:string`, which is a resource as well, is applied.

There are two main differences between the RDF abstract syntax and our generic graph data model: first, we assign URI identifiers to graphs. We require this feature because we want graphs on each meta-level (metadata descriptions, metadata schemes) to be accessible by dereferencing their globally unique identifiers. For RDF there exists an extension called *Named Graphs* [CBHS05], which extends the RDF abstract syntax in a similar manner and permits a set of triples (i.e., a graph) to be named by an URI. Second, we introduce an explicit type relationship for resources and an explicit datatype relationship for literals. This enables the navigation to the corresponding typing nodes one meta-level above the respective model. In RDF, the `rdf:type` property fulfils the same purpose for RDF resources. For literals, RDF concatenates the respective datatype directly to the literal's string representation (e.g., 5^xsd:integer).

5.3.1 Formal Definition

After the intuitive description given above, we now provide a formal definition of the generic mapping data model. First we define the basic symbols that will be used throughout the rest of this work.

Definition 5.1 *[Symbols]*

Let

- $\mathbb{N}$, with $\mathbb{N} = \mathbb{R} \cup \mathbb{L}$ and $\mathbb{R} \cap \mathbb{L} = \emptyset$, *be the set of all nodes in a graph,*
- $\mathbb{R} \subseteq \mathbb{N}$ *be the set of all resource nodes,*
- $\Theta \subseteq \mathbb{R}$ *be the set of all types that can be assigned to resource nodes,*
- $\mathbb{L} \subseteq \mathbb{N}$ *be the set of all literal nodes,*
- $\mathbb{D} \subseteq \mathbb{R}$ *be the set of all data types that can be assigned to literal nodes,*
- $\mathbb{T}$ *be the set of all triples, and*
- $\mathbb{G}$ *be the set of all graphs.*

Further, let

- STR *be the set of strings, which are finite sequences of characters from a literal alphabet* α*, and*
- $\text{URI} \subset \text{STR}$ *be the set of all Uniform Resource Identifiers (URIs) represented as strings according to [NWG05].*

Finally, if we let A be an arbitrary set, we denote $\mathcal{P}(A)$ *the powerset of A, i.e., the set of all subsets of A.*

Now we can precisely define the model elements that build up the generic mapping model and provide the basis for further language-specific extensions.

Definition 5.2 *[Node, Resource, Literal, Triple, Graph]*

- *A node* $n \in \mathbb{N}$ *is a pair* $n = (k_n, t_n)$ *with* $(k_n \in \text{URI} \wedge t_n \in \Theta) \vee (k_n \in \text{STR} \wedge t_n \in \mathbb{D})$.
- *A resource* $r \in \mathbb{R}$ *is a pair* $r = (u_r, \Theta_r)$*, where* $u_r \in \text{URI}$ *denotes the associated identifier and* $\Theta_r \subseteq \Theta \wedge \Theta_r \neq \emptyset$ *the set of associated types.*
- *A literal* $l \in \mathbb{L}$ *is a pair* $l = (c_l, d_l)$*, where* $c_l \in \text{STR}$ *denotes the literal's string value and* $d_l \in \mathbb{D}$ *the associated data type.*
- *A triple* $t \in \mathbb{T}$ *is a triple* $t = (s_t, p_t, o_t)$*, where* $s_t \in \mathbb{R}$ *denotes the subject,* $p_t \in \mathbb{R}$ *the predicate, and* $o_t \in \mathbb{N}$ *the object of a triple.*
- *A graph* $g \in \mathbb{G}$ *is a pair* $g = (u_g, T_g)$*, where* $u_g \in \text{URI}$ *denotes a graph's unique URI identifier and* $T_g \subseteq \mathbb{T}$ *the unordered set of triples in a graph.*

The following constraints enforce that the URIs assigned to resources and graphs are unique and that literals are distinct from resources.

$$\forall a, b \in \mathbb{R} : u_a = u_b \longrightarrow a = b$$
$$\forall a, b \in \mathbb{G} : u_a = u_b \longrightarrow a = b$$

To access the information represented in terms of the generic graph model we define a set of operators denoted as *accessors*:

Definition 5.3 *[Accessors]*

- *uri* : $\mathbb{R} \cup \mathbb{G} \longrightarrow \mathbb{URI}$, *defined as* $uri(x) := u_x$, *returns the identifier of a resource or a graph.*
- *type* : $\mathbb{R} \longrightarrow \mathcal{P}(\Theta)$, *defined as* $type(r) := \Theta_r$, *returns the set of all types of a resource node.*
- *value* : $\mathbb{L} \longrightarrow \mathbb{STR}$, *defined as* $value(l) = c_l$, *returns the string value of a literal.*
- *datatype* : $\mathbb{L} \longrightarrow \mathbb{D}$, *defined as* $datatype(l) := d_l$, *returns the data type of a literal node.*
- *subject* : $\mathbb{T} \longrightarrow \mathbb{R}$, *defined as* $subject(t) := s_t$, *returns the subject of a triple.*
- *predicate* : $\mathbb{T} \longrightarrow \mathbb{R}$, *defined as* $predicate(t) := p_t$, *returns the predicate of a triple.*
- *object* : $\mathbb{T} \longrightarrow \mathbb{N}$, *defined as* $object(t) := o_t$, *returns the object of a triple.*
- *triples* : $\mathbb{G} \times \mathbb{R} \times \mathbb{R} \times \mathbb{N} \longrightarrow \mathcal{P}(\mathbb{T})$, *defined as* $triples(g, s, p, o) = \{t \mid t \in T_g \land uri(subject(t)) = uri(s) \land uri(predicate(t)) = uri(p) \land (\exists o \in \mathbb{R} \mid uri(object(t)) = uri(o) \lor \exists o \in \mathbb{L} \mid value(object(t)) = value(o))\}$, *returns all triples within a graph that match the given criteria.*

5.4 Abstract Mapping Model Specification

A mapping model defines the language primitives required to reconcile the structural and semantic heterogeneities among metadata information objects. In our design, we let mappings also be directed labelled graphs and therefore construct the *abstract mapping model* on the basis of the previously specified *generic graph model*.

Since mapping requires semantic constructs for the definition of mapping relationships, we introduce the mapping model's elements as extensions of the elements defined in the generic graph model. Therefore, we can define a mapping model M as being a specialisation of a directed labelled graph G, where M is a triple $M = <V_M, E, L_M>$, with V_M being the set of mapping elements, E the set of edges between distinct nodes, and L_M the set of labels taken from a fixed set of labels expressing mapping semantics. In Figure 5.4, we present the generic mapping model from a static perspective using UML notation.

Chapter 5. Abstract Mapping Model

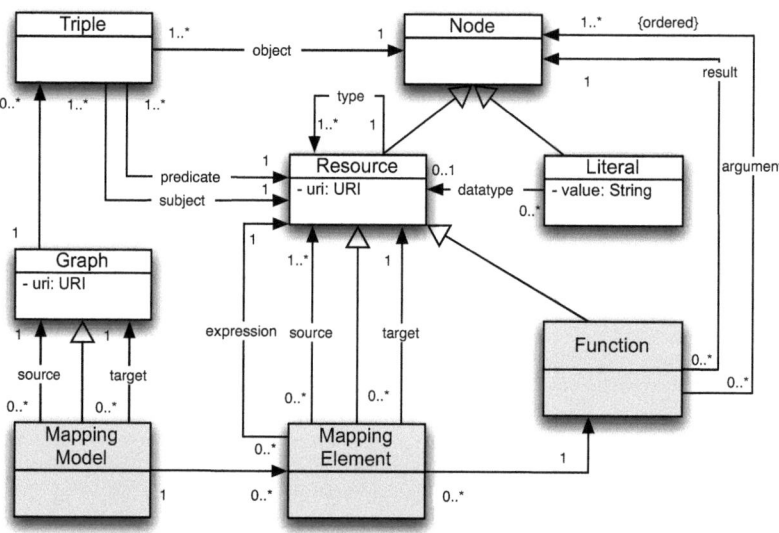

Figure 5.4: The abstract mapping model from a static perspective

A `MappingModel` is a specialisation of a `Graph` and reconciles the heterogeneities among exactly one source and one target graph. It comprises a set of mapping elements, whereas each `MappingElement` is a specialisation of a `Resource` and defines a mapping relationship between one or more distinct source resources and one target resource. This implies that a mapping element can either represent an 1:1 or n:1 mapping relationship[1]. For reconciling the heterogeneities on the instance level, a mapping element can contain a instance transformation function, represented by the class `Function`. A function takes an ordered set, i.e., a list, of nodes as `argument` and returns a single node as `result`. Since a function is a specialisation of a `Resource`, which in turn is a specialisation of a `Node`, a function can also take other functions as input arguments, which allows nesting of instance transformation functions.

A mapping element carries an `expression`, which is a resource that defines the semantics of a mapping element. As part of the abstract model, we provide the set of mapping expressions we have already defined in Section 3.1. They have the following meaning:

- `equivalent`: the interpretation of the source and target resources is equivalent.

- `sourceInclude`: the interpretation of the source resource(s) includes the interpretation of the target resource.

- `targetInclude`: the interpretation of the target resource includes the interpretation of the source

---
[1]The cardinality of mapping relationships has been discussed in Section 3.1

5.4. Abstract Mapping Model Specification

resource(s).

- `overlap`: the interpretation of the source and target resources overlap but do not include each other.

We do not require an `exclude` expression, because we can assume that, if the interpretations of two elements exclude each other, no mapping relationship will be defined among these elements.

5.4.1 Formal Definition

In the following, we extend the definition of the generic graph data model with mapping semantics. First we introduce the required additional symbols and then we provide a definition for the abstract mapping model's main conceptual entities.

Definition 5.4 *[Symbols]*
Let

- $\mathbb{M} \subseteq \mathbb{G}$ *be the set of all mapping models,*
- $\mathrm{FUN} \subseteq \mathbb{R}$ *be the set of all instance transformation functions,*
- $\mathbb{P} \subseteq \mathbb{R}$ *be the set of all mapping expressions, and*
- $\mathbb{E} \subseteq \mathbb{R}$ *be the set of all mapping elements.*

Definition 5.5 *[Mapping Model, Function, Mapping Element]*

- *A mapping model* $m \in \mathbb{M}$ *is a 5-tuple* $m = (u_m, T_m, s_m, t_m, E_m)$, *where* $u_m \in \mathrm{URI}$ *denotes the mapping model's unique URI identifier,* $T_m \subseteq \mathbb{T}$ *the unordered set of triples in a mapping model,* $s_m \in \mathbb{G}$ *the source graph,* $t_m \in \mathbb{G}$ *the target graph, and* $E_m \subseteq \mathbb{E}$ *the set of associated mapping elements.*

- *A function* $f \in \mathrm{FUN}$ *is a quadruple* $f = (u_f, \theta_f, A_f, n_f)$, *where* $u_f \in \mathrm{URI}$ *denotes instance transformation function's unique identifier,* $\theta_f \in \Theta \wedge \theta_f = \{\texttt{Function}\}$ *its fixed type,* $A_f \subseteq \mathbb{N}$ *the ordered set of argument nodes, and* $n_f \in \mathbb{N}$ *the result node of an instance transformation function.*

- *A mapping element* $e \in \mathbb{E}$ *is a 6-tuple* $e = (u_e, \theta_e, S_e, t_e, f_e, p_e)$, *where* $u_e \in \mathrm{URI}$ *denotes a mapping element's unique identifier,* $\theta_e \in \Theta \wedge \theta_e = \{\texttt{MappingElement}\}$ *its fixed, mapping-specific type identified by a URI,* $S_e \subseteq \mathbb{R} \wedge S_e \neq \emptyset$ *the set of source elements,* $t_e \in \mathbb{R}$ *the target element,* $f_e \in \mathrm{FUN}$ *the associated instance transformation function, and* $p_e \in \mathbb{P}$ *the associated mapping expression.*

In order to be able to access the information provided by a mapping model, we define the following accessors:

Definition 5.6 *[Accessors]*

- *sourceGraph* : $\mathbb{M} \longrightarrow \mathbb{G}$, defined as $sourceGraph(m) := s_m$, provides access to the source graph of a mapping model.

- *targetGraph* : $\mathbb{M} \longrightarrow \mathbb{G}$, defined as $targetGraph(m) := t_m$, provides access to the target graph of a mapping model.

- *elements* : $\mathbb{M} \longrightarrow \mathcal{P}(\mathbb{E})$, defined as $elements(m) := E_m$, returns the set of associated mapping elements.

- *arguments* : $\mathbb{FUN} \longrightarrow \mathcal{P}(\mathbb{N})$, defined as $arguments(f) := A_f$, returns the ordered set of all arguments of a function.

- *result* : $\mathbb{FUN} \longrightarrow \mathbb{N}$, defined as $result(f) := n_f$, returns the result node of an instance transformation function.

- *sourceElements* : $\mathbb{E} \longrightarrow \mathcal{P}(\mathbb{R})$, defined as $sourceElements(e) := S_e$, returns a mapping element's source elements.

- *targetElement* : $\mathbb{E} \longrightarrow \mathbb{R}$, defined as $targetElement(e) := t_e$, returns a mapping element's target element.

- *expression* : $\mathbb{E} \longrightarrow \mathbb{P}$, defined as $expression(e) := p_e$, returns a mapping element's mapping expression.

- *function* : $\mathbb{E} \longrightarrow \mathbb{FUN}$, defined as $function(e) := f_e$, returns the instance transformation function assigned to a mapping element.

5.5 The Dynamic Aspects of the Generic Mapping Model

We have defined mapping as being a cyclic process consisting of four subsequent phases: mapping discovery, mapping representation, mapping execution, and mapping maintenance. As shown in Figure 5.5, we can depict that perception in the dynamic, behavioural aspect of the abstract mapping model.

The operation `findMappings():MappingElement[]` is a core function during the mapping discovery phase and determines a set of mapping elements for a given source and target graph. The matching algorithm used in that process depends on the implementation of that operation on a concrete, language-specific level and is out of the scope of this work.

The mapping representation phase does not need to be reflected in the dynamic behaviour of the mapping model. The model itself, with its previously specified elements, provides the required primitives for specifying mappings. Consequently, if no dynamic behaviour is implemented, our mapping approach supports at least the mapping representation phase.

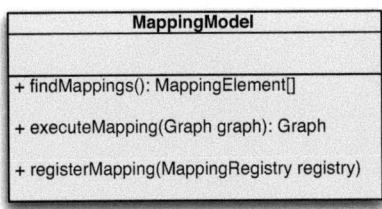

Figure 5.5: Reflecting the four mapping phases in the abstract mapping model

As discussed earlier, the characteristics of the mapping execution phase largely depend on the mapping model's language binding. If it is defined for XML, one can generate XQuery code or XSL stylesheets from mapping specifications. For RDFS or OWL mappings one can generate SPARQL queries. Therefore, mapping execution operations can hardly be generalised and should be provided at the level of a concrete language binding (see Figure 5.1). Nevertheless, a minimum requirement that all concrete, language-specific mapping model implementations should fulfil, is the possibility to transform a source instance graph to a target instance graph according to the mapping specification. This kind of transformation is covered by the operation with the signature `executeMapping(Graph):Graph`.

The necessary features for mapping maintenance are usually provided by a mapping registry, which keeps track of available schemes and mappings between them. Therefore, the mapping model defines an operation `registerMapping(MappingRegistry registry)`, which publishes the respective mapping model in a mapping registry. If we assume that the mapping registry is Web-based, a `MappingRegistry` object passed as parameter to such an operation should contain all relevant parameters (e.g., URL-endpoint, security-credentials) required for publishing mappings on the Web.

5.6 Summary

In this chapter, we have illustrated and specified our abstract mapping model. It is based on a generic directed labelled graph data model that is flexible enough to represent metadata models of on any abstraction level. The mapping model itself is a specialisation of that graph and allows for the expression of mapping-specific semantics, i.e., to model mapping relationships between source and target models. The dynamic aspects of the abstract mapping model reflect the four mapping phases.

The abstract mapping model already provides the basic building blocks required for integrating mappings with the Web architecture: each graph, all nodes within a graph except literals, and therefore also all mapping specifications including their mapping elements and instance transformation functions are identified by URIs. In order to apply our Web-based integration architecture in a real-world integration scenario, we must bind the abstract mapping model to a concrete schema definition language that allows us to treat URIs as dereferencable HTTP URIs.

Part III

Implementation and Proof of Concept

Chapter 6
An RDFS Binding of the Mapping Model

The abstract mapping model presented in the previous chapter defines the main concepts that are required in order to deal with semantic and structural heterogeneities among incompatible metadata objects. Due to its generic nature, it cannot be directly applied in a productive mapping solution because it is not bound to a concrete M2 schema definition language.

In this chapter, we present a language-specific RDFS binding of the *abstract mapping model* described in the previous section. Step-by-step we extend the model by language-specific elements to allow the expression of mapping relationships among metadata schemes defined in RDFS. We start this chapter by giving a brief overview of RDFS in Section 6.1 and then, in Section 6.2, describe how existing metadata schemes, such as those presented in the illustrative examples in Section 2.1, can be lifted to the level of RDFS. In Section 6.3, we provide an informal specification of the first step of the RDFS-specific extension of the abstract mapping model. In Section 6.4, as a second step of the RDFS-specific extension of the abstract mapping model, we describe how RDFS mappings can be processed in the mapping execution phase. In Section 6.5, we discuss how an RDFS-tailored mapping registry can complete the cyclic mapping process by supporting the mapping maintenance phase. Finally, in Section 6.6, we focus on the implementation details of the RDFS binding of the abstract mapping model.

6.1 RDFS Overview

The Resource Description Framework (RDF) is a model for representing metadata descriptions on the Web. RDF Schema (RDFS) is the adjacent language that allows the definition of M1-level metadata schemes[1].

RDFS is a semantic extension of RDF and provides language primitives to describe groups of related resources and their relationships [W3C04a]. The primitives themselves are also RDF resources and therefore uniquely identified by URIs. RDFS metadata schema descriptions comprise *classes* and *properties*.

---
[1] In the context of RDF, metadata schemes defined in terms of RDFS are called *vocabularies*.

Classes define groups of semantically related resources (e.g., Person, Event) and the resources associated with a class, called the extension of a class, represent its *instances*. This relationship is expressed using the `rdf:type` property. A class can be a subclass of (`rdfs:subClassOf`) multiple other classes, which means that all instances of a certain class are also instances of all its super-classes. Datatypes (e.g., integer) are also classes and instances of datatypes (e.g., the integer value 5) are the members of the domain of the respective datatype.

Properties in RDFS can be compared with attributes and relationships in other schema definition languages (e.g., object-oriented model) but take a different role because they are first-class objects and not defined within the scope of a class. In order to define an RDFS class in terms of the properties its instances may have, properties can be assigned to a class using the `rdfs:domain` property. This permits the dynamic extension of classes with properties and the assignment of the same property to multiple classes. When a property is assigned to a class using the `rdfs:domain` property, then any instance resource having that property assigned is also an instance of that class. The `rdfs:range` property assigned to property states that the values of a property are instances of one or more classes (e.g., integer values). Furthermore, a property can be defined as sub-property (`rdfs:subPropertyOf`) of another property, meaning that all instance resources related by one property are also related by the other.

Since RDFS is an extension of RDF, metadata schemes defined in RDFS can be serialised using any available RDF syntax. The RDF standard proposes RDF/XML [W3C04d], which is a serialisation into XML. In practice, however, other syntaxes such as N3 [BL98] or Triple [SD02] are frequently used due to better readability and known shortcomings[2] of RDF/XML.

6.2 Lifting and Normalising Metadata Schemes to RDFS

As discussed in Section 3.1, metadata mapping postulates that all metadata schemes to be mapped are expressed in the same schema definition language. In the following we lift and normalise the schema definitions presented in the illustrative examples (see Section 2.1) to the level of RDF Schema and use these schemes in the subsequent sections for a stepwise introduction to the RDFS mapping model. The precise algorithm for lifting models expressed in other schema definition languages is out of the scope of this work. Here, we refer to the works conducted by others on that topic (see Section 2.4.3).

For the following examples, we have chosen the N3 syntax for representing schema-excerpts in a serialised format. Here we only concentrate on the definition of classes and properties and omit any additional schema information such as human readable documentation, which is usually assigned to classes and properties using the `rdfs:label` or `rdfs:comment` properties.

The first example is the RDFS representation of the metadata schema used in the XML program information retrieved from the BBC TV-Anytime Service. When expressing the adjacent metadata schema,

---

[2]A detailed discussion of the major problems with RDF/XML is available at: http://www.dajobe.org/2003/11/new-syntaxes-rdf/paper.html

6.2. Lifting and Normalising Metadata Schemes to RDFS

we can omit purely structural elements such as `ProgramInformationTable` and concentrate on the elements that express real-world semantics. In fact, the example describes a certain `Program` having amongst others a `title`, belonging to a certain `Genre` with an associated `genreName`, and gives `credits` to a `Person` having a `givenName` and a `familyName`. Example 6.1 illustrates how this metadata schema can be expressed in RDFS:

Example 6.1 *Parts of the TV-Anytime schema (TVA) lifted to RDFS*

```
@prefix rdfs: <http://www.w3.org/2000/01/rdf-schema#> .
@prefix xsd:  <http://www.w3.org/2001/XMLSchema#>.
@prefix tva:  <http://www.example.com/schema/tva#>.

tva:Program a rdfs:Class;
    .
tva:title a rdfs:Property;
    rdfs:domain tva:Program;
    rdfs:range xsd:string;
    .
tva:genre a rdfs:Property;
    rdfs:domain tva:Program;
    rdfs:range tva:Genre;
    .
tva:credits a rdfs:Property;
    rdfs:domain tva:Program;
    rdfs:range tva:Person;
    .
tva:Genre a rdfs:Class
    .
tva:genreName a rdfs:Property;
    rdfs:domain tva:Genre;
    rdfs:range xsd:string;
    .
tva:Person a rdfs:Class
    .
tva:givenName a rdfs:Property;
    rdfs:domain tva:Person;
    rdfs:range xsd:string;
    .
tva:familyName a rdfs:Property;
    rdfs:domain tva:Person;
```

```
rdfs:range xsd:string;
.
```

The next example illustrates the RDFS representation of the ONB metadata schema used for describing digital images. From the tables of the relational database where the description is stored, we can derive the schema information which can then be represented in RDFS. In Example 6.2 we show the RDFS representation of the `ImageData` table with some of its attributes. In fact, the metadata describe an `Image` having amongst others a `title` and an `author`. The image depicts a certain `Person` having a `firstname` and a `lastname`.

Example 6.2 *Parts of the Austrian National library (ONB) schema lifted to RDFS*

```
@prefix onb: <http://www.example1.com/schema/onb#>.

onb:Image a rdfs:Class;
.
onb:title a rdfs:Property;
    rdfs:domain onb:Image;
    rdfs:range xsd:string;
.
onb:author a rdfs:Property;
    rdfs:domain onb:Image;
    rdfs:range xsd:string;
.
onb:depictedPerson a rdfs:Property;
    rdfs:domain onb:Image;
    rdfs:range onb:Person;
.
onb:Person a rdfs:Class;
.
onb:firstname a rdfs:Property:
    rdfs:domain onb:Person;
    rdfs:range xsd:string;
.
onb:lastname a rdfs:Property:
    rdfs:domain onb:Person;
    rdfs:range xsd:string;
.
```

The third example is an RDFS representation of the elements defined in the Dublin Core metadata standard. Since a definition of its elements in RDFS is already available as part of the Dublin Core Element Set specification[3], Example 6.3 does not mirror the complete RDFS element definitions but just focuses on the elements required in our further discussion:

Example 6.3 *Parts of the Dublin Core schema (DC) represented in RDFS*

```
@prefix dc: <http://purl.org/dc/elements/1.1/>.

dc:title a rdfs:Property.
dc:creator a rdfs:Property.
dc:format a rdfs:Property.
dc:coverage a rdfs:Property.
dc:date a rdfs:Property.
dc:description a rdfs:Property.
dc:type a rdfs:Property.
dc:subject a rdfs:Property.
```

6.3 RDFS Mapping Model Specification

Mapping incompatible RDFS metadata schemes requires the abstract mapping model to be extended by elements that take RDFS-specific language primitives into account. In the following, we will introduce these extensions with respect to existing heterogeneities in the above examples.

6.3.1 ClassMapping

We can see that Example 6.1 and Example 6.2 both define a class `Person` but identify them with distinct URIs. Hence, we can say that there exist an *identification* conflict between two semantically related classes. In order to reconcile that kind of conflict, we extend the abstract mapping model by an element `ClassMapping`, which is a subclass of `MappingElement` and restricts the domain and range of a mapping relationship to instances of `rdfs:Class`, i.e., to class declarations in RDFS metadata schemes.

Classes in RDFS — as in most other schema definition languages — can be arranged in a subsumption hierarchy using the `rdfs:subClassOf` property, which means that all subclasses of a certain class inherit all its properties. Hence, if a `ClassMapping` is established between a class A and a class B, and C is a subclass of A, then there is also a mapping between class B and C.

---

[3] http://dublincore.org/2008/01/14/dcelements.rdf

Example 6.4 shows a mapping between the two `Person` classes in N3 notation. The namespaces used in the example have the following meanings: `http://www.example1.com/schema/onb#` and `http://www.example.com/schema/tva#` identify the context of the source and target schemes, the abstract mapping model is defined in the namespace `http://www.mediaspaces.info/mapping/abstract_mapping#`, the RDFS mapping elements are defined in the namespace `http://www.mediaspaces.info/mapping/rdfs_mapping#`, and also the concrete mapping instance, i.e., the mapping between the two schemes, is bound to a specific context identified by the namespace `http://www.institution.com/mapping/onb_tva#`.

Example 6.4 *Sample ClassMapping*

```
@prefix onb: <http://www.example1.com/schema/onb#>.
@prefix tva: <http://www.example.com/schema/tva#>.
@prefix am:  <http://www.mediaspaces.info/mapping/abstract_mapping#>.
@prefix mm:  <http://www.mediaspaces.info/mapping/rdfs_mapping#>.
@prefix map: <http://www.institution.com/mapping/onb_tva#>.

map:Person2Person a mm:ClassMapping;
    am:expression am:equivalent;
    am:sourceElement onb:Person;
    am:targetElement tva:Person;
    .
```

6.3.2 PropertyMapping

Also related properties with different URIs and names must be mapped with each other. In our examples, the ONB schema defines a property `author` while the DC schema represents the semantically equivalent information using the property `creator`. To resolve that kind of conflict, we introduce another mapping element `PropertyMapping`, which is also a subclass of `MappingElement` and restricts the domain and range of a mapping relationship to instances of `rdf:Property`. If a mapping is defined between the properties a and b, and the property c is a `rdfs:subPropertyOf` of a, then there also exists a mapping relationship between properties c and b.

Properties in RDFS are defined as first-class objects and are semantically bound to classes using the `rdfs:domain` and `rdfs:range` properties. This allows properties to be related with multiple classes, which means that resources having a certain property are also instances of multiple classes. In our example, the property `author` could also have other classes, such as `Book` or `Composition`, as domain. In that case, it is necessary to define property-mappings in the context of a certain class, because the author of a book might be related differently to a target model than the author of an image. Therefore,

6.3. RDFS Mapping Model Specification

we introduce the properties `sourceClassContext` and `targetClassContext` both with `rdfs:domain` `mm:PropertyMapping` and `rdfs:range` `rdfs:Class`.

So far, a `PropertyMapping` can only reconcile naming, identification and terminological conflicts between distinct properties. For more complex incompatibilities such as multilateral correspondences or scaling/unit conflicts, we must provide the possibility to assign *instance transformation functions* to property mappings. An instance transformation function is an instance of a `Function`, as defined in the abstract mapping model. It can provide any computational functionality for a set of input nodes, and is identified via a unique URI. In practice, mapping experts can resort to existing functions and operators such as those defined in the XQuery and XPath Functions and Operators specification [W3C07]. If none of the existing functions provides the desired functionality, they can define and implement additional functions with arbitrary functional behaviour. One could, for instance, even define mapping functions that incorporate information from external services (e.g., data providers, online thesauri) into the mapping process.

Example 6.5 illustrates how the properties `onb:firstname` and `onb:lastname`, both defined as part of the ONB schema, can be mapped to the DC property `dc:creator` in the context of the ONB source schema class `onb:Person`. According to the semantic definition of `dc:creator`[4], the instance values of the ONB properties (e.g., firstname=Willy, lastname=Bogner) must be concatenated into a single string separated by a comma and a space (e.g., Bogner, Willy). We can apply the XQuery Function `fn:concat` to achieve such an instance transformation.

Example 6.5 *Sample PropertyMapping between ONB and DC properties with class context and instance transformation function*

```
@prefix onb:  <http://www.example1.com/schema/onb#>.
@prefix dc:   <http://purl.org/dc/elements/1.1/>.
@prefix am:   <http://www.mediaspaces.info/mapping/abstract_mapping#>.
@prefix mm:   <http://www.mediaspaces.info/mapping/rdfs_mapping#>.
@prefix map:  <http://www.institution.com/mapping/onb_dc#>.
@prefix fn:   <http://www.w3.org/2005/xpath-functions#>.

map:fnln2creator a mm:PropertyMapping;
    am:expression am:targetInclude;
    mm:sourceClassContext onb:Person;
    am:sourceElement onb:firstName;
    am:sourceElement onb:lastName;
    am:targetElement dc:creator;
```

---

[4]The Dublin Core Usage Guide (http://dublincore.org/documents/usageguide/elements.shtml) says that *personal names should be listed surname first, followed by forename or given name*

```
am:transFunction map:fnlnConcat;
.


map:fnlnConcat a am:Function;
    am:URI fn:concat;
    am:argument (onb:lastname, ", ", onb:firstname);
    am:result dc:creator;
    .
```

The power of instance transformation functions lies in the possibility of nesting functions, i.e., in the use of functions as input of other functions. In that way, mapping experts have the possibility to include complex computational behaviour into mappings. Example 6.6 illustrates how the mapping in Example 6.5[5] could be defined the other way round, thus from the DC to the ONB schema. This requires the instances of onb:firstname and onb:lastname to be extracted from a comma-separated instance value of dc:creator. To achieve that we apply the following functions:

- fn:substring(string, start, length), fn:substring(string, start): a predefined XQuery/XPath function that returns the substring of a given string from the start position to the specified length. If the length parameter is omitted, the function returns the substring from the start position to the end. The first character in a string has index one. For example:

    - fn:substring("Bogner, Willy", 1, 6) returns Bogner.
    - fn:substring("Bogner, Willy", 9) returns Willy.

- op:numeric-add(arg1, arg2) and op:numeric-subtract(arg1, arg2): are both predefined XQuery/XPath operators, whereas numeric-add returns the arithmetic sum of its operands (arg1 + arg2) and numeric-subtract returns the arithmetic difference of its operands (arg1 - arg2).

- fx:index-of-string(string, char): is a user-defined function, which we have introduced and is not part of the XQuery/XPath functions and operators. It determines the index of the first occurrence of a certain character (char) in a given string. As the fn:substring function, fx:index-of-string starts counting the characters in a given string from index one. For example:

    - fx:index-of-string("Bogner, Willy", ",") returns 7.

---

[5]In this and also in the following examples we omit namespace declarations that have already been introduced in previous examples.

6.3. RDFS Mapping Model Specification

Example 6.6 *Sample PropertyMapping between DC and ONB properties with class context and instance transformation function*

```
@prefix fx:   <http://www.functx.com#>.
@prefix op:   <http://www.w3.org/2002/08/xquery-operators>.
@prefix map:  <http://www.institution.com/mapping/dc_onb#>.

map:creator2ln a mm:PropertyMapping;
    am:expression am:sourceInclude;
    am:sourceElement dc:creator;
    am:targetElement onb:lastName;
    mm:targetClassContext onb:Person;
    am:transFunction map:lnExtract;
    .

map:creator2fn a mm:PropertyMapping;
    am:expression am:sourceInclude;
    am:sourceElement dc:creator;
    am:targetElement onb:firstName;
    mm:targetClassContext onb:Person;
    am:transFunction map:fnExtract;
    .

map:lnExtract a am:Function;
    am:URI fn:substring;
    am:argument (dc:creator, "1", map:lnEnd);
    am:result onb:lastname;
    .

map:lnEnd a am:Function;
    am:URI op:numeric-subtract;
    am:argument (map:commaIndex, "1");
    am:result xsd:int;
    .

map:fnExtract a am:Function;
    am:URI fn:substring;
    am:argument (dc:creator, map:fnStart);
    am:result onb:firstname;
    .
```

```
map:fnStart a am:Function;
    am:URI op:numeric-add;
    am:argument (map:commaIndex, "2");
    am:result xsd:int;
    .

map:commaIndex a am:Function;
    am:URI fx:index-of-string;
    am:argument (dc:creator, ",");
    am:result xsd:int;
    .
```

Example 6.6 also demonstrates the usage of the `result` relationship that has been defined in the abstract mapping model specification in Section 5.4. The outermost function (e.g., `map:lnExtract`, `map:fnExtract`) that is embedded into a `PropertyMapping` element defines a reference to the target element of a `PropertyMapping`. Functions that serve as arguments for instance transformation functions and define a certain processing behavior on node values (e.g., `map:lnEnd`, `map:fnStart`, `map:commaIndex`) define the datatype (e.g., `xsd:int`) of the function's return value, which will be required for internal processing during the mapping execution phase.

In the previous examples, for each property mapping we defined either a `mm:sourceClassContext` or a `mm:targetClassContext` property, which bind a property mapping specification to a certain class (and its subclasses) either in the source or in the target model. However, if we assume that there already exists a `mm:ClassMapping` between two models and property mappings need to be defined within the context of these classes, we can directly bind the property mappings to the class mappings and omit any class context declaration. Therefore, we introduce an additional property `mm:classMappingContext` with `rdfs:domain mm:PropertyMapping` and `rdfs:range mm:ClassMapping`. Example 6.7 shows such a declaration in a mapping between the TVA and ONB schema.

Example 6.7 *Sample PropertyMapping between ONB and TVA properties bound to the context of a ClassMapping*

```
map:Person2Person a mm:ClassMapping;
    am:expression am:equivalent;
    gm:sourceElement onb:Person;
    gm:targetElement tva:Person;
    .

map:fn2gn a mm:PropertyMapping;
```

6.3. RDFS Mapping Model Specification

```
    am:expression am:equivalent;
    gm:sourceElement onb:firstname;
    gm:targetElement tva:givenName;
    mm:classMappingContext map:Person2Person;
.

map:ln2fn a mm:PropertyMapping;
    am:expression am:equivalent;
    gm:sourceElement onb:lastName;
    gm:targetElement tva:familyName;
    mm:classMappingContext map:Person2Person;
.
```

After having introduced the RDFS-specific mapping model by example, we now provide a definition in UML notation in Figure 6.1, leaving out some of the classes and associations that have already been illustrated in Figure 5.4 to maintain readability. The classes `Property` and `Class` represent an RDFS-specific extension of our generic graph data model. Both are specialisations of the class `Resource` and can therefore be identified by URIs and be described with further triples. In order to represent RDFS-specific mapping relationships, we introduce two `MappingElement` extensions: first, a class `ClassMapping` and second, a class `PropertyMapping`, which can either be bound to the context of a set of source classes (`sourceClassContext`), a set of target classes (`targetClassContext`), or to the context of already specified `ClassMappings` via the (`classMappingContext`) property. Additionally, the `PropertyMapping` and `ClassMapping` classes refine the `source` and `target` associations defined by the general `MappingElement` class: `ClassMapping` restricts the range of the source and target resources to `Class` instances, while `PropertyMapping` restricts the range of the source and target resources to `Property` instances.

After having described our proposed RDFS binding of the abstract mapping model, we specify it formally as follows:

Definition 6.1 *[Symbols]*

Let

- $\text{CLASS} \subseteq \text{R}$ *be the set of all RDFS classes as defined in [W3C04a]* ,

- $\text{PROPERTY} \subseteq \text{R}$ *be the set of all RDFS properties as defined in [W3C04a],*

- $\text{CM} \subseteq \text{E}$ *be the set of all class mappings, and*

- $\text{PM} \subseteq \text{E}$ *be the set of all property mappings.*

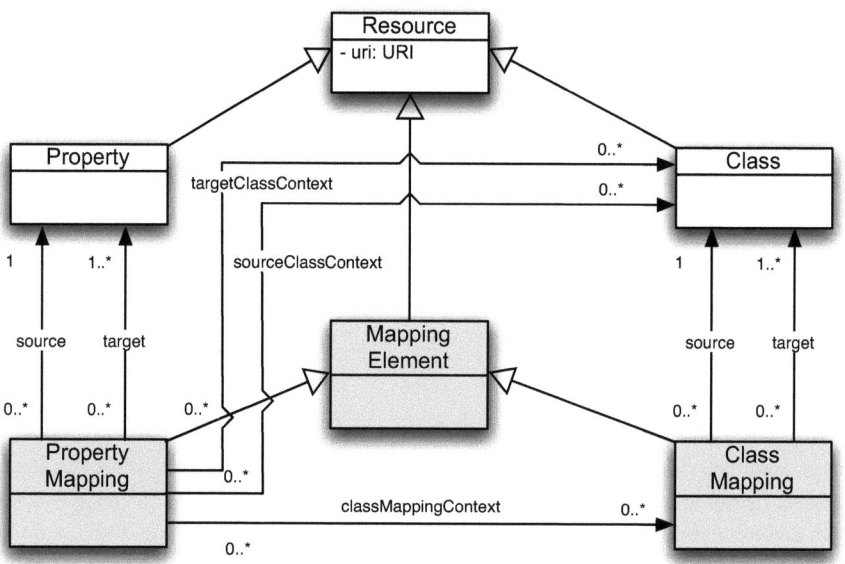

Figure 6.1: An RDFS binding of the abstract mapping model

Definition 6.2 *[Class Mapping, Property Mapping]*

- *A class mapping $cm \in \mathbb{CM}$ is a 6-tuple $cm = (u_{cm}, \theta_{cm}, S_{cm}, t_{cm}, f_{cm}, p_{cm})$, where u_{cm} denotes its unique identifier, $\theta_{cm} \in \Theta \wedge \theta_{cm} = \{\texttt{ClassMapping}\}$ its fixed type identified by a URI, $S_{cm} \subseteq \mathbb{CLASS}$ the set of source classes, $t_{cm} \in \mathbb{CLASS}$ the target class, $f_{cm} = \texttt{null}$ indicates that instance transformations cannot be applied for class mappings, and $p_{cm} \in \mathbb{P}$ the associated mapping expression.*

- *A property mapping $pm \in \mathbb{PM}$ is a 9-tuple $pm = (u_{pm}, \theta_{pm}, S_{pm}, t_{pm}, f_{pm}, p_{pm}, SC_{pm}, TC_{pm}, CM_{pm})$, where u_{pm} denotes its unique identifier, $\theta_{pm} \in \Theta \wedge \theta_{pm} = \{\texttt{PropertyMapping}\}$ its fixed type identified by a URI, $S_{pm} \subseteq \mathbb{PROPERTY}$ the set of source properties, $t_{pm} \in \mathbb{PROPERTY}$ the target property, $f_{pm} \in \mathbb{FUN}$ the associated instance transformation function, $p_{pm} \in \mathbb{P}$ the associated mapping expression, $SC_{pm} \subseteq \mathbb{CLASS}$ the set of classes defining a property mapping's source context, $TC_{pm} \subseteq \mathbb{CLASS}$ the set of classes defining a property mapping's target context, and $CM_{pm} \subseteq \mathbb{CM}$ the set of class mappings defining a property mapping's context.*

In order to be able to access the information provided by the RDFS-binding of the abstract mapping model, we extend Definition 5.6 by the following accessors:

6.4. Executing RDFS Mappings

Definition 6.3 *[Accessors]*

- *sourceClassContext* : PM $\longrightarrow$ $\mathcal{P}(\text{CLASS})$, *defined as sourceClassContext(pm) := SC_{pm}, provides access to the set of classes defining a property mapping's source context.*

- *targetClassContext* : PM $\longrightarrow$ $\mathcal{P}(\text{CLASS})$, *defined as targetClassContext(pm) := TC_{pm}, provides access to the set of classes defining a property mapping's target context.*

- *classMappingContext* : PM $\longrightarrow$ $\mathcal{P}(\text{CM})$, *defined as classMappingContext(pm) := CM_{pm}, provides access to the set of class mappings defining a property mapping's target context.*

6.3.3 Integrating Mapping Specifications with the Web Architecture

The central idea behind our mapping architecture is that the major artefacts required for integrating metadata from heterogeneous sources become part of the Web. Therefore, schema definitions as well as mapping specifications should become Web-accessible resources that are interpretable by humans and machines. In that way, they become part of an open and inter-linked information network instead of technical specifications that define the structures of closed information systems, such as relational databases.

For schema definitions lifted to the level of RDFS this implies that they must be published in some Web-accessible location. A straight-forward solution is to assign them a dereferencable URL-namespace. The elements of the ONB-namespace could be defined in the namespace http://www.onb.ac.at/schema/onb#. If a client, which can either be a human using a web browser or an application, resolves that URI it should obtain the schema definition in an appropriate data format, which could be (X)HTML for web browsers and RDF/XML for applications.

Mappings between RDFS schemes are published in a similar manner. They map two metadata schemes such as http://www.onb.ac.at/schema/onb# and http://www.bbc.org/schema/tva# by defining a set of mapping elements within the context of a certain namespace, e.g., http://www.mediaspaces.info/mapping/onb_tva#. Consequently, also all mapping elements are uniquely identified by a certain dereferencable context and like mapping specification also read- and interpretable by human agents and applications.

In that way, RDFS schema definitions as well as mappings between them become *sharable, readable*, and subsequently also *reusable*. Furthermore, through the assignment of namespaces, they are unambiguously bound to a certain context.

6.4 Executing RDFS Mappings

For the mapping execution phase, previously defined mapping specifications must be transformed into executable code. The type of code to be generated depends on the applied language binding. In the case of an RDFS-binding, i.e., when schemes and mappings are defined in RDFS and the metadata instances are available in RDF, one would generate SPARQL query templates to access source metadata and return the results expressed according to the target metadata schema.

In the following, after a brief introduction of SPARQL, we will present an algorithm which allows us to transform RDFS mapping representations to SPARQL query templates and describe how these templates are executed during run-time in order to deliver metadata results expressed in terms of a target metadata schema.

6.4.1 An Introduction to the SPARQL Query Language

The *SPARQL Query Language for RDF* [W3C08] allows query formulation across diverse RDF data sources and returns either results sets or RDF graphs. Here we briefly introduce the basic structure of the SPARQL query language and concentrate on those parts we require in the context of metadata mappings.

A SPARQL query contains a *basic graph pattern* made up of a set of *triple patterns*, whereby the subject, predicate, and object of each triple pattern may be variables. Its main building blocks are the SELECT clause, which defines the variables to appear in the query results, and the WHERE clause, which defines the basic graph pattern to be matched against a *data graph*. Example 6.8 shows a sample SPARQL query that selects all images (onb:Image) taken by the author (onb:author) Ruebelt Lothar. The WHERE clause contains two triple patterns, whereas the subject of each triple pattern corresponds to the variable defined in the SELECT clause. As a result, it returns the URIs of the matching image resources.

Example 6.8 *Sample SPARQL Query*

```
@prefix onb: <http://www.example1.com/schema/onb#>.

SELECT ?img
WHERE
{
    ?img rdf:type onb:Image .
    ?img onb:author 'Ruebelt Lothar' .
}
```

Executing a SPARQL query results in a sequence of solutions. To modify results, the SPARQL query language provides so called *solution sequence modifiers* which can be applied to create another sequence used to generate the final query results:

- ORDER BY: establishes an order in the solution sequence. Can either be ascending (ASC) or descending (DESC).

- DISTINCT: eliminates duplicates in solution results set.

6.4. Executing RDFS Mappings

- LIMIT: puts an upper bound to the number of solutions returned.
- OFFSET: causes the solutions generated to start after a specified number of solutions.

Besides the SELECT query form, SPARQL also defines the CONSTRUCT form, which does not return the variable bindings in a matching pattern but returns an RDF graph constructed by substituting variables in a set of triple patterns. Hence, it returns a single RDF graph specified by a graph *template*.

With FILTER expressions one can restrict the matching graph patterns to a given expression. This eliminates any solution that returns *false* when being substituted into the expression. SPARQL provides a mapping of FILTER expressions to a subset of the functions and operators defined by XQuery; i.e., the evaluation of an function is defined by XQuery functions. SPARQL extensions may provide additional FILTER expressions and mappings to implementing functions.

Example 6.9 shows a SPARQL CONSTRUCT query template that returns all metadata about persons available in the ONB data set expressed in terms of the TVA metadata schema. Because of the LIMIT solution modifier, only the first ten matching results are returned. The FILTER expression restricts the matching graph patterns to those that define a triple with any subject, predicate onb:firstname, and an object literal value starting with letter 'A'. In other words, the query returns the first ten arbitrary persons, whose firstnames start with letter 'A'. The results are represented compliant to the TVA metadata schema.

Example 6.9 *Sample SPARQL CONSTRUCT Query*

```
@prefix onb: <http://www.example1.com/schema/onb#>.
@prefix tva: <http://www.example.com/schema/tva#>.

CONSTRUCT
{
    ?x rdf:type tva:Person .
    ?x tva:givenName ?y
}
WHERE
{
    ?x rdf:type onb:Person .
    ?x onb:firstName ?y .
    FILTER regex(?y, 'A')
}
LIMIT 10
```

For expressing n-ary mapping relationships between properties in SPARQL (e.g., firstname and lastname to name), we require a SPARQL extension called *Property Functions*[6]. This extension is not

---
[6]Property functions in ARQ: http://jena.sourceforge.net/ARQ/extension.html#propertyFunctions

part of the current specification but is supported by SPARQL query engines such as ARQ[7]. A property function causes a triple match to happen by executing some function that performs a calculation on input values and binds the result to a given output variable. Example 6.10 shows a query that uses a property function upper-case to convert the object node of a matching triple to uppercase. The matched triples are determined by the pattern ?x onb:lastName ?ln., the final binding of the variable ?y, however, is calculated by the property function ext:upper-case, with input argument ?ln and result variable ?y.

Example 6.10 *Sample SPARQL CONSTRUCT Query with Property Function*

```
CONSTRUCT
{
    ?x tva:familyName ?y.
}
WHERE
{
    ?x onb:lastName ?ln.
    ?y ext:upper-case ?ln.
}
LIMIT 10
```

Before we focus on the algorithms for transforming mapping representations into executable queries, we introduce a formal notation for the major constituents of the SPARQL query language:

Definition 6.4 *[Symbols]*

Let

- $\mathbb{V}$ *be the set of all variables,*

- $\mathbb{PF}$ *be the set of all property functions,*

- $\mathbb{TP}$ *be the set of all triple patterns,*

- $\mathbb{Q}$ *be the set of all SPARQL queries, and*

- $\mathbb{Q}^C \subseteq \mathbb{Q}$ *the set of all SPARQL CONSTRUCT query templates.*

Now we can precisely define the constituents of a SPARQL query, which we will refer to later in this section.

---

[7] ARQ — A SPARQL Processor for Jena: http://jena.sourceforge.net/ARQ/

6.4. Executing RDFS Mappings

Definition 6.5 *[Variable, Property Function, Triple Pattern, Query Template]*

- A variable $v \in \mathbb{V}$ is a pair $v = (n_v, \theta_v)$, where $n_v \in \mathbb{STR}$ denotes the variable's name and $\theta_v \in \Theta \wedge \theta_v = \{\texttt{Variable}\}$ its fixed, variable-specific type identified by a URI.

- A property function $pf \in \mathbb{PF}$ is a triple $pf = (r_{pf}, f_{pf}, A_{pf})$, where $r_{pf} \in \mathbb{V}$ denotes the result variable of a function, $f_{pf} \in \mathbb{R}$ a resource identifying the function, and $A_{pf} \subseteq \mathbb{N} \cup \mathbb{V}$ the ordered set of arguments.

- A triple pattern $tp \in \mathbb{TP}$ is a pair $tp = (T_{tp}, PF_{tp})$, where T_{tp} denotes the set of triples and PF_{tp} the set of property functions in the respective triple pattern. Since SPARQL allows the subject and object of a triple to be variables, we extend the original definition of a triple $t \in T_{tp}$, as specified in Definition 5.2, to $t = (s_t, p_t, o_t)$, where $s_t \in \mathbb{R} \cup \mathbb{V}$, $p_t \in \mathbb{R}$, and $o_t \in \mathbb{N} \cup \mathbb{V}$.

- A query template[8] $q \in Q^C$ is a pair $q = (c_q, w_q)$, where $c_q \in \mathbb{TP}$ denotes the CONSTRUCT clause, and $w_q \in \mathbb{TP}$ denotes the WHERE clause of a query template.

Further, we define the following operations required for the specification of subsequent transformation algorithms:

Definition 6.6 *[Operations and Accessors]*

- $nodeVar : Q^C \longrightarrow \mathbb{V}$, defined as $nodeVar(q) := v_q$, generates a new query variable for an existing template.

- $varBinding : Q^C \times \mathbb{R} \longrightarrow \mathbb{V}$, defined as $varBinding(q, p) := v_p$, accesses the object-variable binding of a certain property p. If a query template q contains a triple $t = (?x, \texttt{onb}:\texttt{firstname}, ?y)$ and $p = \texttt{onb}:\texttt{firstname}$, the operation $\texttt{varBinding(q,p)}$ results[9] in $v_p = ?y$.

- $resultVar : \mathbb{PF} \longrightarrow \mathbb{V}$, defined as $resultVar(pf) := r_{pf}$, returns a property function's result variable.

- $functionURI : \mathbb{PF} \longrightarrow \mathbb{R}$, defined as $functionURI(pf) := f_{pf}$, returns the resource identifying the function.

- $argList : \mathbb{PF} \longrightarrow \mathcal{P}(\mathbb{N} \cup \mathbb{V})$, defined as $argList(pf) := A_{pf}$, returns the ordered set of arguments of a property function.

---

[8] Although SPARQL CONSTRUCT queries can contain solution sequence modifiers (ORDER BY, DISTINCT, LIMIT, OFFSET), we can omit them in this specification. This is because the RDFS mapping specifications that serve as input for the transformation algorithms, which are presented later in this section, are specified independently of any solution modification operations.

[9] The result of the `varBinding` operation is always unique because the mapping elements that serve as input for the transformation have distinct `source` and `target` resources assigned (see Section 5.4).

6.4.2 Transforming Mappings to SPARQL Query Templates

In the previous section, we have specified a mapping model that allows the declaration of semantic and structural correspondences between source and target metadata schemes. For the query execution phase we need to translate mapping specifications into a machine-processable representation, in order to deliver metadata information objects available in a certain source schema in terms of a given target schema.

The mapping model is designed for representing mapping relationships among RDFS schemes. With such a mapping specification as input, a machine should be able to retrieve metadata information objects expressed in RDF. Since SPARQL is the means for accessing RDF data, we need to transform mapping representations to SPARQL queries which allows a SPARQL processor to deliver metadata in terms of the defined target schema.

We introduce this transformation capability by extending and redefining the previously specified RDFS binding of the abstract mapping model as given in Figure 6.1 with behaviour that allows the generation of SPARQL CONSTRUCT query templates from existing mapping representations. Figure 6.2 shows how that behaviour is implemented: we assign an abstract operation `toSPARQLTemplate()`: `SPARQLTemplate` to the abstract class `RDFSMappingElement`, which is a specialisation of a generic `MappingElement`, and provide element-specific operation implementations in `ClassMapping` and in the `PropertyMapping`. We also specialise the class `MappingModel` and add the class `RDFSMappingModel` defining the operation `generateSPARQL()`: `SPARQLTemplate[]` for the mapping execution phase.

Algorithm 1 presents the pseudo-code for the `toSPARQLTemplate` operation, which is defined within the scope of a `ClassMapping`. It takes a `ClassMapping` declaration as input and delivers the corresponding SPARQL CONSTRUCT template, by adding one triple pattern to the CONSTRUCT clause c_q, and one to the WHERE clause w_q. The resulting template transforms all resources that have the source class as `rdf:type`, to resources having the target class as `rdf:type`. If a `ClassMapping` has multiple source elements, i.e., source classes, the algorithm generates multiple templates, one for each source class.

Algorithm 1: *toSPARQLTemplate*. Transforms ClassMappings to SPARQL construct templates.

Data: a ClassMapping element $cm \in \mathbb{CM}$
Result: a set of SPARQL CONSTRUCT query templates $Q \in \mathbb{Q}^C$

1 **begin**
2     $result \longleftarrow \emptyset$
3   **foreach** $s \in sourceElements(cm)$ **do**
4        $q \longleftarrow new()$;
5        $x \longleftarrow nodeVar(q)$;
6   add $(x, \text{rdf:type}, targetElement(cm))$ to c_q;
7   add $(x, \text{rdf:type}, s)$ to w_q;
8   add q to $result$;
9   **end**
10   return $result$;
11 **end**

6.4. Executing RDFS Mappings

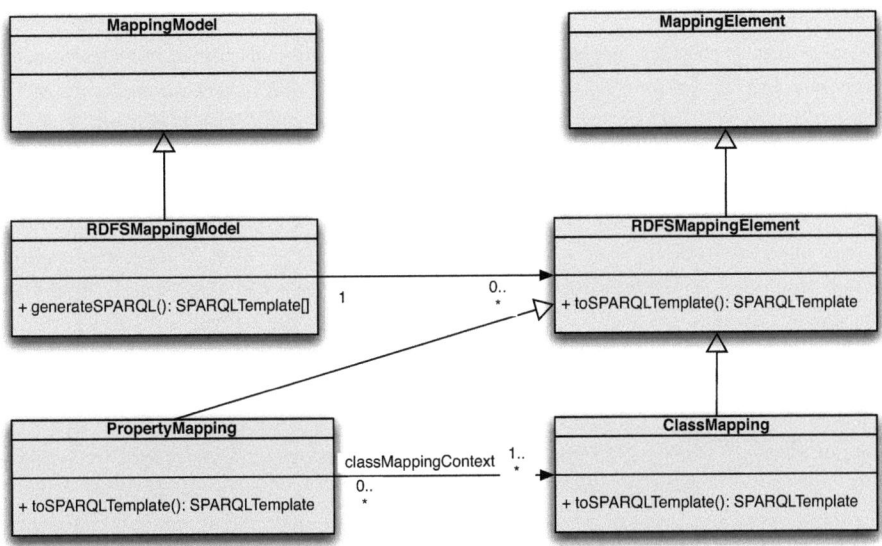

Figure 6.2: Extending and redefining the RDFS binding of the abstract mapping model with mapping execution behaviour

Example 6.11 shows how the `ClassMapping` instance defined in Example 6.4 results in a SPARQL query template after applying the transformation algorithm.

Example 6.11 *SPARQL template generated from the sample ClassMapping in Example 6.4*

```
@prefix onb: <http://www.example1.com/schema/onb#>.
@prefix tva: <http://www.example.com/schema/tva#>.

CONSTRUCT
{
    ?x rdf:type tva:Person.
}
WHERE
{
    ?x rdf:type onb:Person.
}
```

Algorithm 2 shows how `PropertyMapping` elements are transformed to SPARQL query templates. It first generates an empty query template and two variables, one subject-variable x and one object-variable y. It uses these variables to formulate the triple pattern in the CONSTRUCT clause c_q, which corresponds to the target property in the mapping specification. Then the algorithm distinguishes between two cases: in the simple case, there is no instance transformation function, which implies that there is a 1:1 mapping between properties, i.e., that only a single source property has been specified. In that case (line 14), the algorithm takes that single element from the set of source properties and simply adds a triple pattern with the same subject- and object-variables to the WHERE clause w_q. If there is an instance transformation function defined as part of a mapping element (($f \longleftarrow function(pm)) \neq$ null), it iterates through the defined source elements, generates a new object-variable for each source element, and adds a triple pattern with subject-variable x and the respective object-variable to the WHERE clause w_q. Thereafter, it determines the object-variable binding of the result property defined as part of a instance transformation declaration and invokes the operation `toPropertyFunction`, which transforms a given instance transformation function f to a SPARQL property function and adds this function to the given query template q with the previously determined result variable binding *resultVar*. Finally, the algorithm considers `sourceClassContext`, `targetClassContext`, and `classMappingContext` declarations and adds the appropriate `rdf:type` triples to the CONSTRUCT and WHERE clauses of the query template.

Algorithm 3 transforms a specified instance transformation function to a SPARQL property function. It is defined recursively because an instance transformation function can have other transformation functions as arguments. Starting at the *root* function, it traverses the operator tree as far as possible and starts the transformation process with those operators that do not have any child operators, i.e., other functions as arguments. Then the algorithm backtracks and generates property functions for the instance transformation functions that have not been transformed yet. As input, the algorithm takes an instance transformation function f, a query template q, and a property function's result variable v. First it creates an empty ordered set (line 2) for the arguments to be assigned to the generated property function. Then (line 3) it examines each argument *arg* defined in the instance transformation function declaration. If an argument is another instance transformation function (line 4), the algorithm generates a new result variable x and recursively calls the *toPropertyFunction* operation (line 6) with the function argument *arg*, the given query template q, and the newly generated result variable x as input. Then it adds the result variable x to the argument list of the property function that has been created in the context of this recursion level (line 2). If an argument is not another function but another property (line 9), the algorithm determines the object-variable binding for this property and adds that variable to the argument list *argList*. Otherwise (line 12) the argument is treated as literal node (e.g., "2") and directly added to the argument list. Finally (line 16) the algorithm generates the property function and assigns the given result variable v, the given instance transformation function's URI identifier $uri(f)$ and the generated argument list *argList*. The property function is then (line 17) added to the WHERE clause w_q of the given query template q.

6.4. Executing RDFS Mappings

Algorithm 2: *toSPARQLTemplate*. Transforms PropertyMappings to SPARQL construct templates.

Data: a PropertyMapping element $pm \in \mathbb{PM}$
Result: a SPARQL CONSTRUCT query template $q \in \mathbb{Q}^C$

1 **begin**
2     $q \longleftarrow new()$;
3     $x \longleftarrow nodeVar(q)$;
4     $y \longleftarrow nodeVar(q)$;
5   add $(x, targetElement(pm), y)$ to c_q;
6   **if** $((f \longleftarrow function(pm)) \neq \text{null})$ **then**
7   **foreach** $s \in sourceElements(pm)$ **do**
8           $z \longleftarrow nodeVar(q)$;
9   add (x, s, z) to w_q;
10   **end**
11        $resultVar \longleftarrow varBinding(q, result(f))$;
12        $toPropertyFunction(f, q, resultVar)$;
13   **else**
14   add $(x, elementOf(sourceElements(pm)), y)$ to w_q;
15   **end**
16   **foreach** $tc \in targetClassContext(pm)$ **do**
17   add $(x, \text{rdf:type}, tc)$ to c_q;
18   **end**
19   **foreach** $sc \in sourceClassContext(pm)$ **do**
20   add $(x, \text{rdf:type}, sc)$ to w_q;
21   **end**
22   **foreach** $cm \in classMappingContext(pm)$ **do**
23   add $(x, \text{rdf:type}, targetElement(cm))$ to c_q;
24   add $(x, \text{rdf:type}, sourceElements(cm))$ to w_q;
25   **end**
26   return q;
27 **end**

Example 6.12 shows how the mapping specification from Example 6.5, between the Dublin Core property `dc:creator` and the ONB properties `onb:firstName` and `onb:lastName` with the assigned instance transformation function `map:fnlnConcat`, is transformed to a SPARQL query template. The definition of `sourceClassContext` results in an additional `rdf:type` definition in the WHERE clause of the template.

Algorithm 3: *toPropertyFunction*. Transforms instance transformation declarations to property functions in SPARQL templates.

Data:
1. An instance transformation function $f \in \mathbb{FUN}$;
2. A SPARQL query template $q \in \mathbb{Q}^C$;
3. A result variable $v \in \mathbb{V}$

Result: the given SPARQL query template q including a set of property functions $PF \subseteq \mathbb{PF}$

```
 1  begin
 2      argList ⟵ ∅;
 3      foreach arg ∈ arguments(f) do
 4          if arg ∈ FUN then
 5              x ⟵ nodeVar(q);
 6              toPropertyFunction(arg, q, x);
 7              add x to argList;
 8          else
 9              if arg ∈ ℝ then
10                  add varBinding(q, arg) to argList;
11              else
12                  add arg to argList;
13              end
14          end
15      end
16      pf ⟵ (v, uri(f), argList);
17      add pf to w_q;
18  end
```

Example 6.12 *SPARQL template generated from the sample PropertyMapping in Example 6.5*

```
@prefix onb: <http://www.example1.com/schema/onb#>.
@prefix dc:  <http://purl.org/dc/elements/1.1/>.
@prefix fn:  <http://www.w3.org/2005/xpath-functions#>.

CONSTRUCT
{
    ?x dc:creator ?y.
}
WHERE
{
    ?x onb:firstName ?a.
    ?x onb:lastName ?b.
    ?y fn:concat (?b ", " ?a).
    ?x rdf:type onb:Person.
}
```

6.4. Executing RDFS Mappings

mapping defined in Example 6.6. Since the specification defines two `PropertyMapping` instances, this would also result in two SPARQL CONSTRUCT templates. Here we show only the one for the mapping between the properties `onb:firstName` and `dc:creator`. The example clearly demonstrates how nested instance transformation functions are transformed to property functions and a `targetClassContext` definition results in an additional `rdf:type` definition in the template's CONSTRUCT clause.

Example 6.13 *SPARQL template generated from the sample PropertyMapping in Example 6.6*

```
@prefix onb:   <http://www.example1.com/schema/onb#>.
@prefix dc:    <http://purl.org/dc/elements/1.1/>.
@prefix fn:    <http://www.w3.org/2005/xpath-functions#>.
@prefix fx:    <http://www.functx.com#>.

CONSTRUCT
{
    ?x onb:firstName ?y.
    ?x rdf:type onb:Person.
}
WHERE
{
    ?x dc:creator ?a.
    ?b fx:index-of-string (?a ", ").
    ?c op:numeric-add (?b "2").
    ?y fn:substring (?a ?c).
}
```

6.4.3 Run-time Execution of SPARQL Templates

The overall goal of metadata mapping is to provide uniform access to heterogeneous metadata located in distributed, autonomous sources. An application on behalf of a user should have the possibility to access these sources via a single, uniform interface. The predominant architectural approach applied to fulfil this requirement is the mediator-wrapper architecture [Wie92], where the mediator provides the single interface — typically a query interface — and transparently handles the translation between the involved, incompatible metadata information objects. Mapping specifications, which are provided by domain experts, give the mediator the necessary information to reconcile structural and semantic heterogeneities.

In our approach, we follow a Web-based approach, where schema information, as well as mapping specifications are defined in RDFS and published on the Web. The underlying metadata are represented in

RDF and the query language to access these data in a structured way is SPARQL. Therefore, we must give the user the possibility to set up a mediator based on previously defined RDFS mapping specifications. The mediator can then integrate metadata from a given set of data sources, provide a SPARQL interface as uniform metadata access point, and internally handle the retrieval and reconciliation of incompatible RDF metadata information objects.

Figure 6.3 illustrates the main components involved in the mapping execution phase at runtime. The user expresses a SPARQL query Q over a certain target schema S_T and executes it at the SPARQL mediation endpoint, which then retrieves the metadata from a set of given SPARQL endpoints, each exposing a certain source schema (S_A and S_B). Based on the mapping specifications between the source schema of SPARQL Endpoint A and the target schema (M_{AT}) as well as the mapping specification between the schema of Endpoint B and the target schema (M_{BT}), the mediator formulates the queries Q_A and Q_B in order to retrieve the requested metadata. The results R_A and R_B are then merged into R and returned to the user.

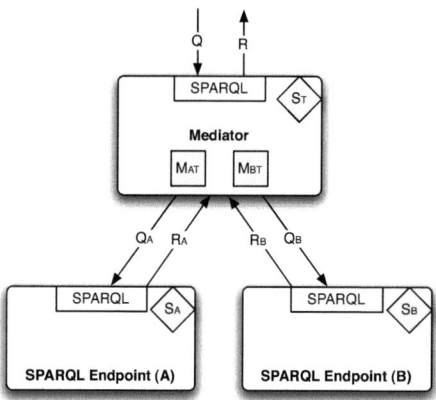

Figure 6.3: Run-time execution of SPARQL templates — Overview

To achieve the goal of uniform accessibility, the mediation endpoint has to perform the following computational steps:

1. Analyse the incoming, user-formulated SPARQL query and select the relevant query templates for each data source (query template selection).

2. Execute the user-query against the query templates, collect the results and deliver them to the user (query unfolding and result collection).

6.4. Executing RDFS Mappings

Query template selection

For each data source, the mediator maintains an RDFS mapping specification that defines the structural and semantic correspondences between the mediator's schema, i.e., the target schema, and a data source's schema. After applying the transformation process described in Section 6.4.2, the mediator obtains a set of SPARQL query templates for each data source.

From the set of generated query templates, the mediator must now decide, which ones to execute for an incoming user query. This decision is taken by comparing the triple patterns in the WHERE clause of the SPARQL user query, with those defined in the CONSTRUCT clauses of the generated SPARQL query templates. Figure 6.4 illustrates the basic strategy of the query template selection algorithm. The left-hand side symbolises the triple pattern defined in the WHERE clause of an incoming SPARQL query, the right-hand side the available SPARQL query templates that have been generated from an RDFS mapping specification. The goal of the query template selection algorithm is to find the minimal number of matching query templates for a given query triple pattern. Regarding the example, we can see that template T_1 matches the triple pattern, which connects the nodes A, B, and D in the incoming query. Template T_2 matches the triple connecting nodes B and C, and template T_3 the triple connecting A and B.

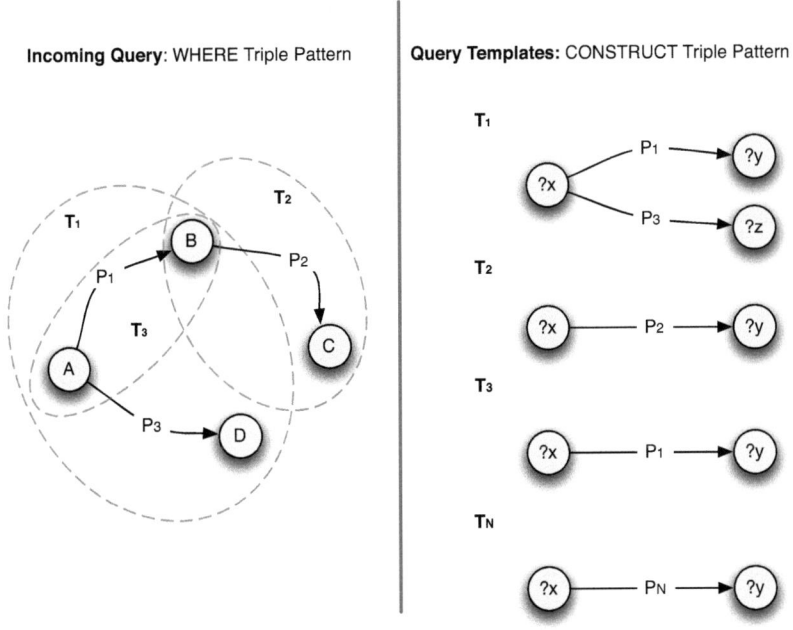

Figure 6.4: SPARQL query template selection

We could now proceed and execute the query templates T_1, T_2, and T_3 in order to retrieve the data required to answer the query from the data source. However, there is an opportunity for a first optimisation step: regarding the query templates, we notice that T_3 matches a subset of the result graph matched by template T_1. Hence, the query result triples template T_3 delivers are *contained* in the resulting triples of template T_1. Based on that, we can infer that there is no need to execute T_3 to answer the query and simply omit the execution of that template.

Example 6.14 shows a sample user query expressed over the ONB metadata schema, asking for all resources that identify a person with a certain first-name. For metadata sources that maintain metadata using a different scheme (e.g., Dublin Core), the mediator must apply mapping specifications and select the appropriate SPARQL query templates. In the case of this query, the template presented in Example 6.13 is selected, because its CONSTRUCT clause triple pattern matches the one in the WHERE clause in the user query.

Example 6.14 *Sample user query executing the query template shown in Example 6.13*

```
@prefix onb: <http://www.example1.com/schema/onb#>.

SELECT ?x
WHERE
{
    ?x onb:firstName "David".
    ?x rdf:type onb:Person.
}
```

If the user query included an additional triple pattern referring to the property onb:lastName, this would result in the selection of a second query template, which maps the property dc:creator to onb:lastName. The template selection process can further be improved by considering basic query optimisation strategies such as query containment. Since query optimisation is out of the scope of this work, we refer to the related work described elsewhere (see e.g., [MLF00]).

Query unfolding and result collection

After the relevant templates have been selected, the mediation component must execute them in order to retrieve the requested metadata information objects. Similar to *views* (see [Hal01]) in relational database management systems, the SPARQL query templates deliver dynamic virtual graphs collected from the data sources' data graphs, expressed in terms of the user-selected target schema. The incoming user queries are then executed against these virtual graphs, i.e., against the template execution results. From a data integration perspective, we follow a *Global-As-View (GAV)* approach for specifying mappings, where each concept of the global view is mapped to a query over the data source (see [Len02]).

6.4. Executing RDFS Mappings

In our current approach, the mediation component executes the selected templates as they result from the translation of the previously defined mapping specifications, which leads to high latency. It does, for instance, not consider that only a subset of the metadata in a data source should be selected during template execution if a specific restriction on an object node is formulated in the user query (e.g., ?x onb:firstname "David"). Nor does it consider the possibility to combine relevant query templates in order to reduce the overall amount of query template executions. We can identify the following optimisation possibilities:

- Template adaption
- Template combination
- Persisting virtual graphs
- Capability-based optimisation

We can reduce the overall amount of metadata that is transferred between the wrapper and mediator components by adapting the templates to be executed according to restrictions provided in the user query. If for instance, the user query asks for "all persons having 'David' as firstname" and we know that there is a mapping relationship between onb:firstname and dc:creator and we also know that the object restriction "David" is a literal of datatype xsd:string, we can add an appropriate SPARQL FILTER expression (see Example 6.9) to the WHERE clause of the query template to be executed and thereby reduce the overall amount of metadata being returned from the involved wrapper components. Example 6.15 shows how the SPARQL query template presented in Example 6.13 can be adapted according to the object restriction given in the user query presented in Example 6.14.

Example 6.15 *The query template presented in Example 6.13 adapted to the user query shown in Example 6.14.*

```
CONSTRUCT
{
     ?x onb:firstName ?y.
     ?x rdf:type onb:Person.
}
WHERE
{
     ?x dc:creator ?a.
     ?b fx:index-of-string (?a ", ").
     ?c op:numeric-add (?b "2").
     ?y fn:substring (?a ?c).
     FILTER regex(?y, "David")
}
```

Template combination denotes the possibility to create additional templates from existing ones. Without optimisation, the query engine in the mediator executes the set of selected query templates, whereas each template leads to one query to be executed. We can reduce the number of required query executions by creating additional templates from the set of generated templates. The resulting templates should cover a larger part of the triple pattern in the WHERE clause of the user query than the templates that are generated directly from the mapping specification. If we regard Example 6.13 and assume that there exists another template generated for the mapping between dc:creator and onb:lastName, we could, as illustrated in Example 6.16, combine these templates into a single one. A user query, asking for a certain resource that identifies a person with a certain first- and lastname, would then trigger that template instead of two separate templates. For a more profound discussion of template based mapping approaches we refer to [RSU95].

Example 6.16 *Sample combined query template.*
```
CONSTRUCT
{
    ?x onb:firstName ?y.
    ?x onb:lastName ?z.
    ?x rdf:type onb:Person.
}
WHERE
{
    ?x dc:creator ?a.

    ?b fx:index-of-string (?a ", ").

    ?c op:numeric-add (?b "2").
    ?y fn:substring (?a ?c).

    ?d op:numeric-subtract (?b "1").
    ?z fn:substring (?a "1" ?d)
}
```

Another optimisation technique for reducing the query answering latency in the data sources is to persist query results as virtual graphs. Analogous to *materialised views* (see [LW95]) known from the relational database domain, we can cache the result of a query template execution as a concrete graph and update that graph in a certain time interval. The drawback of this optimisation technique is that the persistence of virtual graphs requires additional storage space. Therefore, the domain expert must decide for which templates this trade-off between reduced latency and additional storage spaces is beneficial.

Since metadata are integrated from distributed, autonomous data sources, the mediator can also optimise the order and timing of query execution. While closed database management systems can estimate the cost of each query and deduce an optimised query plan, this is hardly possible in open, distributed environments. The mediator, which executes the unfolded queries at the data source wrappers, has little or no knowledge about the data sources' internal query processing behaviour. Thus, the mediator must select a query plan based on the *capabilities* of the involved data sources. For a more detailed discussion on capability-based optimisation in mediators, which also explains how such capabilities could be described, we refer to [PGH96]. DARQ [QL08], a query engine for executing federated SPARQL queries, implements such a query optimisation approach, which is based on data source capability descriptions. A general strategy for query federation in SPARQL-based mediator-wrapper architectures is described in [LWB08].

All these optimisation techniques are currently out of the scope of our work. We neither provide any further technical specification nor consider these techniques in our implementation. In our future work, however, we must consider these issues in order to provide efficiency and low latency also for the mapping execution phase.

6.5 Maintaining RDFS Mappings

For the mapping maintenance phase, we require a registry that enables the discovery of and access to existing metadata schemes and mappings between them. The availability of a registry is an essential step towards metadata interoperability because domain experts can reuse existing schemes and mappings rather than designing new ones. This is the main reason why we defined *metadata mapping* as being a cyclic process where the fourth phase, *mapping maintenance*, is followed by the first phase *mapping discovery*.

A noteworthy mapping solution, which supports the mapping maintenance phase, is Altova SchemaAgent [Alt07b]. It provides a registry for analysing and managing relationships among XML Schemes, XML instance documents, and other XML based files. Domain experts working on data integration projects, can use this tool to view existing schemes and mappings and reuse existing components in a modular development approach. The drawback of this solution is that it operates in a closed-world environment, i.e., within an institution hosting an Altova Schema Agent installation.

In contrast to existing stand-alone mapping solutions, we continue the approach we have followed also for the preceding mapping phases and integrate our mapping maintenance solution with the architecture of the World Wide Web. So far, we have defined metadata schemes and mappings between them as simply being Web resources identified via URIs. For the concrete language-specific RDFS binding, we can define these components as being *dereferencable* Web resources. In that way, we can regard the data maintained by registries as dereferencable Web-resources. Therefore, in our approach, we are not building a mapping maintenance solution but simply use the Web infrastructure for these tasks.

6.5.1 Mapping Registry Architecture

The central idea of our mapping registry approach is that all components involved in the mapping process become dereferencable Web resources. Figure 6.5 illustrates the basic architecture of such a mapping registry: the clouds represent the domains within the Web that a certain registry covers. Each registry is aware of a certain amount of registered schemes (e.g., S_A, S_B, S_T) and metadata mappings (e.g., M_{AT}, M_{BT}) and also maintains links to other registries.

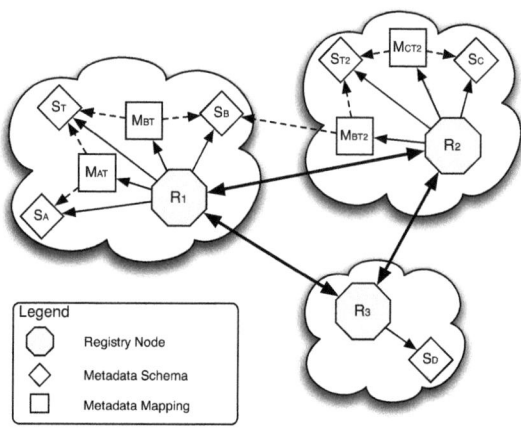

Figure 6.5: Mapping registry architecture

Metadata schema definitions, such as those presented in Examples 6.1-6.3, and also their elements are accessible by dereferencing their URLs. For the Dublin Core schema elements, this is already the case. If a client (e.g., a Web browser) requests the element http://purl.org/dc/elements/1.1/title, it obtains the definition of the schema element. Since Dublin Core is defined in RDFS, the client retrieves the schema information in RDF/XML. Analogously to the DC schema, also all other involved metadata schemes must be published in some Web-accessible location. The Austrian National Library could assign a URL to their schema, which is within their domain, e.g., http://www.bildarchiv.com/schema/onb#. The BBC could use the URL http://www.bbc.co.uk/tvradio/programmes/schema/tva# for publishing their RDFS metadata schema definition.

Also the RDFS mapping specifications are published on the Web and made accessible via a URL that also defines the context of a mapping. If, for instance, domain experts create a mapping between the Dublin Core and the TV-Anytime metadata schema for a specific institution, they can publish that mapping within the domain of that institution. For Example 6.4, that URL would be http://www.institution.com/mapping/onb_tva#. It could, however, be any other Web accessible, dereferencable URL.

6.5. Maintaining RDFS Mappings

If we assume that all metadata schema definitions and all mapping specifications are available on the Web, we require a mapping registry that can inform domain experts about their availability and location. For that purpose, we set up a network of linked mapping registries, each of which maintains the relevant information for a set of schemes and mappings. A registry node is also simply a Web accessible URL (e.g., http://www.institution.com/registry), which delivers that information to a requesting client application. On top of a registry node, one can build schema and mapping search applications that analyse the available registry data and follow the links to other registry nodes for retrieving remote registry information.

A drawback of using dereferencable URLs as identifiers for schemes and mappings is their sensitivity regarding changes in their physical location. If, for instance, the Austrian National Library decides to change the domain-name of its Image Archive to http://www.imagearchive.at, without further maintaining their current domain, all URL references pointing to schema http://www.bildarchiv.com/schema/onb# become invalid. One well known approach for solving that problem is the introduction of a logical level for identifiers that transparently handles changes in the physical location of schemes and mappings. Persistent Uniform Resource Locators[10] (PURLs) and Digital Object Identifiers[11] (DOIs) are example technologies that address this issue and introduce a link-resolver that returns the actual physical URL location for a given logical URL. The proposed registry component could provide such a link-resolver mechanism, but this is out of the scope of this work.

6.5.2 Mapping Registry Data Model

For maintaining data about registered schemes and mappings, the registry nodes require a common data model. Previously, in the description of the abstract mapping model (see Section 5.4), we presented the three-layered, directed labelled graph architecture and defined metadata schemes as simply being *schema graphs*. Also a mapping specification is in fact a specialisation of a graph (see Section 5.4). From this perspective, it appears to be natural to define the mapping registry data model on the basis of a general graph data model too.

Figure 6.6 illustrates the conceptual design of the mapping registry data model. Analogously to the MappingModel class, we define a SchemaModel as being a specialisation of a generic Graph. In the case of a language-specific binding, a mapping model then has one target and one source schema model each of which is identifiable via a URI. Also the RegistryModel is simply a specialisation of a graph and provides the links to a set of known metadata schemes (registeredSchema), mappings (registeredMapping) among them, and other known mapping registries (linkedRegistry).

Example 6.17 shows an example mapping registry entry. It references all known metadata schemes (e.g., http://purl.org/dc/elements/1.1/) and a mapping specification between the Dublin Core Element Set and the TV-Anytime schema available at http://www.institution.com/mapping/onb_

---

[10]Persistent URL website: http://purl.org/
[11]Digital Object Identifier (DOI) System website: http://www.doi.org/

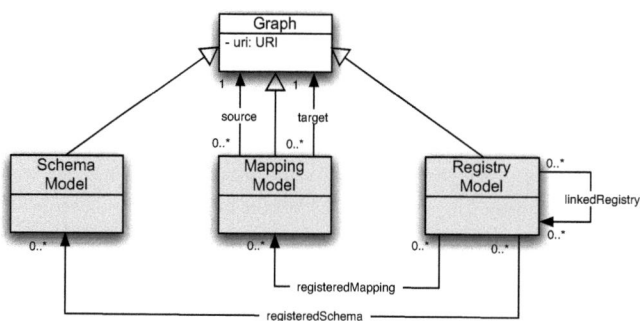

Figure 6.6: Mapping registry model

tva. Furthermore, it contains a link to another mapping repository, which is deployed at http://www.institutionY.com/registry/r2.

Example 6.17 *Sample Mapping Registry Entry*

```
@prefix rm: <http://www.mediaspaces.info/mapping/registry#>.
@prefix am: <http://www.mediaspaces.info/mapping/abstract_mapping#>.
@prefix reg: <http://www.institutionX.com/registry/>.

reg:r1 a rm:RegistryModel;
    rdfs:label "Institution X Metadata Registry";
    rm:linkedRegistry <http://www.institutionY.com/registry/r2>;
    rm:registeredSchema <http://purl.org/dc/elements/1.1/>;
    rm:registeredSchema <http://www.bildarchiv.com/schema/onb>;
    rm:registeredSchema <http://www.bbc.co.uk/tvradio/programmes/schema/tva>;
    rm:registeredMapping <http://www.institution.com/mapping/onb_tva>;
    .

http://purl.org/dc/elements/1.1/ a am:SchemaModel;
    rdfs:label "Dublin Core Metadata Element Set, Version 1.1";
    .

http://www.bildarchiv.com/schema/onb a am:SchemaModel;
    rdfs:label "Austrian National Library Metadata Schema";
    .
```

```
http://www.bbc.co.uk/tvradio/programmes/schema/tva a am:SchemaModel;
    rdfs:label "BBC TV-Anytime Metadata Schema";
    .

http://www.institution.com/mapping/onb_tva am:MappingModel;
    rdfs:label
        "Mapping between the Dublin Core Element Set and TV-Anytime";
    am:source <http://www.bildarchiv.com/schema/onb>;
    am:target <http://www.bbc.co.uk/tvradio/programmes/schema/tva>;
    .
```

6.6 Implementation Considerations

The technical realisation of the previously described metadata mapping approach can be divided into two main areas: first, we must specify guidelines for *deploying schemes and mappings on the Web* so that they are accessible via dereferencable URLs and readable for both humans and machines. Second, we must provide a *mediation service* that allows domain experts to set up configurable mediation endpoints, which provide SPARQL query access to a set of distributed and autonomous SPARQL data sources via a single query interface.

6.6.1 Deploying Schemes and Mappings on the Web

The various serialisation formats of RDF (e.g., RDF/XML, N3) are not primarily meant to be read or interpreted by humans. The RDF representation of metadata, schema definitions, and mappings among schemes is a purely machine-oriented format, i.e., it describes data to be parsed and interpreted by machines. Humans, who use a certain application (e.g., a Web browser) for accessing information on the Web, require an HTML or XHTML representation of that data. Since we want our mapping architecture to be integrated with the Web architecture and all schema information and mappings between schemes to be comprehensible for humans *and* machines, we must consider this in the deployment of schemes and mappings on the Web.

The Semantic Web Deployment Working Group has already defined best-practice guidelines for publishing schemes on the Web [BP08]. In order to be interoperable also with other Semantic Web applications we follow these guidelines and adopt them to our needs.

For serving information in various formats when dereferencing a certain URL, the guidelines propose to apply *content negotiation*, which is a built-in HTTP protocol feature. A client attempting to dereference a URL, can specify which type of content it would prefer to receive in the response. It can do this by including an Accept field in the header of a HTTP request message and specifying the preferred content types in terms of a MIME type. When a client prefers to receive the response in XHTML or HTML, it issues a HTTP request that includes the field `Accept:application/xhtml+xml,text/xml`. For the same response in RDF/XML, it issues an `Accept:application/rdf+xml` request.

Since metadata schemes as well as metadata mappings are deployed on the Web in a machine- and human-readable format, the domain experts require the following artefacts:

- A machine-readable RDF/XML (e.g., `onb.rdf` and `onb2dc.rdf`) representation of each schema- and mapping definition

- A renderable[12] (X)HTML representation (e.g., `onb.html` and `onb2dc.html`) of each schema and mapping definition.

Deploying and serving resources on the Web typically requires a Web server — and there exists a variety of implementations (e.g., Microsoft Internet Information Services (IIS)[13], Apache HTTP Server[14]). The following technical details for schema and mapping deployment are Apache HTTP Server specific. For other Web Servers, one has to consult the respective content negotiation documentation.

The Apache HTTP Web Services relies on the `mod_rewrite`[15] module, which is a rule-based URL rewriting engine, to rewrite requested URLs on the fly. If, for instance, the client requests the URL `http://www.example1.com/schema/onb` with the HTTP header field `Accept:application/xhtml+xml, text/xml`, the engine can redirect the request to the physical location of the (X)HTML file (e.g., `http://www.example1.com/schema/content/onb.html`), which provides a human-readable definition of that schema. In that same way, it is possible to redirect an `Accept: application/rdf+xml` request to the physical location of the RDF/XML schema definition (e.g., `http://www.example1.com/schema/content/onb.rdf`).

Internally, the redirection process works as depicted in Figure 6.7. The client sends an HTTP request to the server. The server determines the `Accept` field in the request's HTTP header and returns an HTTP `303 See Also` response which redirects to the location of the appropriate physical representation of the schema definition. The client follows that URL and receives the schema definition in the desired format.

For the mapping definitions we apply exactly the same mechanism. Physically they are deployed in some Web accessible location (`http://www.institution.com/mapping/content/onb_tva.rdf`) and a set of `mod_rewrite` rules handles the rewriting of the virtual URLs to the physical location of the files to be served.

---

[12]In fact, (X)HTML is not really human-readable; its rather read- and processable by applications, which can render the provided information in a human-friendly presentation format
[13]Microsoft Windows Server 2003: `http://www.microsoft.com/WindowsServer2003/IIS/Default.mspx`
[14]Apache Web Server: `http://httpd.apache.org/`
[15]Apache Mod_Rewrite Module: `http://httpd.apache.org/docs/1.3/mod/mod_rewrite.html`

6.6. Implementation Considerations 143

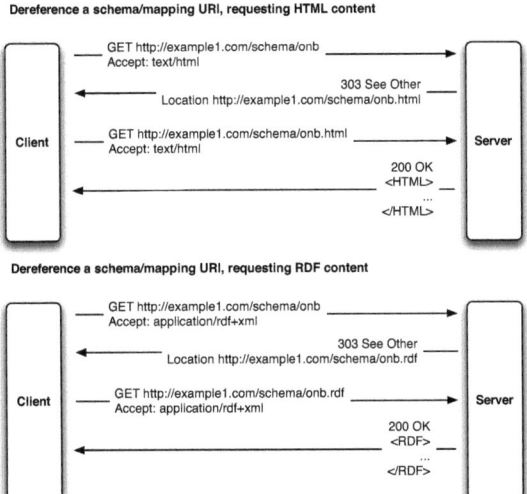

Figure 6.7: Serving schemes and mapping using HTTP Content Negotiation (adapted from [BP08])

6.6.2 Mediation Service

The mapping execution phase is covered by a *mediation service*, that transforms mapping specifications as described in Section 6.4.2 and support the run-time execution of SPARQL templates, as describe in Section 6.4.3. Domain experts can use the service to easily set up new SPARQL mediation endpoints for a selected set of data sources.

Simplicity and light-weigthness were the main design goals for that service. The domain experts should have the possibility to create and publish sharable mediation endpoints without purchasing and installing any heavy-weight standalone solution. Therefore we provide a Web-based solution, which allows to set up SPARQL mediation endpoints using an ordinary Web-browser. In order to set up a new SPARQL endpoint, a domain expert must perform the following steps:

1. Enter the URL of the SPARQL endpoint (e.g., http://www.mediaspaces.info/mediation/endpoint1/sparql) within the domain (e.g., http://www.mediaspaces.info/mediation) of a mediation service instance. If the endpoint does not exist yet, the user is prompted to create a new SPARQL endpoint.

2. In a configuration screen, the user then defines the SPARQL endpoints of the data sources to be integrated (e.g., http://www.institution1.com/sparql and http://www.institution2.com/sparql).

3. For each data source, the URL location of the previously defined and published RDFS source

schemes must be defined. Also for the mediation endpoint, the domain expert must provide the URL of the target or mediation schema.

4. Finally, for each source- and target schema pair, the domain experts must create an appropriate, Web-accessible mapping entry.

After these steps have been performed properly, an additional SPARQL endpoint is created and provides a single, uniform query interface to a set of distributed and autonomous data sources.

The *mediation service* is implemented as a Web application, which handles the incoming HTTP requests and performs the appropriate processing in the back-end. The Web-application uses the Jena RDF API[16] and ARQ[17] for advanced SPARQL query processing functionality. The information to be persisted is handled by Jena and stored in an underlying Apache Derby[18] database, whereas the database back-end can be switched to any Jena-supported RDBMS.

Since we have implemented the *mediation service* in Java, which is platform-independent, it can be installed on any platform which provides a Java Runtime Environment and a Java Servlet Container. By default, we use the Jetty[19], a simple, scalable, and efficient Web Server and Servlet Container.

6.6.3 Mapping Registry Service

As elaborated on earlier (see Section 6.5), the mapping registry is a network of registry nodes, where each node provides metadata about a set of known metadata schemes and mappings between them. Each registry node is identified by a dereferencable URL and exposes its metadata in a human- and machine-interpretable way.

For users and applications who access a registry node by dereferencing a registry node's URL, we must deliver an appropriate representation. For metadata schemes and mappings, we have already described how this can be realised. In fact, for registry metadata we can apply the same mechanism: we deploy registry metadata in some Web-accessible location using a Web server and rely on content negotiation to deliver the appropriate representation. This implies that for each registry node, the maintainer of such a node must provide two data files (e.g, registry.rdf and registry.html) and define URL rewriting rules to route incoming HTTP requests from a virtual URL (e.g., http://www.institution.com/registry), based on the value of the HTTP Accept header field, to the appropriate representation format.

The obvious problem domain experts are facing with such an approach is that they do not know which registry nodes to contact when searching for schemes or mapping between schemes. To overcome this limitation, we have implemented a simple *mapping registry service* which provides basic search and

---

[16] Jena — A Semantic Web Framework for Java: http://jena.sourceforge.net/
[17] ARQ — A SPARQL Processor for Jena: http://jena.sourceforge.net/ARQ/
[18] Apache Derby: http://db.apache.org/derby/
[19] Jetty: http://www.mortbay.org/jetty-6/

discovery functionality for domain experts. It is again realised as Java Web application, can be installed on any platform, and can process the metadata provided by the registry nodes.

To set up a registry service instance, the domain experts need to provide a single registry node URL; we assume that within a certain domain there exists at least one known node. The registry service can then fetch the metadata from that node, follow the links to other, linked registry nodes and process the metadata. If domain experts search for a specific schema or schema mapping by entering a URL identifier or search strings into a Web form, the registry service delivers a list of results pointing to relevant registry nodes.

6.7 Summary

In this chapter, we have described the conceptual design and the implementation of the RDFS binding of the abstract mapping model presented earlier. We have illustrated how to lift schemes expressed in other schema definition languages to the level of RDFS, provided a precise specification of the RDFS mapping model, described how to translate mapping specifications to SPARQL query templates, and described how these templates are processed in the mapping execution phase. For the mapping maintenance phase, we have designed a lightweight, but functional mapping registry architecture.

The clear advantage of our approach, in contrast to other existing mapping solutions, is its simplicity and light-weightness. All mapping artefacts (schemes, mappings, registry data) and also the supporting services (mediation service, registry service) are Web-based and do not require the installation or purchase of any standalone, heavy-weight mapping solution or data integration suite. For defining and publishing schemes, mappings and registry data, domain experts require only an RDF-supporting editor. For setting up a mediation endpoint, they can simply enter URLs into a Web application and provide the necessary metadata integration information.

The focus of our approach is mainly on the mapping representation and maintenance phase, as well as on the transition from the representation to the execution phase. The mapping discovery phase is out of the scope of this work because it is a too broad research area for being discussed extensively in this work. Our mapping model does, however, provide the necessary means to integrate schema mapping algorithms that deliver a set of potentially related schema elements.

Since the discovery phase is out of the scope of this work and the execution phase is a too broad research area for being discussed extensively in this work, there is still much future work to be conducted in these areas.

One limitation in our proposed approach is the fact that the mapping representation phase requires the definition of two separate representations, one in RDF and the other in HTML. At the moment, there exists no RDF counterpart to XSL stylesheets, which would allow the rendering of a single document in various representation formats.

Chapter 7

The OAI2LOD Server — Wrapping OAI-PMH Data Sources

For including data source in an integration context, we require wrapper components that expose schema information on the Web and make the contained metadata accessible via SPARQL. In this chapter, we provide — as a proof of concept — an example for such a wrapper according to our architecture. For this purpose, we describe the OAI2LOD Server, which is a wrapper component for the Open Archives Initiative Protocol for Metadata Harvesting (OAI-PMH) [LdS02].

The OAI-PMH protocol is utilised for the exchange and sharing of metadata for digital and non-digital items and enjoys growing popularity in the domain of digital libraries and archives. Currently, we know of more than 1700 OAI-PMH compliant repositories exposing metadata descriptions for several millions of items. The design of OAI-PMH is based on the Web Architecture [JW04], but it does not treat its conceptual entities as dereferencable resources. The selective access to metadata is out of its scope too. One can, for instance, retrieve metadata for a certain digital item, but one cannot retrieve all digital items that have been created by a certain author.

In Section 7.1, we will give a brief introduction into the technical characteristics of OAI-PMH. Then, in Section 7.2, we describe how the OAI2LOD Server builds a bridge between the OAI-PMH and the Linked Data principles. In Section 7.3, we provide the implementation details, and finally, in Section 7.4, we discuss how the Linked Data concepts have already influenced protocol development in the digital libraries domain.

7.1 What is OAI-PMH?

Client applications can use the OAI-PMH protocol to harvest metadata from *Data Providers* using open standards such as URI, HTTP, and XML. Institutions taking the role of data providers can easily expose their metadata via OAI-PMH by implementing light-weight wrapper components on top of their existing metadata repositories.

7.1.1 Technical Details

The main conceptual entities in the OAI-PMH specification are Item, Record, and MetadataFormat. An item represents a digital or non-digital resource and is uniquely identified by a URI. It can be described by an arbitrary number of metadata records, each of which is bound to a certain metadata format, which can freely be chosen by the data provider. To guarantee a basic level of interoperability, all data providers *must* support the unqualified Dublin Core [DC06] format. Further, OAI-PMH provides the concept of a Set for grouping related items and their associated metadata.

OAI-PMH is implemented on top of HTTP and defines a set of *verbs* to request different information types: an Identify request retrieves administrative metadata (e.g., name, owner) about a repository as a whole. GetRecord is used to fetch an individual record for a certain item in a given format, whereas the request ListRecords harvests all metadata for all available items in a certain metadata format. ListIdentifiers returns the identifiers (URIs) of all available items, ListMetadataFormats the formats in which the data provider exposes metadata, and ListSets returns the available sets in an OAI-PMH repository.

Figure 7.1 shows a sample GetRecord request for a Dublin Core metadata record exposed by the Library of Congress and the corresponding response. The request URI contains the address of the repository, the verbs, and required parameters like the item URI. The response consists of a <header> section, which contains the item's URI, and a <metadata> section encapsulating the metadata record.

7.1.2 Spreading and Future of OAI-PMH

There exist a number of OAI Data Provider Registries[1], from which we know that currently 1765 institutions worldwide maintain OAI-PMH repositories. Regarding their application domain, we can observe that the protocol has been implemented in a variety of institutions, ranging from small research facilities to national libraries that have integrated this protocol with their catalogue systems. Examples are the *Institute of Biology of the Southern Seas*, exposing 403 records, and the *U.S. National Library of Medicine's digital archive*, exposing 1,272,585 records.

In order to estimate the amount and the characteristics of metadata one can retrieve via OAI-PMH, we have carried out an analysis on the 915 registered repositories that delivered valid responses. Figure 7.2 illustrates the size of these repositories using a logarithmic scale on the Y-axis. The results show that 843 or 92% of all repositories expose metadata for less than 20,000 items. With 14,303 being the average number of items, the total number of 13,087,842 items is made up of a large number of smaller OAI-PMH repositories.

In total, the analysed repositories expose 161 different metadata formats. Figure 7.3 illustrates the top ten metadata formats and clearly shows, that besides unqualified Dublin Core, which is required to be implemented by definition, RFC1807 (12%), MARC (11.8%) and MARC-21 (10.3%), MODS (7.5%),

---

[1] Available OAI Data Provider Registries: http://www.openarchives.org/Register/BrowseSites, http://gita.grainger.uiuc.edu/registry/

7.1. What is OAI-PMH?

```
REQUEST:

http://memory.loc.gov/cgi-bin/oai2_0?
  verb=GetRecord&
  identifier=oai:lcoal.loc.gov:loc.gdc/gcfr.0018_0163&
  metadataPrefix=oai_dc

RESPONSE:

<OAI-PMH xmlns="http://www.openarchives.org/OAI/2.0/" ... >
...
<GetRecord>
 <record>

 <header>
  <identifier>
    oai:lcoal.loc.gov:loc.gdc/gcfr.0018_0163</identifier>
  <setSpec>ascfrbib</setSpec>
  ...
 </header>

 <metadata>
  <oai_dc:dc
    xmlns:oai_dc="http://www.openarchives.org/OAI/2.0/oai_dc/"
    xmlns:dc="http://purl.org/dc/elements/1.1/" ...>

  <dc:title>Don Christopher Columbus to his friend, Don Louis de Santangel, on his arrival
     from his first voyage. At the Azores, Feb. 15, 1493.
  </dc:title>
  <dc:creator>Columbus, Christopher.</dc:creator>
  <dc:subject>America--Discovery and exploration--Spanish--Early works to 1800.</dc:subject>
  <dc:identifier>http://hdl.loc.gov/loc.gdc/gcfr.0018_0163</dc:identifier>
  <dc:coverage>America</dc:coverage>
  ...
  </oai_dc:dc>
 </metadata>

 </record>
</GetRecord>

</OAI-PMH>
```

Figure 7.1: Sample OAI-PMH communication

and METS (5.7%) are most frequently used[2]. The large gap between Dublin Core and the other metadata formats reveals that most data providers do not follow the OAI-PMH standard's suggestion of exposing metadata in a semantically richer format than unqualified Dublin Core.

We expect the number of institutions that expose metadata via OAI-PMH to grow even further. Major attempts of building union catalogues, e.g., the *The European Library (TEL)* project[3], rely on this protocol for indexing metadata originating from remote sources. Currently, that initiative integrates 47 national libraries and gives access to approximately 150 millions of metadata records. Since the OAI-PMH endpoints of these libraries are not yet listed in the before mentioned OAI Data Providers Registry, we could not consider them in our analysis.

---

[2]Further information about these standards: http://www.loc.gov/standards and http://rfc.net/rfc1807.html
[3]The European Library (TEL): http://www.theeuropeanlibrary.org

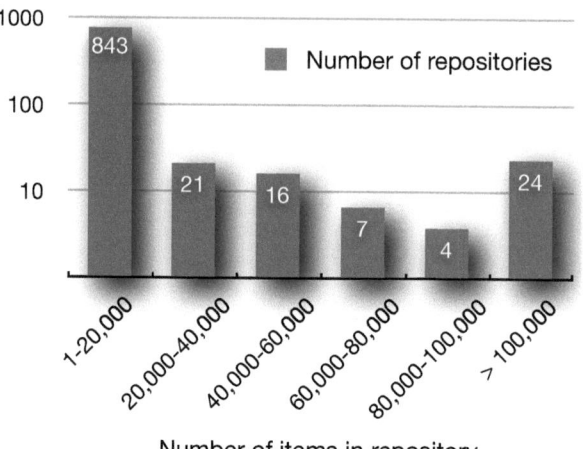

Figure 7.2: Size of OAI-PMH repositories

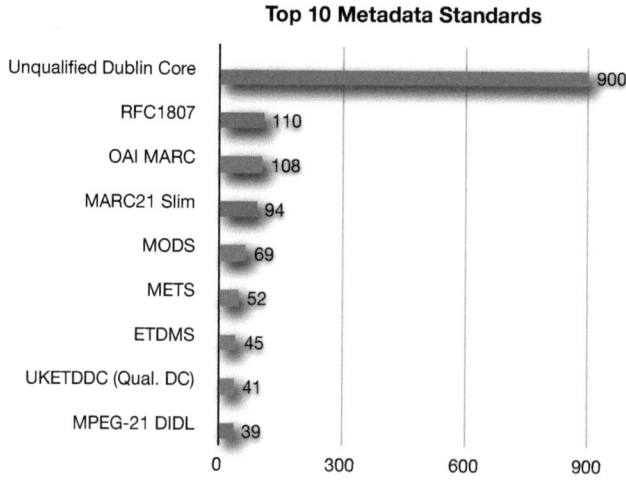

Figure 7.3: Top 10 metadata formats

Another reason why we expect the number of OAI-PMH endpoints to grow is that popular open source

7.2. Design Considerations

digital library systems, such as Fedora[4], DSpace[5], and EPrints[6], provide OAI-PMH support by default. In recent years, these systems have found widespread adoption in various small and medium institutions (e.g., universities or museums) and will foster the global distribution of open and Web accessible metadata even more.

7.1.3 Shortcomings of OAI-PMH

The OAI-PMH protocol has been designed for transferring large amounts of metadata from a server to a client over the Web. From that perspective, it provides a reasonable solution for clients that need to aggregate or index metadata. However, it has two significant drawbacks:

- *Non-dereferencable identities*: although OAI-PMH is built on the Web infrastructure, we believe that it does not yet make use of its full potential. To retrieve information from a repository, a client must execute an HTTP GET request on an OAI-PMH specific URI (see Figure 7.1). This prevents Web clients, which are unaware of the protocol specifics, from accessing the repository.

- *Restricted selective access to metadata*: the record selection criteria in the OAI-PMH harvesting process are restricted to item identifiers, metadata formats, sets, and record creation date intervals. However, some clients might only be interested in records matching certain criteria (e.g., *all records describing items created by X*) or even just a subset of the available metadata values (e.g., *all authors of all books in a library*).

One could argue that these features are out of the scope of OAI-PMH and already implemented by other digital library protocols such as Z.39.59[7] or SRU[8]. However, because of the popularity and widespread adoption of OAI-PMH in contrast to other protocols, we believe that it should be enhanced in order to solve the above mentioned drawbacks. Institutions, which employ the OAI-PMH, could then provide powerful metadata access functionality by implementing just a single protocol.

7.2 Design Considerations

At a first glance, the OAI2LOD server is a wrapper that exposes metadata of OAI-PMH compliant data sources as Linked Data on the Web and provides a SPARQL query interface to these metadata. During design time we have noticed that it also covers large parts of the OAI-PMH features by simply following the Linked Data rules [BL06] and provides solutions for the shortcomings mentioned in the previous section.

---

[4] http://www.fedora.info
[5] http://www.dspace.org
[6] http://www.eprints.org
[7] http://www.loc.gov/z3950/agency/Z39-50-2003.pdf
[8] http://www.loc.gov/standards/sru/specs/

The first Linked Data rule says that things should have URIs. In the context of OAI-PMH, items and sets are such things. By definition, items already fulfil that rule because, according to the OAI-PMH specification, each item must be identified by a URI (e.g., `oai:lcoa1.loc.gov:loc.gdc/gcfr.0018_0163`). This not the case for sets as they are identified by arbitrary strings consisting of any valid URI unreserved characters (e.g. `ascfrbib`). However, such strings are no valid URIs.

According to the second rule, URIs that identify resources should be resolvable HTTP URLs. In OAI-PMH it is common to use non-resolvable URNs to identify items. The OAI2LOD server bridges this gap by wrapping item URNs and set identifiers with resolvable HTTP URLs. Continuing the above example, the item's URI becomes `http://example.com/resources/item/oai:lcoa1.loc.gov:loc.gdc/gcfr.0018\_0163`, and the set's identifier becomes `http://example.com/resources/set/ascfrbib`.

The third Linked Data rule proposes to deliver useful information whenever a URL is dereferenced. The OAI-PMH protocol delivers useful information for harvesting clients that can parse and process OAI-PMH responses. We believe that the provided metadata might also be valuable for applications that are unaware of the OAI-PMH protocol specifics. For humans we should provide the possibility to browse, display, and search metadata using an ordinary Web browser. Applications such as Web crawlers should be able to access OAI-PMH metadata without knowing the protocol details. We fulfil this requirement (i) by assuring that the responses delivered to a client contain only resolvable HTTP URLs, and (ii) by exposing data in various representations.

When delivering metadata records to the client, we must assure that each field (e.g., creator) within a record has assigned a resolvable URL. For some formats (e.g., Dublin Core) this is the case by definition (e.g., `http://purl.org/dc/elements/1.1/creator`), for others we must publish a machine-readable representation (e.g., in RDF/S or OWL) on the Web. Further, we have defined a machine-processable vocabulary[9] defining OAI-PMH specific concepts such as `Item` and `Set`.

XHTML and RDF serialisation formats, i.e., RDF/XML and N3, are the data representations the OAI2LOD Server currently supports. While Web browsers can process the former and display the returned information to humans, the latter can be processed by machines. The server uses content negotiation, as explained in [BCH07], to decide which representation to deliver.

In the context of OAI-PMH, the forth Linked Data rule recommends that metadata records should contain links to other related resources. One kind of link that should be included in a record delivered to a client is a reference to its origin, i.e., the OAI-PMH endpoint and all relevant protocol parameters required to retrieve the corresponding XML representation of an item and its records. We express this information using the OAI2LOD specific `oai2lod:origin` property, which is defined as a sub-property of `rdfs:seeAlso`.

Searching other OAI2LOD Server instances for equivalent or similar metadata records, is another strategy for adding links. If we refer to the example presented in Figure 7.1, it is quite likely that other

---

[9]`http://www.mediaspaces.info/vocab/oai-pmh.rdf`

7.3. Implementation

institutions also have a copy of this book. This fact can be captured by adding an `owl:sameAs`[10] property to the metadata record. Currently we do this by regarding metadata records originating from distinct server instances and comparing the values of a set of manually selected metadata fieles according to their lexical similarity using the Levensthein string distance [Lev66]. If the similarity of two entries is above a certain threshold, two records are linked. We ask the server administrator to specify (i) remote OAI2LOD Servers that expose relevant data sets for the linking process, (ii) pairs of source and target fields to be analysed, and (iii) a similarity threshold for each pair.

Figure 7.4 shows the RDF/XML representation of our example metadata record as it is returned by the OAI2LOD Server. It contains the same metadata as the record in Figure 7.1 but represents them according to the Linked Data principles. The `owl:sameAs` property points to a fictive URL which maintains metadata about the same book. We can see that by following the Linked Data rules, we have bridged the problem of non-dereferencable identities and support access to metadata repositories for a variety of Web agents.

7.3 Implementation

The OAI2LOD Server, as illustrated in Figure 7.5, is a stand-alone server implemented in Java and based on the architecture of the D2RQ Server [BS04]. It can be configured to expose all metadata records from a specific OAI-PMH endpoint in a certain metadata format according to the principles described above. A scheduled process regularly harvests metadata from the given endpoint, transforms them into RDF/XML using a format-specific XSL style-sheet, stores the transformed metadata in a built-in triple store, and exposes the metadata to various kinds of clients. The built-in Request Handler/Dispatcher analyses the `Accept` property in the HTTP headers and delivers metadata either in RDF/XML (`Accept:application/rdf+xml`) or in XHTML (`Accept:application/xhtml+xml`). Then it forwards the client requests to the OAI2LOD Server's entry point that provides metadata in the appropriate representation using the `HTTP 303 See Other` response.

We use URI paths to expose information in different representations. The `/resource` path holds the URIs of all items and sets exposed by the server. When a client requests such a URI, the OAI2LOD Server examines the `Accept` property and points to the URI path that delivers information in a representation suitable for the client: the `/data` path provides access to all machine-readable RDF descriptions for a certain resource; the `/page` path returns the same information in XHTML. Further, the `/directory` path lists what types of resources (e.g., items, sets) are available in an XHTML representation. Analogously, the `/all` path delivers that information in a machine readable RDF representation. Figure 7.6 shows examples of OAI2LOD Server requests and the corresponding OAI-PMH requests that return the same information.

---

[10]The `owl:sameAS` property, which is defined as part of the Web Ontology Language OWL, indicates that two URI references actually refer to the same real-world thing.

```
<rdf:RDF
...
xmlns:oai2lod="http://www.mediaspaces.info/vocab/oai-pmh.rdf#">

<rdf:Description
  rdf:about="http://www.mediaspaces.info:2020/resource/item/
  oai:lcoa1.loc.gov:loc.gdc/gcfr.0018_0163">

<rdf:type rdf:resource=
  "http://www.mediaspaces.info/vocab/oai-pmh.rdf#Item"/>

<oai2lod:setSpec rdf:resource=
  "http://www.mediaspaces.info:2020/resource/set/ascfrbib"/>
<oai2lod:origin rdf:resource= "http://memory.loc.gov/cgi-bin/
  oai2_0?verb=GetRecord&identifier=oai:lcoa1.loc.gov:loc.gdc/
  gcfr.0018_0163&metadataPrefix=oai_dc"/>
<owl:sameAs rdf:resource=
  "http://example.com/resource/item/oai:example.com/itemX"/>

<dc:title>Don Christopher Columbus to his friend, Don Louis
de Santangel, on his arrival from his first voyage.
At the Azores, Feb. 15, 1493.
</dc:title>
<dc:creator>Columbus, Christopher.</dc:creator>
<dc:subject>America--Discovery and exploration--Spanish--
Early works to 1800.
</dc:subject>
<dc:identifier rdf:resource=
  "http://hdl.loc.gov/loc.gdc/gcfr.0018_0163"/>
<dc:coverage>America</dc:coverage>

</rdf:Description>

</rdf:RDF>
```

Figure 7.4: Sample OAI2LOD Server response

7.3.1 Preliminary Experiences

The OAI2LOD Server version 0.2 serves records from an in-memory Jena RDF model, which is fed with metadata records exposed by a certain OAI-PMH endpoint. The number of records a server instance can host, depends on the amount of memory assigned to the Java Virtual Machine.

In our test environment[11], we have exposed 25,000 records in a JVM having 128 megabytes of RAM assigned. This indicates that a large fraction of existing OAI-PMH repositories (see Figure 7.2) could use the OAI2LOD Server for exposing their metadata according to the Linked Data rules with a very low resource effort.

---

[11]http://www.mediaspaces.info:3030/

7.3. Implementation

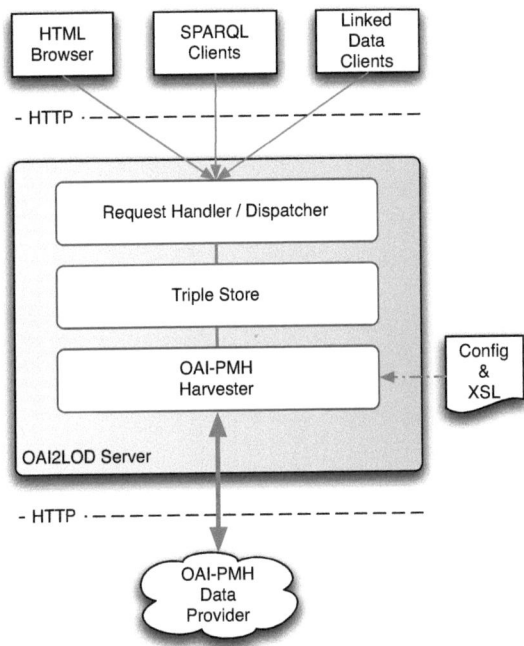

Figure 7.5: The OAI2LOD Server architecture

7.3.2 Open Issues

Currently, the OAI2LOD Server exposes metadata records only in a single pre-defined format. When setting up a server instance for a specific OAI-PMH repository, the administrator decides in which format the metadata records are harvested. Since this approach contradicts a central idea of OAI-PMH we will further investigate how the OAI2LOD Server could serve metadata in multiple formats. One potential solution is to define mappings between formats.

Another important OAI-PMH feature is batch retrieval of metadata records. Using the ListRecords request, a client can iteratively retrieve a chunk of records. The OAI2LOD Server currently supports these features through SPARQL and its LIMIT and OFFSET clauses. However, we believe that alternatively we could offer that feature via a dereferencable URI.

The OAI2LOD Server's capabilities of linking items with other resources on the Web are limited and still rely on human intervention. We need to experiment with further duplicate detection algorithms and similarity metrics, in order to achieve better and scalable results.

	OAI2LOD Request	OAI-PMH Request
All available resource types	/ (in HTML) /all (in RDF)	N/A
All item identifiers	/directory/Item (in HTML) /all/Item (in RDF)	/oai?verb=ListIdentifiers& metadataPrefix=oai_dc
The metadata record describing a certain item	/resource/item/oai:lcoa1.loc.gov:loc.gdc/gcfr.0018_0163 -- /page/item/oai:lcoa1.loc.gov:loc.gdc/gcfr.0018_0163 (XHTML) /data/item/oai:lcoa1.loc.gov:loc.gdc/gcfr.0018_0163 (RDF)	/oai?verb=GetRecord& identifier=oai:lcoa1.loc.gov:loc.gdc/gcfr.0018_0163& metadataPrefix=oai_dc

Figure 7.6: Comparison of OAI2LOD and corresponding OAI-PMH requests

7.4 The Future of OAI-PMH

The Open Archives Initiative Object Reuse and Exchange (OAI-ORE) [LVJ+07] specification is the latest standardisation effort driven by the designers of the OAI-PMH protocol. Although the standards are still in an alpha release status, we can already notice strong similarities with the ideas of Linked Data and the OAI2LOD Server respectively.

OAI-ORE is a set of standards for the *description and exchange* of *aggregations* of Web resources. A resource can be anything that is identified with a URI such as Web sites, online multimedia content, or items stored in institutional digital library systems. In the ORE data model, an aggregation is an instance of the conceptual entity `Resource Map` and is identified by a URI. A resource map describes the encapsulated resources as a set of machine readable RDF statements, which makes them readable for a variety of Web applications. Clients can retrieve aggregations by executing an HTTP GET request on a resource map's URI. The ATOM Syndication Format[12] is specified as the primary serialisation format for delivering resource maps to clients. However, since the ORE data model is defined in RDF, resources can not only be mapped to the ATOM format but also serialised in other RDF exchange formats such as RDF/XML or N3.

Regarding the OAI-ORE specification from the perspective of Linked Data, we can observe that the first two Linked Data rules are fundamental building blocks of the standard: all *things*, i.e., resource maps and the aggregated resources, are identified by dereferencable URIs. Further, all terms used for describing aggregations have a well-defined semantics, published in terms of a Web accessible vocabulary

---

[12]RFC 4287 — The Atom Syndication Format, available at http://www.ietf.org/rfc/rfc4287.txt

definition. It also considers the third rule because resolving the URIs returns *useful*—i.e., processable and interpretable—information for both human and machines. Finally, OAI-ORE also follows the fourth rule by providing several possibilities to link resources: first, an aggregation of resources is by definition a collection of linked (`ore:aggregates`) resources; second, the ORE model uses the `owl:sameAs` property to denote that two identifiers refer to the same information object; third, it supports the concepts of nested aggregations.

OAI-PMH and OAI-ORE overlap in the fact that Resource Maps can be included as metadata records in OAI-PMH responses, which allows batch retrieval and harvesting of aggregation information. We believe that there lies a great potential in a tighter integration of these two standards: if OAI-PMH metadata repositories expose their items as Web resources by assigning them HTTP-dereferencable URIs, these items could take part in OAI-ORE aggregations. One possible strategy could be to define a common core data model that links these two standards so that the ORE specification builds on top of the OAI-PMH protocol. Meanwhile, the OAI2LOD Server can serve as a bridge between these two standards.

7.5 Summary

In this chapter, we have presented the OAI2LOD Server as a proof of concept for a wrapper component. It allows us to expose metadata and schema information provided by OAI-PMH endpoints as dereferencable Web resources and provides selective, structured access to these data via a SPARQL query interface. We have designed the OAI2LOD Server according to the Linked Data Principles, which makes OAI-PMH metadata accessible also for (Web) clients that are not aware of the OAI-PMH protocol specifics. Although the linking of related metadata sets is not a requirement imposed by our Web-based metadata integration architecture, the OAI2LOD Server provides rudimentary support for this feature. Improving the linking capabilities and interlinking OAI2LOD Server instances with other data sets exposed according to the Linked Data principles is on our future research agenda.

Chapter 8
Qualitative Evaluation and Case Study

In the preceding chapters, we have presented the methodology and concepts of a Web-based metadata mapping approach and described its implementation for the RDFS schema definition language. In this chapter, we compare it with other existing mapping solutions and demonstrate its feasibility and practical benefit in an example metadata integration scenario.

Section 8.1 provides an in-depth analysis of the requirements our approach implements and compares them with those of other mapping solutions. Thereafter, in Section 8.2, we present a case study we have performed on the basis of the illustrative examples presented earlier in this work.

8.1 Comparison with Existing Mapping Solutions

Previously, in Section 3.4, we have performed an analysis of existing mapping solutions against the requirements framework we have set up based on an extensive literature study. Now, in this section, we will do the same for our proposed Web-based metadata mapping solution and point out the areas where our approach exceeds existing ones, but also show yet remaining limitations of our work.

For the analysis, we follow the same structure as in the analysis of existing tools (see Section 3.4) and discuss, for each mapping phase, to what extent our approach fulfils a certain requirement in that phase.

8.1.1 General Requirements

This category contains all requirements that cannot be assigned to any of the four mapping phases. They are, however, essential for any mapping solution.

Uniform Accessibility

If a mapping solution provides uniform accessibility, a domain expert can access a set of autonomous, distributed, and heterogeneous data sources via a single query interface, using a specific query language and by formulating queries over a certain target (mediation) schema.

Different from *pure* mapping solutions, our approach goes beyond the formulation and representation of mappings and provides the means to translate them into executable query templates. User queries, received at the mediator interface, trigger these templates, fetch the requested metadata expressed in terms of the target metadata schema from the integrated data sources, and return the results to the requesting client. Therefore, our approach clearly supports the uniform accessibility requirement.

Modularity

For adding an additional, incompatible data source to an integration context, i.e., to a certain mediation endpoint, it is not necessary to change the implementation of the already existing, productive endpoint. While other solutions require the redefinition and redeployment of previously created integration (mapping) specifications, in our approach the domain expert can simply add additional data sources, by (i) installing a wrapper component for that data source, (ii) defining and publishing a mapping between the newly created, wrapped data source, and (iii) registering the data source at a mediation endpoint by providing its configuration (data source-, schema-, and mapping-URI) via a Web-interface. Since adding another data source does not require any modification of existing system components, our solution fulfils that requirement.

Flexibility in Lifting and Normalisation

Lifting metadata, which are expressed in different schema definition languages, to a common metadata meta-model, which is in our case RDFS, is the wrapper components' task. In fact, one can build wrappers for any data source, ranging from industry standard databases (e.g., RDBMS) over Web-service adapters, to wrappers for spreadsheet data. Therefore, in our architecture, lifting and normalisation is the task of the wrapper designer and implementers. They must guarantee that the schema is defined in RDFS and published on the Web, that the metadata themselves are delivered in RDF, and that both are accessible via a SPARQL query interface.

However, in contrast to other works, our approach currently does not provide any automatic means for transforming schema definitions to RDFS; for that part we referred to work conducted by others. Therefore, we consider this feature to be partially supported by our approach.

Mapping GUI

Providing a fully-fledged, user-friendly mapping GUI that supports domain experts in creating mapping specifications, especially in drawing mapping relationships, is an important feature that must be supported by any industrial mapping solution, be it a standalone or Web-based approach. In Web environments, such a GUI should run in an ordinary Web browser and must therefore be based on Web front-end technologies (JavaScript, CSS, Ajax). The main challenge lies in dealing with the limited interaction possibilities (e.g., drag-and-drop) current Web technologies offer.

8.1. Comparison with Existing Mapping Solutions

So far, our approach provides a simple Web GUI for setting up mediation endpoints and for searching metadata registry nodes. The design and implementation of a Web-based front-end has been outside the scope of this thesis and is subject of our future work. Hence, in the context of this work, we can rate this requirement as being supported partially.

8.1.2 Mapping Discovery

The mapping discovery phase is concerned with matching metadata schemes, i.e., with determining mapping relationships between the element of two distinct metadata schemes — if possible automatically. Here we briefly discuss to what extend our approach supports this phase.

Schema Matching / Alignment Support

At the beginning of our thesis, we have excluded the development of new matching algorithms from the scope of this work, because this would shift its focus into a completely different direction. Schema matching, and — to use recent terminology — ontology alignment, has been an active research area over decades, but the results still cannot produce reliable mappings without the supervision of domain experts. This is the main reason why schema matching algorithms have not found widespread adoption in commercial mapping solutions.

Although we do not provide schema matching algorithms, we have considered that there could be a need to integrate them into our mapping approach and provided an adequate interface (see Section 5.5). The requirement itself, however, is not supported by our solution.

Consensus Building Features

Our analysis of existing solutions revealed that currently only Yahoo Pipes partially supports building consensus on conflicting requirements, simply by providing user and community features. We could say that these features do not provide but *enable* consensus building.

Regarding our metadata mapping approach, the same is the case: we do not provide but enable consensus building. Simply by the fact that we publish mapping specifications on the Web and providing the possibility of copying and adopting mappings for similar integration scenarios, we enable domain experts to agree on a set of common mapping relationships. This would not be possible when mapping specifications are held in closed system environments. Therefore, we consider this requirement as being partially fulfilled.

8.1.3 Mapping Representation

Previously we stated that the aim of a mapping model is to provide the language primitives required to reconcile the structural and semantic heterogeneities among metadata information objects. It should be expressive enough to bridge the various groups of heterogeneities described in 2.3.2. In the following, we will analyse to what extend the mapping model presented in Section 6.3 fulfils that requirement.

Model-Level Structural Heterogeneity Reconciliation

This group of heterogeneities occurs because domain experts arrange model elements that reflect the constituents of a certain domain in various ways and detail. The presented mapping model can resolve these heterogeneities as follows:

- *Naming conflicts:* if classes or properties in distinct models are related but have different names assigned (e.g., `lastname` vs. `surname`), one can easily represent that fact by a `ClassMapping` or a `PropertyMapping` respectively.

- *Identification conflicts:* different (URI) identifiers in related classes or properties can be resolved the same way as naming conflicts.

- *Constraints conflicts:* if two distinct models apply incompatible constraints on their properties (e.g., datatypes, enumeration values), one can introduce a dedicated `Function` that, for instance, performs datatype conversion or maps a broader range of literal values to a given set of enumeration values.

- *Abstraction Level Incompatibilities:* such heterogeneities occur, for instance, when model A defines the concepts `Person` and `Organisation`, while model B subsumes these classes in a single concept `Agent`. In such cases, one can apply a `ClassMapping` to relate the concepts and split up or merge the properties of the involved concepts using `PropertyMappings` and appropriate `Functions`.

- *Meta-Level Discrepancy:* if one model defines a property to capture certain information (e.g., `creator`) and another model defines a certain class (e.g., `Person`) and several properties (e.g., `firstname`, `lastname`) for a more fine-grained representation of the same information, one can resolve that as illustrated in Example 6.5 by introducing a `PropertyMapping` bound to the respective class using the `classContext` property.

- *Domain Coverage:* different models usually describe one and the same domain in different levels of detail. As a result, it frequently occurs that no mapping relationships between model elements can be determined, because either the source or the target model simply does not define any explicit elements covering a specific domain aspect. If the information is implicitly available in the instance values of other elements, one can introduce `Functions` that extract that information or even contact external services in order to obtain the necessary information. For instance, if a source model defines a property `location` with instance location denominators in natural language (e.g., Vienna) and the target model represents location information using GIS-coordinates, one could introduce

… a function `location2gis` that contacts an external service to retrieve the corresponding GIS-coordinates. If the required information is not even available implicitly, domain coverage conflicts cannot be resolved by any mapping solution.

Model-Level Semantic Heterogeneity Reconciliation

Semantic heterogeneities occur because of differences in the semantics of models on the M1 level, i.e., due to differences in the elements defined by a metadata schema:

- *Domain Conflicts:* if two models describe two completely incompatible domains (e.g., electronic billing vs. multimedia contents), mappings can hardly be determined. We can, however, assume that mappings will only be created in a specific integration context within a certain domain. If domains subsume each other, or overlap one can apply the above mentioned mapping model primitives.

- *Terminological Mismatches:* synonym or homonym conflicts between model elements can easily be resolved by creating mapping relationships between semantically related model elements. Also on the instance level, one can handle such mismatches using `Functions`. One could even introduce a function that looks up synonyms or homonyms in external thesauri to determine if there is a semantic correspondence between two instance values.

Instance-Level Semantic Heterogeneity Reconciliation

Semantic heterogeneities can also occur because of semantic discrepancies on the M0 level, i.e., due to differences in the content values of metadata information objects:

- *Scaling/Unit Conflicts:* can easily be resolved by introducing `Functions` that convert from one scale/unit to the other.

- *Representation Conflicts:* as scaling/unit conflicts, this kind of heterogeneity can be resolved by introducing a `Function` that converts content values from one encoding scheme to another.

Context Representation

The semantics of a mapping relationship depends on the interpretation context of the domain expert who has created the mapping specification. For other experts, the interpretation could be completely different. For the purpose of representing a domain expert's interpretation context after having created a mapping specification, we rely on URI namespaces. Since each mapping model is a specialisation of a generic graph, which in turn is identified by a URI, we have a mechanism we can use for context representation. Thus, each mapping URI represents a certain context and we can say that this requirement is fulfilled.

Flexible Language Binding

The core of our mapping solution relies on a generic, graph-based abstract mapping model that reflects the mapping problem independent of any M2 schema definition language. In this thesis, we have implemented an RDFS language binding, but in principal, bindings can be created for any schema definition languages that can be reduced to a basic graph structure. XML, for instance, is based on a hierarchical tree model, which is in fact a specialisation of a graph (see Section 2.2.2) and could therefore also be bound to the abstract mapping model. The same is the case for the object-oriented model, which allows the definition of object graphs. The clear disadvantage of our approach is the increased complexity and the additional implementation effort for each schema definition language binding. The *flexible language binding* requirement, however, is fulfilled.

8.1.4 Mapping Execution

The mapping execution phase is concerned with processing previously defined mapping specifications at run-time and with delivering the desired results to the requesting application. In the following, we analyse how and to what extent our solution fulfils the requirements we have identified for this phase.

Query Reformulation

In the context of virtually integrated systems, this requirement demands that a mapping solution can reformulate queries received by a mediation endpoint according to a mapping specification. We follow an approach that can be compared to *views* in relational databases: a mapping specification compiles to a set of query templates, which provide source-schema transparent access to a data source's metadata. An incoming user query is executed against these templates, which in turn return the results in the appropriate representation. Therefore, our query template approach fulfils the query reformulation requirement.

Query Plan / Optimiser

Query optimisation has not been the main focus of this thesis and is therefore still a major construction area in our mapping solution. In Section 6.4.3, we have described a first, basic optimisation strategy that selects the query templates to be executed by analysing if the graph structure defined in the CONSTRUCT clause of a template is contained in another template. As a result, the total number of templates and consequently also the total number of queries to be executed against the wrapped data sources is reduced. The development of a fully fledged query plan and optimisation strategy is not available yet. Therefore, we rate this requirement as partially fulfilled.

Integration Component Generation

Via a Web-based front-end, domain experts can easily set up new mediation endpoints by providing the URLs of the data sources to be integrated and the respective mapping specifications. The mapping execution logic is handled transparently by the mediation component and does not require any further development effort by the domain expert. Therefore, this requirement is fulfilled.

8.1.5 Mapping Maintenance

For supporting the mapping maintenance phase, we have introduced the concept of a Web-based mapping registry, which allows the discovery of available metadata schemes and mapping specifications. As we will see in the following, it does not fully cover all but at least one essential mapping maintenance requirement.

Mapping Verification

The validity of a mapping specification can be determined only within a specific context because it depends on the interpretation of one or more domain experts. However, even within a certain context there could be inconsistencies. One could for instance reference non-existing schema elements or map the same schema elements several times but differently within one and the same mapping specification. So far, also commercial solutions and academic prototypes provide only limited means for mapping verification. In our approach, this aspect is not yet covered, but definitely subject of future work.

Mapping Reusability

The *reusability* requirement has been a major motivation for lifting the mapping process to the level of the Web. We believe that domain experts can benefit from the work of others and reuse mapping specification in their own integration context by tailoring them to their application specific needs. Analogous to human-readable Web sites, where anyone can view and reuse — as long as there are no legal restrictions — the source code of (X)HTML pages, we want to achieve the same for mapping specifications. Via the registry service, domain experts can search for already existing mappings among specific metadata schemes, decide if they are relevant, and modify them according to their own needs. Therefore, we support the requirement of mapping reusability.

Mapping Inference

The requirement *mapping inference* denotes the ability to derive additional mapping relationships from existing ones. One could, for instance, exploit transitive mapping relationships among metadata schemes and semi-automatically obtain input for additional mapping specifications. As all mapping solutions we have analysed so far, we do not yet support this requirement.

8.1.6 Summary of Qualitative Evaluation

In Table 8.1, in the right-most column, we have summarised the results of our qualitative evaluation and compared them against the requirements other existing mapping solutions fulfil. At a first glance, we can see that the strength of our approach lies in the mapping representation and in the mapping execution phase.

From the general requirements category, we fulfil uniform accessibility and modularity, which are two requirements only provided by large Enterprise Information Integration (EII) and Enterprise Application Integration (EAI) suites as well as by the StylusStudio mapping tool and Yahoo Pipes. For lifting models expressed in other schema definition languages than RDFS, we referred to related work and provided examples for the three illustrative scenarios presented at the beginning of this thesis. A first mapping GUI prototype version is available, but in a still very rudimentary status.

Developing schema matching algorithms for the mapping discovery phase has been out of the scope of this thesis and is therefore, as in most commercial mapping applications, not supported. However, by following an open Web-based approach, we at least support consensus building in mapping discovery.

The clear strength of our approach lies in the mapping representation phase. Especially the introduction of instance transformation functions provides mapping capabilities that go beyond those of existing solutions. Additionally, we provide the possibility to represent the context of a mapping specification by means of URIs. By following a generic design approach, we also achieve flexibility in language binding.

Also the mapping execution phase, or more specifically, the transition from the representation to the execution phase, is well supported. We provide a semi-automatic approach for integration component generation, whereas the generated mediation components take over the task of query reformulation and, to a minor extent, also the calculation of a query plan and optimisation strategies.

Finally, by providing a mapping registry, we have also covered an important mapping maintenance requirement: mapping reusability. The other features are subject to future work.

8.2 Example Metadata Integration Scenario

In order to demonstrate the feasibility and practical benefits of our mapping solution, we have implemented a sample metadata integration scenario, which provides uniform access to three autonomous, distributed and heterogeneous library catalogues. In particular, we realised an advanced search interface that allows users to search for resources (images, documents, etc.) in the integrated catalogues by entering search criteria for a set of given metadata fields. One could, for instance, formulate a query which searches for all library resources from a certain author and have a certain keyword in their title. The search form translates the search criteria into SPARQL query requests and executes them at a predefined mediation endpoint, which a domain expert has set up beforehand.

Since we want to give users a simple user interface with a comprehensible set of metadata fields, we have chosen the Dublin Core metadata element set to be the target schema, i.e., the mediation endpoint

8.2. Example Metadata Integration Scenario

		EII Suites		EAI Suites			Mapping Tools			Other Solutions			Proposed Mapping Solution
		BEA Liquid Data 8.1	Sybase Data Integration Suite - Avaki (Studio/Server) 7.0	Microsoft BizTalk Server 2006	Cape Clear 7 (Studio/Server)	IBM WebSphere Integration Developer	Altova MapForce / SchemaAgent	COMA++	Clio	StylusStudio / DataDirect XML Converters	TopBraid Composer	Yahoo Pipes	
General	Uniform Accessibility	■	■	■	■	■	□	□	□	■	□	■	■
	Modularity	■	■	■	■	■	□	□	□	■	□	■	■
	Lifting & Normalisation	□	□	■	■	■	□	□	□	■	□	□	◨
	Mapping GUI	■	■	■	■	■	■	■	■	■	■	■	◨
Mapping Discovery	Schema Matching / Alignment Support	□	□	■	□	◨	◨	■	■	□	□	□	□
	Consensus Building Features	□	□	□	□	□	□	□	□	□	□	◨	◨
Mapping Representation	Model-Level Structural Heterogeneity Reconciliation	■	■	■	■	■	■	◨	■	■	■	■	■
	Model-Level Semantic Heterogeneity Reconciliation	◨	◨	◨	◨	◨	◨	□	□	◨	◨	◨	■
	Instance-Level Semantic Heterogeneity Reconciliation	■	■	■	■	■	■	■	■	■	■	◨	■
	Context Representation	□	□	□	□	□	□	□	□	□	□	◨	■
	Flexible Language Binding	□	■	□	□	□	■	■	■	□	□	□	■
Mapping Execution	Query Reformulation	■	◨	□	□	□	□	□	□	□	□	□	■
	Query Plan / Optimisation	■	□	□	□	□	□	□	□	□	□	□	◨
	Integration Component Generation	■	■	■	■	■	■	□	□	□	□	■	■
Mapping Maintenance	Mapping Verification	□	□	□	□	□	◨	□	◨	□	□	□	□
	Mapping Reusability	□	□	□	□	□	■	□	□	□	□	■	■
	Mapping Inference	□	□	□	□	□	□	□	□	□	□	□	□

■ Supported   □ Not Supported   ◨ Partly Supported

Table 8.1: Qualitative evaluation against existing mapping solutions

can answer queries formulated over the Dublin Core schema and return metadata from other data sources, that do not necessarily describe their metadata using that schema.

8.2.1 Initial Situation

Our case study includes three heterogeneous data sources using the components we have presented in this thesis. These are:

- The Austrian National Library's (ONB) image archive (see Section 2.1.2), which maintains metadata for historical images in a relational database[1] using a **proprietary schema**.

- The Library of Congress (LOC) Open Archives repository[2], which exposes collections of digitised historical material, including photographs, movies, maps, pamphlets, sheet music, and books via the OAI-PMH protocol using the **MODS metadata schema**[3].

- The National Library of Australia's (NLA) Digital Object repository[4] exposing metadata about manuscripts, maps, music, pictures, books, and serials using the **Simple Dublin Core schema**.

As illustrated in Figure 8.1, we have three institutions in three different locations (Austria, Australia, United States), each of them exposing metadata in a different metadata schema (proprietary ONB, MODS, Dublin Core). In total we have two different technical interfaces: one SQL-accessible relational database and two OAI-PMH endpoints. The goal is to make the different kinds data sources, the distributed locations, and the heterogeneities of the metadata provided by these sources transparent to a requesting client.

8.2.2 Wrapping the Data Sources

Wrapping the involved data sources using dedicated wrapper components is the first step to be performed. For the ONB's relational database, we use the D2RQ Server [BS04], a component which publishes metadata residing in relational databases on the Web and provides SPARQL access to these metadata. For wrapping the LOC and NLA OAI-PMH metadata sources, we use the OAI2LOD Server presented earlier in this thesis.

Exposing ONB Metadata using D2RQ

A D2RQ Server instance, which has been set up for a certain relational database, requires a mapping file that defines the correspondences between tables and columns and RDFS classes and properties. Based on that information, it can rewrite incoming SPARQL queries to SQL statements and can transform the metadata to be returned into an RDF representation. Such a mapping file can be generated automatically

---

[1]In fact, the ONB exposes the metadata also via OAI-PMH using the Dublin Core schema. For the purpose of this case study, however, we demonstrate how metadata can be accessed directly from the underlying database.
[2]The LOC OAI-PMH endpoint: http://memory.loc.gov/cgi-bin/oai2_0
[3]The LOC exposes its metadata in three formats: Dublin Core, MODS, and MARC21. For demonstration purposes we request MODS metadata
[4]The NLA OAI-PMH endpoint: http://www.nla.gov.au/apps/oaicat/servlet/OAIHandler

8.2. Example Metadata Integration Scenario

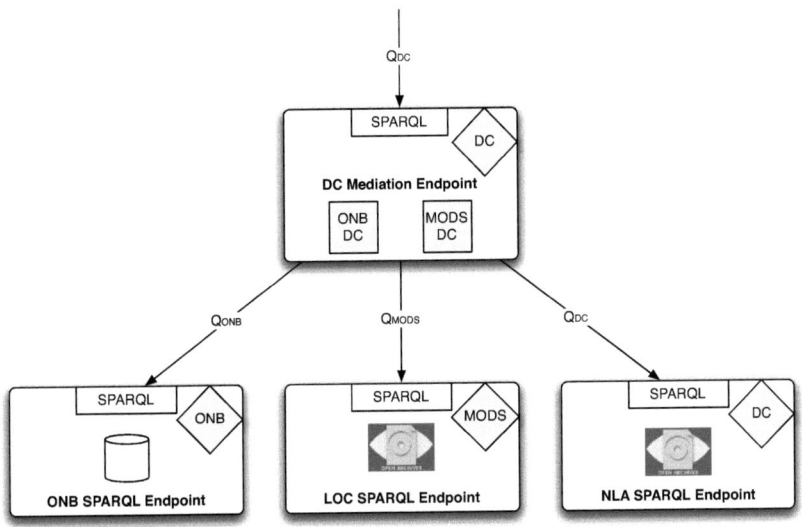

Figure 8.1: Example metadata integration scenario

by running the mapping generation tool, which is part of the D2RQ distribution. A detailed specification of the D2RQ language specification is available elsewhere[5].

Example 8.1 shows an excerpt of the D2RQ mapping file: it provides mapping information[6] for two of the three database tables (IMAGEDATA and IMAGEOBJECT), we have presented in our illustrative example in Section 2.1.2. Due to the lack of space, we only show a small subset of the mapped table columns.

Example 8.1 *Excerpt of the D2RQ configuration file for exposing ONB metadata*

```
@prefix map:   <file:/Users/haslhofer/Desktop/d2r-server-0.4/onb_mapping.n3#> .
@prefix onb:   <http://www.mediaspaces.info/schemes/onb#> .
@prefix d2rq:  <http://www.wiwiss.fu-berlin.de/suhl/bizer/D2RQ/0.1#> .

# DB connection details
map:database a d2rq:Database;
    d2rq:jdbcDriver "oracle.jdbc.OracleDriver";
    d2rq:jdbcDSN "jdbc:oracle:thin:@databaseURL:1521:database";
    d2rq:username "userName";
    d2rq:password "password";
```

---
[5]D2RQ User Manual and Language Specification: http://www4.wiwiss.fu-berlin.de/bizer/D2RQ/spec/
[6]The original database tables and columns are named in German language. Here we translated them to English.

```
# Table IMAGEOBJECT
map:ImageObject a d2rq:ClassMap;
    d2rq:dataStorage map:database;
    d2rq:uriPattern "ImageObject/@@IMAGEOBJECT.ID@@";
    d2rq:class onb:Image;
    .
map:ImageObject_TITEL a d2rq:PropertyBridge;
    d2rq:belongsToClassMap map:ImageObject;
    d2rq:property onb:titel;
    d2rq:column "IMAGEOBJECT.TITLE";
    .

# Table IMAGEDATA
map:ImageData a d2rq:ClassMap;
    d2rq:dataStorage map:database;
    d2rq:uriPattern "Image/@@IMAGEDATA.ID@@";
    d2rq:class onb:ImageObject;
    .
map:ImageData_INFO a d2rq:PropertyBridge;
    d2rq:belongsToClassMap map:ImageData;
    d2rq:property onb:info;
    d2rq:column "IMAGEDATA.INFO";
    .
map:ImageData_IMAGE a d2rq:PropertyBridge;
    d2rq:belongsToClassMap map:ImageData;
    d2rq:property onb:imageObject;
    d2rq:refersToClassMap map:ImageObject;
    d2rq:join "IMAGEDATA.ID = IMAGEOBJECT.BILD_ID";
    .
```

In the D2RQ mapping specification we can see that the tables and columns are mapped to certain RDFS classes and properties that are defined within the http://www.mediaspaces.info/schemes/onb# namespace[7]. To enable other applications to correctly interpret them, we must provide the respective schema definition at the location where the namespace points to. Therefore we create am RDFS schema definition for the ONB metadata schema and deploy it, as described in Section 6.6.1, in the corresponding location.

---

[7]We use the http://www.mediaspaces.info/ namespace only for the purpose of this case study. In a productive environment, the institutions should host their metadata schemes and mapping themselves

8.2. Example Metadata Integration Scenario

Exposing LOC Metadata via the OAI2LOD Server

The metadata provided by the Australian National Library OAI-PMH repository can easily be exposed by setting up an OAI2LOD Server instance. By default, OAI2LOD request metadata in the Dublin Core format from a OAI-PMH endpoint; since in this case study we want to use the MODS metadata schema, we have to provide an adequate OAI2LOD configuration together with an XSL stylesheet that transforms retrieved MODS metadata records from XML to RDF/XML. Example 8.2 shows the configuration file we use to set up our OAI2LOD Server instance.

Example 8.2 *OAI2LOD mapping file for exposing LOC metadata*

```
@prefix rdf:     <http://www.w3.org/1999/02/22-rdf-syntax-ns#> .
@prefix rdfs:    <http://www.w3.org/2000/01/rdf-schema#> .
@prefix oai2lod: <http://www.mediaspaces.info/vocab/oai2lod-server-config.rdf#> .


<> a oai2lod:Server;
    rdfs:label "OAI2LOD Server exposing LOC metadata";
    oai2lod:port 2020;
    oai2lod:baseURI <http://www.mediaspaces.info:4040/>;
    oai2lod:publishes <oai1>;
    .

<oai1> a oai2lod:OAIServer;
    oai2lod:serverURL <http://memory.loc.gov/cgi-bin/oai2_0>;
    oai2lod:metadataPrefix "mods";
    oai2lod:styleSheet "xsl/mods2rdf_xml.xsl";
    .
```

In the XSL stylesheet, where the transformation from MODS XML to RDF/XML is defined, we must refer to classes and properties that are part of an RDFS definition of MODS. Before creating such a definition from scratch, one should always search the Web for already existing definitions. For the MODS schema, such a definition has indeed already been developed as part of the SIMILE[8] project and is now available at http://simile.mit.edu/2006/01/ontologies/mods3.

Exposing NLA Metadata via the OAI2LOD Server

For exposing metadata from the Australian National Library on the Web, we simply have to a set up an OAI2LOD Server instance with default parameters because support for the Dublin Core metadata schema is a built-in OAI2LOD feature. We only need to change the oai2lod:baseURI property to the host (and port) where the instance is running, and the oai2lod:serverURL to http://www.nla.gov.au/apps/oaicat/servlet/OAIHandler, which is the NLA's OAI-PMH endpoint URL.

---
[8]The SIMILE project: http://simile.mit.edu/

8.2.3 Creating the Mapping Specifications

In the next step, we must create mapping specifications for the involved data sources. The target schema is the Dublin Core schema and the two source schemes are the proprietary ONB and the MODS schema. For the NLA data source we do not have to specify mappings because the wrapper already exposes Dublin Core metadata.

Mapping from the ONB schema to Dublin Core

Example 6.5 in Section 6.3 illustrates part of the required mapping specification, which maps the `onb:firstname` and `onb:lastName` properties, in the context of the class `onb:Person`, to the `dc:creator` property. The property mapping uses the `fn:concat` instance transformation function to transform the ONB instances into the representation required by the `dc:creator` property.

In Example 8.3, we present an excerpt of the extension of that mapping specification; basically, we simply introduced additional property mappings. Since the Dublin Core Usage Guide proposes to use RFC8601 date representations (e.g., 2003-07-03) for the `dc:format` property, we introduce a costum instance transformation that transforms the ONB-specific date representation (e.g., 03-JUL-03) to the required format.

Example 8.3 *ONB-DC mapping specification*

```
map:title2title a mm:PropertyMapping;
    am:expression am:equivalent;
    mm:sourceClassContext onb:ImageData;
    mm:sourceElement onb:title;
    mm:targetElement dc:title;
    .
map:info2description a mm:PropertyMapping;
    am:expression am:overlap;
    mm:sourceClassContext onb:ImageData;
    mm:sourceElement onb:info;
    mm:targetElement dc:description;
    .
map:creationDate2date a mm:PropertyMapping;
    am:expression am:equivalent;
    mm:sourceClassContext onb:ImageData;
    mm:sourceElement onb:creationDate;
    mm:targetElement dc:date;
    am:transFunction map:dateConvert;
    .
```

8.2. Example Metadata Integration Scenario

```
map:dateConvert  a  am:Function;
     am:URI  fx:date2rfc8601;
     am:argument(onb:creationDate);
     am:result  dc:date;
     .

map:mimeType2format  a  mm:PropertyMapping;
     mm:sourceClassContext  onb:ImageObject;
     mm:sourceElement  onb:mimeType;
     mm:targetElement  dc:format;
     .
```

Mapping from the MODS schema to Dublin Core

For the metadata provided by the LOC OAI2LOD Server, we must define mapping relationships between the source MODS schema and the target Dublin Core schema. Example 8.4 illustrates an excerpt of that mapping. We can see that MODS defines most properties (e.g., mods:name) in the context of a certain class (e.g., mods:CorporateName), while the Dublin Core element set is simply a flat list.

Example 8.4 *MODS-DC mapping specification*

```
@prefix rdf:   <http://www.w3.org/1999/02/22-rdf-syntax-ns#> .
@prefix rdfs:  <http://www.w3.org/2000/01/rdf-schema#> .
@prefix mods:  <http://simile.mit.edu/2006/01/ontologies/mods3#> .
@prefix dc:    <http://purl.org/dc/elements/1.1/> .

map:title2title  a  mm:PropertyMapping;
     am:expression  am:targetInclude;
     mm:sourceClassContext  mods:Title;
     mm:sourceElement  mods:value;
     mm:targetElement  dc:title;
     .

map:altTitle2title  a  mm:PropertyMapping;
     am:expression  am:targetInclude;
     mm:sourceClassContext  mods:AlternativeTitle;
     mm:sourceElement  mods:value;
     mm:targetElement  dc:title;
     .

map:corporateName2publisher  a  mm:PropertyMapping;
     am:expression  am:targetInclude;
     mm:sourceClassContext  mods:CorporateName;
```

```
    mm:sourceElement mods:name;
    mm:targetElement dc:publisher;
    .
map:abstract2description a mm:PropertyMapping;
    am:expression am:overlap;
    mm:sourceClassContext mods:Item;
    mm:sourceElement mods:abstract;
    mm:targetElement dc:description;
    .
map:topic2subject a mm:PropertyMapping;
    am:expression am:targetInclude;
    mm:sourceClassContext mods:Topic;
    mm:sourceElement mods:name;
    mm:targetElement dc:subject;
    .
```

8.2.4 Deploying a Mediation Endpoint

The deployment of a mediation endpoint is now a straight-forward process and requires the following configuration steps:

- Using a Web browser, we contact the mediation service deployed at http://www.mediaspaces.info/mediation. The service gives us the option to either choose an existing mediation endpoint or to create a new on. We do the latter, create a new mediation endpoint and obtain its URL (e.g., http://www.mediaspaces.info/mediation/ep1).

- At the Web site that appears when contacting the mediation endpoint's URL, we are prompted to enter details about the target schema and the involved data sources. We enter the URLs of the wrapper components we have deployed beforehand, together with the URLs of the source schemes that describe the metadata within these sources.

- Then we deploy the two mapping specifications on the Web (e.g., http://www.mediaspaces.info/mapping/onb_dc and http://www.mediaspaces.info/mapping/mods_dc) and equip our endpoint with these mappings by adding their URI references to the mediation endpoint configuration.

With these few configuration steps, a new mediation endpoint is set up and provides a uniform SPARQL query interface (e.g., http://www.mediaspaces.info/mediation/ep1/sparql) to execute SPARQL queries, formulated over the Dublin Core schema, over three autonomous, distributed metadata sources.

8.3 Summary and Lessons Learned

From the results of the qualitative evaluation, we can clearly see that the strength of our approach lies in the mapping representation and (in the transition to) the execution phase. Mapping discovery has not been the primary focus of this work and for mapping maintenance we have provided a registry solution that covers the basic needs (discovery and reuse of mappings) but still lacks other important features.

The aspect that distinguishes our approach from existing ones, is the focus on the Web architecture: all components (mediators, wrapper) and all involved artefacts (schema definition language, schemes, mappings) are designed in a way, that allows human and machines to access them on the Web. Thereby URIs, and more specifically URLs, play a major role.

The case study we have conducted by implementing an example metadata integration scenario has demonstrated that by using our mapping solution, it requires only a few, basic steps to set up a new mediation endpoint; without the need to install a metadata integration suite in the local system environment. However, it has also unveiled several limitations and areas for improvement in the future:

- *Performance*: we identified two major performance bottlenecks when executing SPARQL queries against a deployed mapping endpoint. First, the template selection and combination algorithms we employ in the mediator requires further optimisation strategies and techniques. For an incoming SPARQL query, the mediator currently executes a set of templates for each data source, whereas each template leads to a separate query to be executed; also if the query targets only a single data source. Combining and merging templates by using a more sophisticated selection algorithm will dramatically increase query performance. Second, the wrappers we use to expose the involved data sources are still academic prototypes and must be further improved in terms of query performance.

- *Mapping GUI*: the domain experts require a mapping GUI for specifying mapping relationships, otherwise it is unlikely that they produce mapping specifications. Since our whole architecture is based on Web technology, we could provide such an application also on the Web.

- *Human readability*: in our examples, we have defined metadata schema and mapping specifications using the N3 notation and deployed them on the Web. Since the N3 language is a format intended to be interpreted by machines, we also need a human-readable representation. Currently, we deploy an HTML representation in parallel and use HTTP content negotiation for delivering the appropriate representation to the requesting client, which means that the specifications must be written twice. A transformation language similar to XSL, which could translate RDF serialisation formats to HTML would solve the problem, but does not exist yet.

Recapitulating, we can say that the mapping solution we have developed so far demonstrates how metadata mappings can be realised in a Web environment. It does, however, require further work be invested in order to eliminate the currently existing limitations.

Chapter 9

Conclusions

9.1 Summary

In this thesis, we have proposed a Web-based metadata mapping technique as a novel approach for establishing metadata interoperability in an open, Web-based environment.

After an introduction to the area of *metadata* and its basic technical building blocks, we have extensively discussed the notion of *metadata interoperability* and provided a categorisation of heterogeneities that can prevent metadata information objects from being interoperable. For resolving these heterogeneities, we can resort to a variety of interoperability techniques, such as metadata standardisation, application profiles, global conceptual models, or schema mapping. An analysis on the quality of these techniques has revealed that especially in metadata integration scenarios, where agreement on a certain metadata standard is not possible, mapping techniques provide the necessary means to resolve a broad range of structural and semantic heterogeneities.

Subsequently, we have defined our conception of *metadata mapping* on a conceptual and technical basis, and identified it as being a cyclic process consisting of four major phases: *mapping discovery*, *mapping representation*, *mapping execution*, and *mapping maintenance*. For each phase, we have developed an extensive set of requirements that should be met by mapping solutions in order to be suitable for the integration of incompatible metadata from a variety of autonomous and distributed data sources. Based on these requirements we have derived an evaluation framework, against which we have analysed a representative set of metadata mapping solutions. Our analysis has revealed, that the majority of existing solutions focuses on closed-world database systems and does not provide means for mapping metadata information objects that are expressed using novel Web-based data models, such as RDF/S. Furthermore, many mapping solutions do not consider metadata mapping as a process, but concentrate only on certain phases: research prototypes primarily focus on mapping discovery and disregard how these mapping could be further processed. Commercial solutions support the representation and execution phase and partially disregard the discovery and maintenance phase. Another limitation of many mapping solutions is the restricted expressiveness of the mapping languages they provide for domain experts in order to express mapping relationships between the elements of distinct metadata schemes.

Facing these deficiencies, this thesis has made three substantial contributions towards a metadata mapping solution that addresses the needs of providing uniform access to incompatible metadata in an open, Web-based environment.

Firstly, we have proposed an *integration architecture* that seamlessly integrates with the architecture of the World Wide Web and a *methodology* that reflects the previously mentioned mapping phases. This enables the deployment of uniform query interfaces to a set of distributed, autonomous, and heterogeneous data sources in a Web-based environment. We can summarise the central characteristics of our approach as follows:

- All involved artefacts are Web resources. Not only the metadata to be integrated and the corresponding metadata schemes, but also the mapping specifications are Web resources and can be dereferenced via their URLs.

- All involved architectural components are Web services. Mediators and Wrappers expose their SPARQL query interfaces as URLs and can be looked up in a registry service, which is a Web service that maintains metadata about existing mediator and wrapper components as well as available schemes and mapping specifications.

- Domain experts can interact with the proposed mapping technique via an easy-to-use Web GUI. They do not need to install any additional mapping software in their local system environment.

Secondly, an *abstract mapping model*, which provides the means for defining mapping relationships among incompatible metadata schemes has been proposed. It has the following characteristics:

- The abstract mapping model is generic and therefore independent of any concrete schema definition language. It does, however, introduce the concept of URIs as identifiers for the model itself and all its elements, and thereby binds the mapping process to the architecture of the World Wide Web.

- The abstract mapping model is built upon a minimal directed labelled graph data model and is therefore applicable for all schema definition languages whose structure is derived from a graph-based grounding structure.

- The abstract mapping model reflects the semantics of a mapping relationship in terms of a mapping expression that is uniquely identified by a URI.

- The abstract mapping model introduces the concept of instance transformation functions, which is an essential feature to reconcile a broad range of heterogeneities occurring in real-world integration scenarios.

Thirdly, we have described an *RDFS binding of the mapping model*, which allows the definition of mapping relationships among metadata schemes expressed in RDFS. Its characteristics can be summarised as follows:

9.2. Future Work

- The RDFS binding extends the abstract mapping model with elements that take into account RDFS-specific characteristics, such as the fact that RDFS properties are first-class objects.

- Although the focus of this thesis has clearly been on the representation and on the (transition to) the execution phase, the RDFS mapping model also reflects the other phases: for the discovery phase, it provides an interface for integrating schema matching and ontology alignment techniques; the maintenance phase is supported by an interface for publishing mappings in a mapping registry.

- RDFS mapping specifications can be transformed into executable SPARQL query templates, which can be processed by the mediator component in order to unfold incoming user queries.

- The execution of the SPARQL templates is slightly optimised by a basic template selection algorithm.

- Discovery and reuse of existing RDFS mapping specifications is supported by a mapping registry that exposes registry metadata on the Web.

The result of these contributions is a metadata integration solution, which resembles a Web-based mediator wrapper architecture. Domain experts can expose the data sources they need to integrate by installing wrappers; the OAI2LOD Server we have provided is such a component. Our solution further enables domain experts to establish uniform SPARQL query access to these sources by deploying a mediation endpoint at the provided mediation service.

9.2 Future Work

The results of this thesis, especially those of the qualitative evaluation and case study we have conducted in Chapter 8, have opened several areas of future research work:

- For lifting and normalisation metadata schemes to the level of RDFS, we have referred to the works provided by others. Our mapping architecture can integrate such algorithms and thereby support users in creating RDFS (or OWL) metadata schemes from existing schema descriptions that are expressed in different schema definition languages.

- The integration of schema matching and ontology alignment algorithms is also possible. We can provide adapters to a variety of algorithms and allow domain experts to select them as support for the mapping discovery phase.

- The realisation of a Web-based mapping GUI, which allows domain experts to interactively create mappings among two metadata schemes, has high priority in our future work. The user interface of Yahoo Pipes shows that such a GUI can be realised with current Web technologies (HTML, CSS, Ajax). We expect that such a mapping GUI will increase the sharing of mapping specifications, because it supports domain experts in interpreting mappings created by others.

- By introducing community features such as tagging, wikis, or annotations, we could improve the process of building consensus on a certain mapping specification, which can lead to higher interoperability.

- Performance improvement is another important area of future work: the mediation component requires more sophisticated distributed query plan algorithms, which additionally take into account the capabilities of involved data sources. We need to consider statistics about the kind of metadata (classes, properties) contained in a data source and about the expected response times. The wrapper components require further optimisation too. The D2RQ Server, for instance, does not yet utilise the full power of the underlying relational database system. Certain SPARQL constructs (e.g., FILTER, LIMIT) are not yet translated to SQL, which leads to high latency and requires extensive data processing in the wrapper component itself. An obvious limitation of the OAI2LOD Server in its current development stage is that the metadata retrieved from OAI-PMH endpoints are replicated in an intermediate triple store — and the performance of triple stores is still a major research area in the Semantic Web community, although commercial database vendors (e.g., Oracle, OpenLink Virtuoso) have already started to work on that issue.

- The OAI2LOD Server currently provides rudimentary capabilities for interlinking OAI-PMH data sets with other data sets (e.g., DBPedia [1]) that have been exposed according to the Linked Data Principles.

- The verification of mappings has been out of the scope of this thesis too. Especially, in an open-world environment it is hard to determine the truth of a statement. However, some basic mechanism, which could evaluate the correctness of mappings, would bring an enormous benefit for domain experts.

- Mapping inference, as for instance, the transitive closure of mapping relationships, is on our list of future research topics.

---

[1] DBPedia is a structured representation of the data provided by Wikipedia. It is accessible at: http://dbpedia.org/About

Bibliography

[Abe01] Karl Aberer. P-grid: A self-organizing access structure for p2p information systems. In *CoopIS '01: Proceedings of the 9th International Conference on Cooperative Information Systems*, pages 179–194, London, UK, 2001. Springer-Verlag.

[Abi97] Serge Abiteboul. Querying semi-structured data. In *ICDT '97: Proceedings of the 6th International Conference on Database Theory*, pages 1–18, London, UK, 1997. Springer-Verlag.

[ACL+07] Mustafa Atay, Artem Chebotko, Dapeng Liu, Shiyong Lu, and Farshad Fotouhi. Efficient schema-based XML-to-relational data mapping. *Inf. Syst.*, 32(3):458–476, 2007.

[ACMHvP04] K. Aberer, P. Cudre-Mauroux, M. Hauswirth, and T. van Pelt. GridVine: Building internet-scale semantic overlay networks. In *International Semantic Web Conference (ISWC)*, volume 3298 of *LNCS*, pages 107–121, 2004.

[ADL07] ADL. *Sharable Content Reference Model (SCORM)*. Advanced Distributed Learning Initative (ADL), 2007. Available at: http://www.adlnet.gov/scorm/index.aspx.

[ADMR05] David Aumueller, Hong Hai Do, Sabine Massmann, and Erhard Rahm. Schema and ontology matching with COMA++. In Fatma Özcan, editor, *SIGMOD Conference*, pages 906–908. ACM, 2005.

[AG08] Renzo Angles and Claudio Gutierrez. Survey of graph database models. *ACM Comput. Surv.*, 40(1):1–39, 2008.

[AJP07] Julie Allinson, Pete Johnston, and Andy Powell. A Dublin Core application profile for scholarly works, January 2007. Available at: http://www.ariadne.ac.uk/issue50/allinson-et-al/.

[ALC00] ALCTS CC:DA. *Task Force on Metadata: Final Report*. Association for Library Collections & Technical Services (ALCTS), 2000. Available at: http://www.libraries.psu.edu/tas/jca/ccda/tf-meta6.html.

[Alt07a] Altova. *Altova MapForce*. Altova, Inc., 2007. Available at: http://www.altova.com/products/mapforce/data_mapping.html.

[Alt07b] Altova. *Altova SchemaAgent*. Altova Inc., 2007. Available at: http://www.altova.com/schemaagent_mapforce.html.

[BBB+02] Thomas Baker, Christophe Blanchi, Dan Brickley, Erik Duval, Rachel Heery, Pete Johnston, Leonid Kalinichenko, Heike Neuroth, and Shigeo Sugimoto. Principles of metadata registries. White paper, DELOS Network of Excellence on Digital Libraries, 2002.

BIBLIOGRAPHY

[BCH07] Chris Bizer, Richard Cyganiak, and Tom Heath. How to publish data on the web, July 2007. Available at: http://www4.wiwiss.fu-berlin.de/bizer/pub/LinkedDataTutorial/.

[BCM+03] Franz Baader, Diego Calvanese, Deborah L. McGuinness, Daniele Nardi, and Peter F. Patel-Schneider. *The description logic handbook: theory, implementation, and applications*. Cambridge University Press, New York, NY, USA, 2003.

[BDH+01] Thomas Baker, Makx Dekkers, Rachel Heery, Manjula Patel, and Gauri Salokhe. What terms does your metadata use? Application profiles as machine-understandable narratives. In *DC '01: Proceedings of the International Conference on Dublin Core and Metadata Applications 2001*, pages 151–159, Tokyo, Japan, 2001. National Institute of Informatics.

[BEA07] BEA. *BEA Liquid Data for WebLogic 8.1*. BEA Systems, Inc., 2007. Available at: http://edocs.bea.com/liquiddata/docs81/index.html.

[BHHK08] Sean Bechhofer, Manfred Hauswirth, Jörg Hoffmann, and Manolis Koubarakis, editors. *The Semantic Web: Research and Applications, 5th European Semantic Web Conference, ESWC 2008, Tenerife, Canary Islands, Spain, June 1-5, 2008, Proceedings*, volume 5021 of *Lecture Notes in Computer Science*. Springer, 2008.

[BHP00] Phillip A. Bernstein, Alon Y. Halevy, and Rachel A. Pottinger. A vision for management of complex models. *SIGMOD Rec.*, 29(4):55–63, 2000.

[BL98] Tim Berners-Lee. Notation 3. Design note, World Wide Web Consortium (W3C), 1998. Available at: http://www.w3.org/DesignIssues/Notation3.

[BL06] Tim Berners-Lee. Linked data, July 2006. Available at: http://www.w3.org/DesignIssues/LinkedData.html.

[BMPQ04] Philip A. Bernstein, Sergey Melnik, Michalis Petropoulos, and Christoph Quix. Industrial-strength schema matching. *SIGMOD Record*, 33(4):38–43, 2004.

[BP08] Diego Berruta and John Phipps. *Best Practice Recipes for Publishing RDF Vocabularies*. W3C Semantic Web Deployment Working Group, January 2008. Available at: http://www.w3.org/TR/swbp-vocab-pub/.

[BS04] Christan Bizer and Andy Seaborne. D2RQ - Treating non-RDF databases as virtual RDF graphs. In *3rd International Semantic Web Conference (ISWC2004)*, Hiroshima, Japan, 2004. Available at: http://www.wiwiss.fu-berlin.de/suhl/bizer/D2RQ/.

[BU04] Gilad Bracha and David Ungar. Mirrors: design principles for meta-level facilities of object-oriented programming languages. In *OOPSLA '04: Proceedings of the 19th annual ACM SIGPLAN conference on Object-oriented programming, systems, languages, and applications*, pages 331–344, New York, NY, USA, 2004. ACM Press.

[BZCS01] Ana B. Benitez, Di Zhong, Shih-Fu Chang, and John R. Smith. MPEG-7 MDS content description tools and applications. In *CAIP '01: Proceedings of the 9th International Conference on Computer Analysis of Images and Patterns*, pages 41–52, London, UK, 2001. Springer-Verlag.

BIBLIOGRAPHY

[Cap07] Cape Clear. *CapeClear Studio / Server*. Cape Clear Software Inc., 2007. Available at: http://www.capeclear.com/products/index.shtml.

[CBHS05] Jeremy J. Carroll, Christian Bizer, Pat Hayes, and Patrick Stickler. Named graphs, provenance and trust. In *WWW '05: Proceedings of the 14th international conference on World Wide Web*, pages 613–622, New York, NY, USA, 2005. ACM.

[CCS02] CCSDS. *Open Archival Information Systems — OAIS*. Council of the Consultative Commitee for Space Data Systems (CCSDS), 2002. Available at: http://public.ccsds.org/publications/archive/650x0b1.pdf.

[CDH+05] Yuhan Cai, Xin Luna Dong, Alon Halevy, Jing Michelle Liu, and Jayant Madhavan. Personal information management with SEMEX. In *SIGMOD '05: Proceedings of the 2005 ACM SIGMOD international conference on Management of data*, pages 921–923, New York, NY, USA, 2005. ACM Press.

[CGMH+94] Sudarshan Chawathe, Hector Garcia-Molina, Joachim Hammer, Kelly Ireland, Yannis Papakonstantinou, Jeffrey D. Ullman, and Jennifer Widom. The TSIMMIS project: Integration of heterogeneous information sources. In *16th Meeting of the Information Processing Society of Japan*, pages 7–18, Tokyo, Japan, 1994.

[Che76] Peter Pin-Shan Chen. The entity-relationship model — toward a unified view of data. *ACM Trans. Database Syst.*, 1(1):9–36, 1976.

[Cod70] E. F. Codd. A relational model of data for large shared data banks. *Commun. ACM*, 13(6):377–387, 1970.

[CW85] Luca Cardelli and Peter Wegner. On understanding types, data abstraction, and polymorphism. *ACM Comput. Surv.*, 17(4):471–523, 1985.

[Cyg05] Richard Cyganiak. A relational algebra for SPARQL. Technical report, HP Labs Bristol, September 2005. Available at: http://www.hpl.hp.com/techreports/2005/HPL-2005-170.html.

[CZ06] Lois Mai Chan and Marcia Lei Zeng. Metadata interoperability and standardization — a study of methodology part I + II. *D-LIB Magazine*, 12(6), June 2006. Available at: http://www.dlib.org/dlib/june06/chan/06chan.html.

[Dat07] DataDirect Technologies. Stylus Studio 2007 and DataDirect XML Converters, 2007. Available at: http://www.stylusstudio.com/.

[DB78] Umeshwar Dayal and Philip A. Bernstein. On the updatability of relational views. In *VLDB'1978: Proceedings of the fourth international conference on Very Large Data Bases*, pages 368–377. VLDB Endowment, 1978.

[DC06] DC. *Dublin Core Metadata Element Set, Version 1.1*. Dublin Core Metadata Initiative, December 2006. Available at: http://dublincore.org/documents/dces/.

[DC07] DC. *Dublin Core Collections Application Profile*. Dublin Core Metadata Initiative (DC), March 2007. Available at: http://dublincore.org/groups/collections/collection-application-profile/.

[DD99]	Ruxandra Domenig and Klaus R. Dittrich. An overview and classification of mediated query systems. *SIGMOD Rec.*, 28(3):63–72, 1999.
[DH05]	AnHai Doan and Alon Y. Halevy. Semantic-integration research in the database community. *AI Magazine*, 26(1):83–94, 2005.
[DMDH02]	AnHai Doan, Jayant Madhavan, Pedro Domingos, and Alon Halevy. Learning to map between ontologies on the semantic web. In *WWW '02: Proceedings of the 11th international conference on World Wide Web*, pages 662–673, New York, NY, USA, 2002. ACM Press.
[DNB07a]	DNB. *Maschinelles Austauschformat für Bibliotheken.* German National Library — Expert group for data formats, 2007. Available at: http://www.d-nb.de/standardisierung/formate/mab.htm.
[DNB07b]	DNB. *Personennormdatei (PND).* German National Library, 2007. Available at: http://www.d-nb.de/standardisierung/normdateien/pnd.htm.
[DR02]	Hong Hai Do and Erhard Rahm. COMA - a system for flexible combination of schema matching approaches. In *VLDB*, pages 610–621. Morgan Kaufmann, 2002.
[EDI07]	EDItEUR. *Online Information Exchange (ONIX).* The EDItEUR Group, 2007. Available at: http://www.editeur.org/onix.html.
[ETS06]	ETSI. *TV Anytime — TS 102 822:1-7.* European Telecommunications Standards Institute (ETSI), 2006. Available at: http://www.etsi.org/etsisite/website/technologies/tvanytime.aspx.
[FHM05]	Michael Franklin, Alon Halevy, and David Maier. From databases to dataspaces: a new abstraction for information management. *SIGMOD Rec.*, 34(4):27–33, 2005.
[GBMS99]	Cheng Hian Goh, Stéphane Bressan, Stuart Madnick, and Michael Siegel. Context interchange: new features and formalisms for the intelligent integration of information. *ACM Trans. Inf. Syst.*, 17(3):270–293, 1999.
[GDDD04]	Dragan Gasevic, Dragan Djuric, Vladan Devedzic, and Violeta Damjanovi. Converting UML to OWL ontologies. In *WWW Alt. '04: Proceedings of the 13th international World Wide Web conference on Alternate track papers & posters*, pages 488–489, New York, NY, USA, 2004. ACM Press.
[Gil05]	Anne J. Gilliland. Introduction to metadata — pathways to digital information, 2005. Available at: http://www.getty.edu/research/conducting_research/standards/intrometadata/index.html.
[GJSB05]	James Gosling, Bill Joy, Guy Steele, and Gilad Bracha. *The Java Language Specification, Third Edition.* Addison-Wesley Longman, Amsterdam, The Netherlands, 3 edition, June 2005.
[Gru93]	Tom Gruber. A translation approach to portable ontology specifications. *Knowledge Acquisitions*, 5:199–220, 1993.

BIBLIOGRAPHY

[HAB+05] Alon Y. Halevy, Naveen Ashish, Dina Bitton, Michael Carey, Denise Draper, Jeff Pollock, Arnon Rosenthal, and Vishal Sikka. Enterprise information integration: successes, challenges and controversies. In *SIGMOD '05: Proceedings of the 2005 ACM SIGMOD international conference on Management of data*, pages 778–787, New York, NY, USA, 2005. ACM Press.

[Hal01] Alon Y. Halevy. Answering queries using views: A survey. *The VLDB Journal*, 10(4):270–294, 2001.

[Has06] Bernhard Haslhofer. A service oriented architecture for integrating metadata from heterogeneous digital libraries. In *The 1st International Workshop "Semantic Information Integration on Knowledge Discovery" (SIIK 2006)*, Yogyakarta, Indonesia, December 2006.

[Has07] Bernhard Haslhofer. Uniform SPARQL access to interlinked (digital library) sources. In *The 6th European Networked Knowledge Organization Systems (NKOS) Workshop*, Budapest, Hungary, September 2007.

[Has08] Bernhard Haslhofer. A comparative study of mapping solutions. Technical report, University of Vienna, January 2008. Available at: http://www.cs.univie.ac.at/publication.php?pid=3886.

[HH05] Bernhard Haslhofer and Robert Hecht. Metadata management in a heterogeneous digital libary. In *eChallenges 2005, Ljubljana, Slowenia*. IOS Press, October 2005.

[HHH+05] Laura M. Haas, Mauricio A. Hernández, Howard Ho, Lucian Popa, and Mary Roth. Clio grows up: from research prototype to industrial tool. In *SIGMOD '05: Proceedings of the 2005 ACM SIGMOD international conference on Management of data*, pages 805–810, New York, NY, USA, 2005. ACM Press.

[HIMT03] Alon Y. Halevy, Zachary G. Ives, Peter Mork, and Igor Tatarinov. Piazza: data management infrastructure for semantic web applications. In *WWW '03: Proceedings of the 12th international conference on World Wide Web*, pages 556–567, New York, NY, USA, 2003. ACM Press.

[HIST05] Y. Halevy, G. Ives, Dan Suciu, and Igor Tatarinov. Schema mediation for large-scale semantic data sharing. *The VLDB Journal*, 14(1):68–83, 2005.

[HK08] Bernhard Haslhofer and Wolfgang Klas. A survey of techniques for achieving metadata interoperability. *ACM Comput. Surv.*, 2008. Accepted for publication.

[HL01] Jane Hunter and Carl Lagoze. Combining RDF and XML schemas to enhance interoperability between metadata application profiles. In *WWW '01: Proceedings of the 10th international conference on World Wide Web*, pages 457–466, New York, NY, USA, 2001. ACM.

[HP00] Rachel Heery and Manjula Patel. Application profiles: mixing and matching metadata schemas, Sep 2000. Available at: http://www.ariadne.ac.uk/issue25/app-profiles/.

[HS08]   Bernhard Haslhofer and Bernhard Schandl. The OAI2LOD Server: Exposing OAI-PMH metadata as linked data. In *International Workshop on Linked Data on the Web (LDOW2008), co-located with WWW 2008*, Beijing, China, April 2008.

[IBM07]   IBM. *IBM WebSphere Integration Developer*. IBM Inc., 2007.

[IEE02]   IEEE WG-12. *IEEE Standard for Learning Object Metadata: 1484.12.1-2002*. IEEE Inc., jul 2002. Available at: http://ltsc.ieee.org/wg12.

[IFL97]   IFLA. *Functional Requirements for Bibliographic Records*. Study Group on the Functional Requirements for Bibliographic Records, International Federation of Library Assocations (IFLA), 1997. Available at: http://www.ifla.org/VII/s13/frbr/frbr.htm.

[ISO03a] ISO TC 211. *Geographic Information Metadata — ISO 19115:2003*. International Standardizaton Organization (ISO), 2003. Available at: http://www.iso.org/iso/iso_catalogue/catalogue_tc/catalogue_detail.htm?csnumber=26020.

[ISO03b] ISO/IEC JTC 1/SC 32. *SQL - ISO/IEC 9075-1:2003*. International Standardizaton Organization (ISO), 2003.

[ISO04]   ISO TC 154. *Data elements and interchange formats — Information Exchange — Representation of dates and times — ISO 8601:2004*. International Standardizaton Organization (ISO), 2004. Available at: http://www.iso.org/iso/catalogue_detail?csnumber=40874.

[ISO05]   ISO/IEC JTC 1/SC 32. *Common Logic (CL) — a framework for a family of logic-based languages - ISO/IEC 24707:2007*. International Standardizaton Organization (ISO), December 2005.

[ISO06a] ISO TC 46. *CIDOC Coneptual Reference Model (CRM) — ISO 21127:2006*. International Standardizaton Organization (ISO), December 2006.

[ISO06b] ISO TC 46. *Codes for the representation of names of countries and their subdivisions — Part 1: Country codes — ISO 3166-1:2006*. International Standardizaton Organization (ISO), 2006. Available at: http://www.iso.org/iso/iso_catalogue/catalogue_tc/catalogue_detail.htm?csnumber=39719.

[ISO06c] ISO/IEC JTC 1/SC 34. *Topic Maps — Part 2: Data model — ISO/IEC 13250-2:2006*. International Standardizaton Organization (ISO), June 2006.

[ISO07a] ISO/IEC JTC 1/SC 29. *MPEG-21 Multimedia Framework — ISO 21000-1-7:2003-2007*. International Standardizaton Organization (ISO), 2007.

[ISO07b] ISO/IEC JTC 1/SC 29. *MPEG-7 Multimedia Content Description Interface — ISO 15938-1-11:2002-2007*. International Standardizaton Organization (ISO), 2007.

[Jav06]   Java Community Process. JSR 269: Pluggable Annotation Processing API, December 2006. Available at: http://jcp.org/en/jsr/detail?id=269.

[JK84]   Matthias Jarke and Jurgen Koch. Query optimization in database systems. *ACM Comput. Surv.*, 16(2):111–152, 1984.

BIBLIOGRAPHY

[Joh04] Pete Johnston. Minerva - technical guidlines for digital cultural content creation programmes. Technical report, UKOLN, University of Bath. MLA The Council for Museums, Libraries and Archives, 2004. Available at: http://www.minervaeurope.org/structure/workinggroups/servprov/documents/techguid1_0.pdf.

[JW04] Ian Jacobs and Norman Walsh. Architecture of the world wide web, volume one, December 2004. Available at: http://www.w3.org/TR/webarch/.

[KHS08] Mirjam Keßler, Bernhard Haslhofer, and Maximilian Schwarzmaier. Umfragereport zur Nutzung von Metadaten. Technical report, KIM - Kompetenzzentrum Interoperable Metadaten, February 2008. Available at: http://www.kim-forum.org/material/pdf/KIM-Umfragereport.pdf.

[Kos03] Harald Kosch. *Distributed multimedia database technologies supported by MPEG-7 and MPEG-21*. CRC Press LLC, Boca Raton, Florida, United States, 2003.

[KQCJ07] David Kensche, Christoph Quix, Mohamed Amine Chatti, and Matthias Jarke. Gerome: A generic role based metamodel for model management. *Journal of Data Semantics*, 8:82–117, 2007.

[KS03] Yannis Kalfoglou and Marco Schorlemmer. Ontology mapping: the state of the art. *Knowl. Eng. Rev.*, 18(1):1–31, 2003.

[LC00] Wen-Syan Li and Chris Clifton. Semint: a tool for identifying attribute correspondences in heterogeneous databases using neural networks. *Data Knowl. Eng.*, 33(1):49–84, 2000.

[LdS02] Carl Lagoze and Herbert Van de Sompel. The open archives initiative protocol for metadata harvesting — version 2.0, 2002. Available at: http://www.openarchives.org/OAI/openarchivesprotocol.html.

[Len02] Maurizio Lenzerini. Data integration: a theoretical perspective. In *PODS '02: Proceedings of the twenty-first ACM SIGMOD-SIGACT-SIGART symposium on Principles of database systems*, pages 233–246, New York, NY, USA, 2002. ACM.

[Lev66] V. I. Levenshtein. Binary Codes Capable of Correcting Deletions, Insertions and Reversals. *Soviet Physics Doklady*, 10, February 1966.

[Lev99] Alon Y. Levy. Logic-based techniques in data integration. In Jack Minker, editor, *Workshop on Logic-Based Artificial Intelligence, Washington, DC, June 14–16, 1999*, College Park, Maryland, 1999. Computer Science Department, University of Maryland.

[LF04] Patrick Lethi and Peter Frankhauser. XML data integration with OWL: Experiences and Challenges. In *2004 Symposium on Applications and the Internet (SAINT 2004)*, pages 160–170, Tokyo, Japan, 2004. IEEE Computer Society.

[LOC07a] LOC. *Library of Congress Authorities*. Library of Congress (LOC), 2007. Available at: http://authorities.loc.gov/.

[LOC07b] LOC. *Library of Congress Subject Headings (LCSH)*. Library of Congress, 2007. Available at: http://www.loc.gov/aba/cataloging/subject/.

[LOC07c] LOC. *MARC 21 Concise Format for Bibliographic Metadata*. Library of Congress' (LOC) Network Development and MARC Standards Office, 2007. Available at: http://www.loc.gov/marc/bibliographic/ecbdhome.html.

[LOC07d] LOC. *Metadata Object Description Schema*. Library of Congress' (LOC) Network Development and MARC Standards Office, 2007. Available at: http://www.loc.gov/standards/mods/.

[LOC07e] LOC. *METS (Metadata Encoding and Transmisson Standard)*. Library of Congress' (LOC) Network Development and MARC Standards Office, 2007. Available at: http://www.loc.gov/standards/mets.

[LVJ+07] Carl Lagoze, Herbert Van de Sompel, Pete Johnston, Michael L. Nelson, Robert Sanderson, and Simeon Warner. Open Archives Initative Object Reuse and Exchange (OAI-ORE). Technical report, Open Archives Initative, December 2007. Available at: http://www.openarchives.org/ore/0.1/toc.

[LW95] David B. Lomet and Jennifer Widom, editors. *Special Issue on Materialized Views and Data Warehousing*, volume 18 of *Bulletin of the Technical Commitee on Data Engineering*. IEEE Computer Society, June 1995.

[LWB08] Andreas Langegger, Wolfram Wöß, and Martin Blöchl. A semantic web middleware for virtual data integration on the web. In Bechhofer et al. [BHHK08], pages 493–507.

[MBDH02] Jayant Madhavan, Philip A. Bernstein, Pedro Domingos, and Alon Y. Halevy. Representing and reasoning about mappings between domain models. In *Eighteenth national conference on Artificial intelligence*, pages 80–86, Menlo Park, CA, USA, 2002. American Association for Artificial Intelligence.

[MBR01] Jayant Madhavan, Philip A. Bernstein, and Erhard Rahm. Generic schema matching with cupid. In Peter M. G. Apers, Paolo Atzeni, Stefano Ceri, Stefano Paraboschi, Kotagiri Ramamohanarao, and Richard T. Snodgrass, editors, *VLDB 2001, Proceedings of 27th International Conference on Very Large Data Bases, September 11-14, 2001, Roma, Italy*, pages 49–58. Morgan Kaufmann, 2001.

[McP02] A.K. McParland. TV-Anytime — using all that extra data. Technical report, BBC, sep 2002. Available at: http://www.bbc.co.uk/rd/pubs/whp/whp-pdf-files/WHP050.pdf.

[MHH+01] Renée J. Miller, Mauricio A. Hernández, Laura M. Haas, Lingling Yan, C. T. Howard Ho, Ronald Fagin, and Lucian Popa. The Clio project: managing heterogeneity. *SIGMOD Rec.*, 30(1):78–83, 2001.

[MHS07] Boris Motik, Ian Horrocks, and Ulrike Sattler. Bridging the gap between OWL and relational databases. In *WWW '07: Proceedings of the 16th international conference on World Wide Web*, pages 807–816, New York, NY, USA, 2007. ACM Press.

[Mic07] Microsoft. *Microsoft BizTalk Mapper*. Microsoft Inc., 2007. Available at: http://www.microsoft.com/biztalk/techinfo/tips/mapper/default.mspx.

BIBLIOGRAPHY

[MIKS00] Eduardo Mena, Arantza Illarramendi, Vipul Kashyap, and Amit P. Sheth. Observer: An approach for query processing in global information systems based on interoperation across pre-existing ontologies. *Distrib. Parallel Databases*, 8(2):223–271, 2000.

[Mil00] Paul Miller. Interoperability. What is it and why should i want it?, June 2000. Available at: http://www.ariadne.ac.uk/issue24/interoperability/intro.html.

[MLF00] Todd Millstein, Alon Levy, and Marc Friedman. Query containment for data integration systems. In *PODS '00: Proceedings of the nineteenth ACM SIGMOD-SIGACT-SIGART symposium on Principles of database systems*, pages 67–75, New York, NY, USA, 2000. ACM Press.

[MMSV02] Alexander Maedche, Boris Motik, Nuno Silva, and Raphael Volz. Mafra — an ontology mapping framework in the semantic web. In *Proceedings of the ECAI Workshop on Knowledge Transformation, Lyon, France, 2002*, 2002.

[NH07] Philipp Nussbaumer and Bernhard Haslhofer. CIDOC CRM in action - experiences and challenges. In László Kovács, Norbert Fuhr, and Carlo Meghini, editors, *ECDL*, volume 4675 of *Lecture Notes in Computer Science*, pages 532–533. Springer, 2007.

[NIS04] NISO. *Understanding Metadata*. National Information Standards Organization (NISO), 2004. Available at: http://www.niso.org/standards/resources/UnderstandingMetadata.pdf.

[NK04] Natalya F. Noy and Michel Klein. Ontology evolution: Not the same as schema evolution. *Knowl. Inf. Syst.*, 6(4):428–440, 2004.

[NLM07] NLM. *Medical Subject Headings*. U.S. National Library of Medicine (NLM), 2007. Available at: http://www.nlm.nih.gov/mesh/.

[NM03] Natalya F. Noy and Mark A. Musen. The prompt suite: interactive tools for ontology merging and mapping. *Int. J. Hum.-Comput. Stud.*, 59(6):983–1024, 2003.

[NM04] Natalya F. Noy and Mark A. Musen. Ontology versioning in an ontology management framework. *IEEE Intelligent Systems*, 19(4):6–13, 2004.

[Noy04] Natalya F. Noy. Semantic integration: a survey of ontology-based approaches. *SIGMOD Rec.*, 33(4):65–70, 2004.

[NP01] Ian Niles and Adam Pease. Towards a standard upper ontology. In *FOIS '01: Proceedings of the international conference on Formal Ontology in Information Systems*, pages 2–9, New York, NY, USA, 2001. ACM Press.

[NWG95] NWG. *A Format for Bibliographic Records (RFC 1807)*. Network Working Group (NWG), jun 1995. Available at: http://rfc.net/rfc1807.html.

[NWG05] NWG. *RFC3986 – Uniform Resource Identifier (URI): Generic Syntax*. Network Working Group (NWG), 2005. Available at: http://www.gbiv.com/protocols/uri/rfc/rfc3986.html.

[NWQ+02]   Wolfgang Nejdl, Boris Wolf, Changtao Qu, Stefan Decker, Michael Sintek, Ambjörn Naeve, Mikael Nilsson, Matthias Palmér, and Tore Risch. Edutella: a P2P networking infrastructure based on rdf. In *WWW '02: Proceedings of the 11th international conference on World Wide Web*, pages 604–615, New York, NY, USA, 2002. ACM Press.

[OCL07]   OCLC. *Dewey Decimal Classification (DDC)*. Online Computer Library Center (OCLC), 2007. Available at: http://www.oclc.org/dewey/.

[OGC04]   OGC. Geography Markup Language. Technical report, Open Geospatial Consortium (OGC), 2004. Available at: http://portal.opengeospatial.org/files/?artifact_id=4700.

[OMG05]   OMG. *Meta Object Facility (MOF) 2.0 Query/View/Transformation Specification*. Object Management Group (OMG), November 2005. Available at: http://www.omg.org/cgi-bin/apps/doc?ptc/05-11-01.pdf.

[OMG06a]   OMG. *Meta Object Facility (MOF) Core Specification - Version 2.0*. Object Management Group (OMG), January 2006. Available at: http://www.omg.org/cgi-bin/apps/doc?formal/06-01-01.pdf.

[OMG06b]   OMG. *Ontology Definition Metamodel Specification (ODM)*. Object Management Group (OMG), 2006. Available at: http://www.omg.org/docs/ptc/06-10-11.pdf.

[OMG06c]   OMG. *UML 2.0 – Infrastructure Specification*. Object Management Group (OMG), 2006. Available at: http://www.omg.org/docs/ptc/03-09-15.pdf.

[OMG07]   OMG. *Unified Modelling Language (UML)*. Object Management Group (OMG), 2007. Available at: http://www.uml.org/.

[OS99]   A. M. Ouksel and A. Sheth. Semantic interoperability in global information systems. *SIGMOD Rec.*, 28(1):5–12, 1999.

[PGH96]   Yannis Papakonstantinou, Ashish Gupta, and Laura Haas. Capabilities-based query rewriting in mediator systems. In *Proceedings of 4th International Conference on Parallel and Distributed Information Systems*, Miami Beach, Flor., 1996.

[PGMW95]   Yannis Papakonstantinou, Hector Garcia-Molina, and Jennifer Widom. Object exchange across heterogeneous information sources. pages 251–260, 1995.

[PL98]   Margaret St. Pierre and William P. LaPlant. Issues in crosswalking content metadata standards. Technical report, National Information Standards Organization (NISO), October 1998. Available at: http://www.niso.org/press/whitepapers/crsswalk.html.

[PNNJ05]   Andy Powell, Mikael Nilsson, Ambjörn Naeve, and Pete Johnston. *DCMI Abstract Model*. Dublin Core Metadata Initiative (DC), March 2005. Available at: http://dublincore.org/documents/abstract-model/.

[PV99]   Yannis Papakonstantinou and Vasilis Vassalos. Query rewriting for semistructured data. In *SIGMOD '99: Proceedings of the 1999 ACM SIGMOD international conference on Management of data*, pages 455–466, New York, NY, USA, 1999. ACM Press.

BIBLIOGRAPHY

[QL08] Bastian Quilitz and Ulf Leser. Querying distributed rdf data sources with sparql. In Bechhofer et al. [BHHK08], pages 524–538.

[RB01] Erhard Rahm and Philip A. Bernstein. A survey of approaches to automatic schema matching. *The VLDB Journal*, 10(4):334–350, 2001.

[RCC05] George G. Robertson, Mary P. Czerwinski, and John E. Churchill. Visualization of mappings between schemas. In *CHI '05: Proceedings of the SIGCHI conference on Human factors in computing systems*, pages 431–439, New York, NY, USA, 2005. ACM Press.

[RGKG+05] Patricia Rodríguez-Gianolli, Anastasios Kementsietsidis, Maddalena Garzetti, Iluju Kiringa, Lei Jiang, Mehedi Masud, Renée J. Miller, and John Mylopoulos. Data sharing in the hyperion peer database system. In *VLDB '05: Proceedings of the 31st international conference on Very large data bases*, pages 1291–1294. VLDB Endowment, 2005.

[RSU95] Anand Rajaraman, Yehoshua Sagiv, and Jeffrey D. Ullman. Answering queries using templates with binding patterns (extended abstract). In *PODS '95: Proceedings of the fourteenth ACM SIGACT-SIGMOD-SIGART symposium on Principles of database systems*, pages 105–112, New York, NY, USA, 1995. ACM Press.

[SD02] Michael Sintek and Stefan Decker. Triple - a query, inference, and transformation language for the semantic web. In Ian Horrocks and James A. Hendler, editors, *International Semantic Web Conference*, volume 2342 of *Lecture Notes in Computer Science*, pages 364–378, Sardinia, Italy, 2002. Springer.

[SE05] Pavel Shvaiko and Jérôme Euzenat. A survey of schema-based matching approaches. *Journal of Data Semantics*, 3730:146–171, 2005.

[Sei03] Ed Seidewitz. What models mean. *IEEE Software*, 20(5):26–32, 2003.

[SHJK08] Karin Schellner, Bernhard Haslhofer, Wolfgang Jochum, and Ross King. Opening annotation systems for multiple content and annotation types. *International Journal on Digital Libraries*, 2008. Submitted for publication.

[SK98] Amit Sheth and Wolfgang Klas. *Multimedia Data Management: Using Metadata to Integrate and Apply Digital Media Media*. Mcgraw-Hill Education, New York, NY, USA, 1998.

[SL90] Amit P. Sheth and James A. Larson. Federated database systems for managing distributed, heterogeneous, and autonomous databases. *ACM Comput. Surv.*, 22(3):183–236, 1990.

[SPD92] Stefano Spaccapietra, Christine Parent, and Yann Dupont. Model independent assertions for integration of heterogeneous schemas. *The VLDB Journal*, 1(1):81–126, 1992.

[Syb07] Sybase. *Sybase Data Integration Suite*. Sybase Inc., 2007. Available at: http://www.sybase.com/products/dataintegration/dataintegrationsuite.

[TEI07] TEI. *TEI P5: Guidelines for Electronic Text Encoding and Interchange*. TEI Consortium, 2007. Available at: http://www.tei-c.org/Guidelines/P5/.

[TH04]   Igor Tatarinov and Alon Halevy. Efficient query reformulation in peer data management systems. In *SIGMOD '04: Proceedings of the 2004 ACM SIGMOD international conference on Management of data*, pages 539–550, New York, NY, USA, 2004. ACM Press.

[The06]   The Rule Markup Iniative. RuleML – version 0.91, October 2006. Available at: http://www.ruleml.org/.

[Til04]   Barbara Tillett. What is FRBR — a conceptual model for the bibliographic universe, 2004. Available at: http://www.loc.gov/cds/FRBR.html.

[Tol06]   Andreas Tolk. What comes after the semantic web - pads implications for the dynamic web. In *PADS '06: Proceedings of the 20th Workshop on Principles of Advanced and Distributed Simulation*, page 55, Washington, DC, USA, 2006. IEEE Computer Society.

[Top07]   TopQuadrant Inc. TopBraid Composer, 2007. Available at: http://www.topbraidcomposer.com/.

[UWGM02] Jeffrey D. Ullman, Jennifer Widom, and Hector Garcia-Molina. *Database Systems - The Complete Book*. Prentice Hall, Inc., 2002.

[vAD04]   Luis von Ahn and Laura Dabbish. Labeling images with a computer game. In *CHI '04: Proceedings of the SIGCHI conference on Human factors in computing systems*, pages 319–326, New York, NY, USA, 2004. ACM Press.

[VJBCS97] Pepjijn R. S. Visser, Dean M. Jones, T. J. M. Bench-Capon, and M. J. R. Shave. An analysis of ontological mismatches: Heterogeneity versus interoperability. In *AAAI 1997 Spring Symposium on Ontological Engineering*, Stanford, USA, 1997. Stanford University.

[VRA07]   VRA. *VRA Core 4.0*. Visual Resources Association's (VRA) Data Standards Commitee, mar 2007. Available at: http://www.vraweb.org/projects/vracore4/index.html.

[W3C01]   W3C. *DAML+OIL*, December 2001. Available at: http://www.w3.org/TR/daml+oil-reference.

[W3C04a] W3C. *RDF Vocabulary Description Language 1.0: RDF Schema*. W3C Semantic Web Activity - RDF Core Working Group, February 2004. Available at: http://www.w3.org/TR/rdf-schema/.

[W3C04b] W3C. *Resource Description Framework (RDF)*. W3C Semantic Web Activity - RDF Core Working Group, 2004. Available at: http://www.w3.org/RDF/.

[W3C04c] W3C. *Web Ontology Language (OWL)*. W3C Semantic Web Activity – Web Ontology Working Group, 2004. Available at: http://www.w3.org/2004/OWL/.

[W3C04d] W3C Semantic Web Activity - RDF Core Working Group. *RDF/XML Syntax Specification (Revised)*, 2004. Available at: http://www.w3.org/TR/2004/REC-rdf-syntax-grammar-20040210/.

[W3C04e] W3C Semantic Web Activity - RDF Core Working Group. *Resource Description Framework (RDF): Concepts and Abstract Syntax*, 2004.

BIBLIOGRAPHY

[W3C06]   W3C. *XML Schema 1.1 Part 1: Structure*. W3C XML Core Working Group, August 2006. Available at: http://www.w3.org/TR/xmlschema11-1/.

[W3C07]   W3C XML Query Working Group. *XQuery 1.0 and XPath 2.0 Functions and Operators*, 2007.

[W3C08]   W3C. *SPARQL Query Language for RDF*. W3C Semantic Web Activity – RDF Data Access Working Group, 2008. Available at: http://www.w3.org/TR/rdf-sparql-query/.

[Wac03]   Holger Wache. *Semantische Mediation für heterogene Informationsquellen*. PhD thesis, University of Bremen, 2003.

[Wie92]   Gio Wiederhold. Mediators in the architecture of future information systems. *Computer*, 25(3):38–49, 1992.

[WK03]   Utz Westermann and Wolfgang Klas. An analysis of XML database solutions for the management of MPEG-7 media descriptions. *ACM Comput. Surv.*, 35(4):331–373, 2003.

[Won03]   WonderWeb Consortium. DOLCE: a descriptive ontology for linguistic and cognitive engineering, 2003. Available at: http://www.loa-cnr.it/DOLCE.html.

[XC06]   Huiyong Xiao and Isabel F. Cruz. Ontology-based query rewriting in peer-to-peer networks. In *In Proceedings of the 2nd International Conference on Knowledge Engineering and Decision Support, 2006*, 2006.

[Yah07]   Yahoo! Inc. Yahoo Pipes, 2007. Available at: http://pipes.yahoo.com.

[ZS06]   Anna V. Zhdanova and Pavel Shvaiko. Community-driven ontology matching. In York Sure and John Domingue, editors, *ESWC*, volume 4011 of *Lecture Notes in Computer Science*, pages 34–49, Berlin, Heidelberg, 2006. Springer.

Die VDM Verlagsservicegesellschaft sucht für wissenschaftliche Verlage abgeschlossene und herausragende

Dissertationen, Habilitationen, Diplomarbeiten, Master Theses, Magisterarbeiten usw.

für die kostenlose Publikation als Fachbuch.

Sie verfügen über eine Arbeit, die hohen inhaltlichen und formalen Ansprüchen genügt, und haben Interesse an einer honorarvergüteten Publikation?

Dann senden Sie bitte erste Informationen über sich und Ihre Arbeit per Email an *info@vdm-vsg.de*.

Sie erhalten kurzfristig unser Feedback!

VDM Verlagsservicegesellschaft mbH
Dudweiler Landstr. 99
D - 66123 Saarbrücken
www.vdm-vsg.de

Telefon +49 681 3720 174
Fax +49 681 3720 1749

Die VDM Verlagsservicegesellschaft mbH vertritt

Printed by Books on Demand GmbH, Norderstedt / Germany